Subject

and

Psyche

Robert M. Doran

Second Edition

Marquette University Press — Milwaukee Wisconsin — 1994

MARQUETTE STUDIES IN THEOLOGY

III

ANDREW TALLON, EDITOR

Cover Design
by
Hommit Zone ©

ISBN 0-87462-627-7
Library of Congress Catalog Card Number 94-79505

Printed in the United States of America
© Marquette University Press, 1994

Table of Contents

Preface to the Second Edition

I am very grateful to Marquette University Press and to its Director, Dr Andrew Tallon, for expressing a keen interest in publishing a second edition of *Subject and Psyche*.

The book, which was originally my doctoral dissertation, represents the first of several protracted arguments on my part to the effect that Bernard Lonergan's intentionality analysis needs to be complemented by a similar process of self-appropriation concerned with the distinct but not separate dimension of interiority that we call the sensitive psyche.

I have limited revisions to those that I considered essential. Thus later nuances in my thinking on the issues covered here are not included in the present edition unless they correct mistaken expressions in the first edition. I have attempted to indicate such corrections in notes. Exclusive language has been eliminated wherever I am speaking in direct discourse. A few new notes point to implications that I did not see when I wrote the original version. And formatting of sections and subsections follows a rubric of enumeration that should make reading easier. Otherwise, except for incidental details, the text remains the same as that which was published by University Press of America in 1977.

I take consolation in the fact that the Press that indicated interest in a second edition is sponsored by the University where the dissertation was written. While revising the manuscript this summer I thought frequently of my days and years as a graduate student at Marquette University, and remembered fondly my professors and fellow students. To all of them I express gratitude for friendship and support during the years when a series of ideas was born that, eventually, brought me to Toronto, to the Lonergan Research Institute, and to the privilege I now share with Frederick Crowe of being general editor of the Collected Works of Bernard Lonergan for University of Toronto Press.

Above all, I remember how the course of events that started at Marquette led me to meet and be befriended by Bernard Lonergan himself. I am deeply moved and humbled when I realize that he thought that the reflections whose early stages are represented here were a valid implementation of his work and a complement that he, too, thought was necessary.

The invitation to a further journey of self-discovery beyond the extensive one on which Lonergan takes us is daunting, and I know that this is surely one of the reasons that not all of his students have been able to accept it. Another reason undoubtedly lies in the poverty of my own expression and explanation. But I am grateful as well to those who, over the years, have heeded the invitation and supported its thrust and intention. May we approach the turn of the century with the hope that, partly because of Bernard Lonergan, we still have the possibility of building a home for the human spirit, despite the monstrous events to which our century has borne witness and the still more murderous potentialities that remain within our capability as a race. The move to the psyche and, through the psyche, to the embodiment of the human spirit is intended as a move into a home. I have no doubt that more remains to be done than is present not only in this book but also in my later work as well, to incarnate in the earth that is our home the spirit that Lonergan differentiated, and to express the theological implications, especially for a religion that professes belief in Incarnation, of what I have, for better or for worse, called psychic conversion. But none of us can take more than one step at a time, and I am grateful that I can present here once again the first step that I took in this direction.

Robert M. Doran
1 September 1993

Preface to the First Edition

Our twentieth century is the scene of a breakthrough in the evolution of human consciousness, a movement to a new stage of meaning in which the self-appropriation of interiority becomes the key to the control of meaning. The writings of Bernard Lonergan, I am convinced, have solidified this breakthrough, made it more than merely coincidental, systematized it, given it a secure foothold, integrated it. But Lonergan's work would have no context, no materials to integrate, were it not for the earlier and less successful but nonetheless essential developments that may roughly be included under the rubric of the 'turn to the subject.' Among these developments has been the discovery and scientific and therapeutic exploration of the psychological depths.

A large part of the work that follows tries to show how Lonergan's analysis of human intentionality allows one to generate categories through which both the human psyche and the science of depth psychology can profitably be understood. The key to my thesis is located in the development of Lonergan's thought from cognitional analysis to intentionality analysis. I accord primary importance to the emergence of a notion of a level of human consciousness distinctly concerned with the issue of value, the *notio valoris*, the human good. Values are primordially apprehended in feelings, and feelings are ascertainable, identifiable, through symbols. From this clue, I employ Lonergan's thought to aid me in developing a metascientific understanding of the psychotherapeutic phenomenon. I utilize basic notions of Jungian analytical psychology, while clarifying some ambiguities in Jung's thought with the aid of both Lonergan's intentionality analysis and Paul Ricoeur's philosophy of the symbol. Especially, I propose the need for moving beyond the framework of Jung's implicit metascience at a certain crucial moment both in Jung's thought and in one's exploration of one's own symbolic interiority.

There is also a second moment to my work. Not only does intentionality analysis clarify and correct depth-psychological understandings of human subjectivity, but a transformed science of the psyche provides to Lonergan's method a needed complement. This complement can be articulated through a careful analysis of Lonergan's understanding of theological foundations. The very dynamic of Lonergan's thought leads inexorably to a depth-psychological analysis that can be integrated with Lonergan's study of human knowledge and human decision. Such an integration greatly expands the foundational resources that are available not only to the theologian but also to the critic of culture, the human scientist, and the philosopher. The turn to the subject, in every instance — philosophical, psychological, theological — has been a search for the foundations of a new epoch in the evolution of human consciousness. I only hope my work is a contribution to the one ongoing foundational quest that is, I dare say, the drama of our age.

I have many debts I should confess, but I will limit myself to only a few acknowledgements. First I must mention the two men most instrumental in mediating the process of self-discovery and personal change that lies behind this work. I has spent seven years on Lonergan's writings before I ever had the pleasure and honor of discussing my own insights with him. But a very happy semester at Regis College in Toronto in the fall and winter of 1973-1974 revealed to me a man as gracious and kind as he is perceptive, insightful, and judicious. Lonergan has been, to put it mildly, most encouraging of my efforts and helpful in promoting my confident hope that I might be on to something. Charles Goldsmith, clinical psychologist and chaplain at Deaconess Hospital in Milwaukee, Wisconsin, skilfully exercised the delicate maieutic art of introducing me to the symbolic process of my own psychological depths.

Next, I wish to thank three friends with whom I have spent many hours discussing various facets of the problems here treated. It is to Vernon Gregson that I owe the term 'psychic conversion,' to Sebastian Moore that I am indebted for the insight that brought me beyond Jung's notion of the self, and to Matthew Lamb that I owe thanks for a sharp clarification of the central issue of the interrelationship of theology, philosophy, and depth psychology.

Introduction

In the following work I attempt a contribution to the analysis of the evaluating, deliberating, deciding, existential subject already begun by Bernard Lonergan, and an elucidation of what this contribution has to do with the theological functional specialty 'foundations.' I use as my key sentence the following statement from Lonergan's *Method in Theology*: 'Besides the immediate world of the infant and the adult's world mediated by meaning, there is the mediation of immediacy by meaning when one objectifies cognitional process in transcendental method and when one discovers, identifies, accepts one's submerged feelings in psychotherapy' (Lonergan 1993, 77). I attempt to understand the second mediation as aiding the self-appropriation of the existential subject in much the same way as the first aids that of the cognitional subject. In my first chapter, I show that such a context for understanding psychotherapy is at least implicit in *Method in Theology*. In the second, third, fourth, and fifth chapters I use Lonergan's thought to aid me in generating appropriate categories for understanding this second mediation of immediacy by meaning. Finally, in the sixth chapter, I state the function of this psychic self-appropriation in relation to the functional specialty 'foundations.'

While I have made use of the writings of Carl Gustav Jung to elucidate the process of psychotherapy, the present work cannot be taken as a thorough statement of Jung's relevance to theology or of the theological pertinence of Jungian analysis. Such a statement, I believe, must take the form of an analysis and critique of Jung's phenomenology of the psyche. I do not undertake this task here, nor do I present an alternative phenomenology—a task that can probably be done only by individual subjects retracing the respective paths of their own psychic development. In the present study, my interest is method, especially theological method. I seek to generate explanatory categories connecting psychotherapy with the self-appropriation of the existential subject and establishing this process as a dimension of theological foundations. I am doing neither depth psychology nor systematic theology, but theological method and foundations.

The statement I have cited from Lonergan places on the same level of discourse the work to which Lonergan devoted his entire career as teacher, scholar, and author, and another movement of self-appropriation achieved in a very different context. It makes these two movements somehow of equal footing, at least in that each is a mediation of immediacy by meaning.[1] What is the significance of this equivalence? In

---

1. The same equivalence is expressed in Lonergan's late paper 'Prolegomena to the Study of the Emerging Religious Consciousness of Our Time.' I quote: 'My book, *Insight*, is an account of human understanding. As a book, it is an outer sociocultural factor providing expression and interpretation of events named insights. But at the same time it is inviting the reader to self-discovery, to performing in and for himself the illustrative insights set forth in successive chapters, to adverting to what happens in himself when the insights occur and, no less, to what is missing when they do not occur, until eventually as is hoped he will be as familiar with his own intelligence in act as he is with his ocular vision.

'What can be done for insights, can also be done for feelings. Feelings simply as felt pertain to an infrastructure. But as merely felt, so far from being integrated into an equable flow of consciousness, they may become a source of disturbance, upset, inner turmoil. Then a cure or part of a cure would seem to be had from the client-centered therapist who

particular, what is its significance for the question of method, for philosophy understood as self-appropriation, and for theology? And what is its significance for depth psychology itself?

Paul Ricoeur cites with approval the insight of Maurice Merleau-Ponty to the effect that a philosophy which starts from an infinite curiosity, from an ambition to see everything, 'must subject its own problematic to the unsettling questions of the body, of time, of intersubjectivity, of the consciousness of things or the world, where being is now "all around (consciousness) instead of laid out before it … oneiric being, by definition hidden"' (Ricoeur 1970, 418, quoting from Merleau-Ponty's Preface to Hesnard 1960, 8). I will start from the cognitional analysis of Lonergan as the philosophy which begins from an infinite curiosity, rather than, as Ricoeur and Merleau-Ponty in this context, from the phenomenology of Edmund Husserl. At my own risk, I will wager that this will be a head start. My wager is encouraged by the fact that for Lonergan being is precisely never laid out before consciousness. Being is always a task, a struggle with the flight from understanding. May we follow this lead and further the work of self-appropriation begun by Lonergan's intentionality analysis? May we show that the movement of self-appropriation instituted by Lonergan extends to the second mediation of immediacy by meaning? Does this extension in

---

provides the patient with an ambiance in which he is at ease, can permit feelings to emerge without being engulfed by them, come to distinguish them from other inner events, differentiate among them, add recognition, bestow names, gradually manage to incapsulate within a suprastructure of knowledge and language, of assurance and confidence, what had been an occasion for disorientation, dismay, disorganization.' (In Lonergan 1985, 58). Here, rather than speaking of the mediation of immediacy, Lonergan talks of raising 'an infrastructure of insights as discoveries or of feelings as felt' to 'a suprastructure of insights as formulated in hypotheses or of feelings as integrated in conscious living' (ibid.).

such a context open upon an appropriation of the dynamics of the moral and religious consciousness which can sublate an intellectually self-appropriating consciousness? In moving to the psychotherapeutic hermeneutic and dialectic of the symbol, does not the existential subject achieve a unity-in-differentiation of three previously disparate and separate disciplines — philosophy, theology, and depth psychology[2] — and in this differentiated unity discover new foundations? These are my questions.

Thus in one sense I do not start simply from Lonergan's cognitional analysis but from the new problematic raised by his later explorations of the evaluative level of intentional consciousness, of the existential subject, of dialectic and foundations.[3] I start from his cognitional analysis as from a secure, massive, and in its essentials irrevocable achievement of the human mind's knowledge of itself. I start from his explorations of value, dialectic, and foundations as from a problem, and attempt to further, if just so slightly, a resolution of that problem by pointing to one direction I believe its resolution may take. I begin with the assumption, then, that there is no going back on chapters 11, 12 and 13 of *Insight* (Lonergan

---

2. Just what I mean by this unity-in-differentiation will be spelled out in chapter 1, in the context of a discussion of Lonergan's notion of method. My clue is the interrelation of philosophy and theology argued in Lonergan's *Philosophy of God, and Theology*). My present work is an attempt to interrelate depth psychology with philosophy and theology on the basis of the same notion of method that allows Lonergan to move toward a unity-in-differentiation of the philosophy of God and the theological functional specialty 'systematics.' As Lonergan argues that the separation but not the distinction between philosophy and theology should be abolished, so I will want to maintain that depth psychology is neither philosophy nor theology but methodologically related to both in the context of the self-appropriation of foundational subjectivity.

3. This problematic is carefully studied by Crowe (1977).

1992) nor on the cognitional structure of theological method derived from the understanding of understanding. I do not attempt to detail this achievement by means of a repetition nor to argue for its conclusiveness. There is simply no substitute for subjecting one's own cognitional activity to the rigorous critique of *Insight* and for discovering for oneself the essentials of the answers to the triad of questions: what am I doing when I am knowing? why is doing that knowing? what do I know when I do that? I accept Lonergan's answers to these questions as correct, that is, as open to refinement but not subject to radical revision, and his elaboration of an operational notion of method on the basis of these answers as valid. I wish to move with Lonergan, then, into the exploration of the evaluating, deliberating, deciding subject and to attempt a contribution to the elucidation of what, in Lonergan's schema, is the fourth level of intentional consciousness.[4]

In the course of my explorations, I have also arrived at the beginnings of a depthpsychological or, more precisely, archetypal appreciation of Lonergan's secure epistemological and methodological achievement and at an understanding of its potential therapeutic value. A sufficiently penetrating scrutiny of the fourth level of intentional consciousness may reveal, I believe, that an elaboration of the semantics of human desire is the meaning of a philosophy understood as self-appropriation. That the phrase 'the semantics of desire' is borrowed from Paul Ricoeur's brilliant study of Freudian discourse (Ricoeur 1970, 5-7, 160, 255, 271, 294, 322, 363, 375, 381, 386) is no indication that I intend to render a psychoanalytic interpretation of Lonergan's writings. If anything, it would be far more accurate to say that I am pointing to a

---

4. For a statement of the levels of consciousness, see *Method in Theology*, chapter 1.

reinterpretation of the psychoanalytic and analytical psychological movements of Freud and Jung, from the standpoint of a philosophy of self-appropriation, from the standpoint of method; that method, then, provides a horizon for understanding both Freudian and Jungian discourse and for locating in being the strange worlds their discoveries open for us. Nonetheless the relationship is reciprocal. The world opened to method by depth psychology affects method's understanding of itself. For depth psychology as praxis is given something of an equivalence with cognitional analysis as praxis, and so, just as cognitional analysis illuminates the truth of depth psychology, depth psychology reveals the archetypal significance of cognitional analysis. If we follow Ricoeur's lead in extending our notion of desire beyond Freud's explicit understanding of it, if we use Jung to help us follow this lead, and if, with Ricoeur and Jung, we interpret the teleological dimension of desire as at least in part an orientation to becoming ever more conscious, then the struggles into which one is plunged by reading Lonergan's work take on an explicitly archetypal dimension, perhaps the most primal archetypal dimension.[5] For Lonergan engages one without mercy in the conflict immanent in human desire itself between the intention of being and the flight from understanding, between the desire to know and the desire not to know. It is this struggle which Ricoeur finds at the heart of the Oedipal drama. I will ask whether this discovery does not call for a new and more inclusive understanding of psychotherapy from its origins. I find, in addition, a different solution to the same struggle in the drama of Orestes, and it is within this drama that I locate the current archetypal situation of method and the archetypal significance of the new

---

5. 1993 note: I would now refer to this dimension as anagogic, on the basis of a later distinction I draw between the archetypal and the anagogic.

directions in Lonergan's explorations of the fourth level of intentional consciousness. Method, on the basis of its resolute and heroic decision in favor of understanding and self-transcendence, is Orestes before his vindication by Athena. The second mediation of immediacy by meaning, when conducted on the basis of the first, and so when engaged in as appropriation at the fourth level of intentional consciousness, will free psyche to be wisdom and to vindicate. For at this level of the existential subject deciding for oneself what one is going to make of oneself, psychic energy and intentionality may become one, may join in a functional unity.

There is a further achievement of philosophy as self-appropriation on which I take my stand. It is the achievement of Paul Ricoeur, who has opened reflective philosophy upon the indispensable requirement of investigating the discoveries of depth psychology and of being instructed and changed by them, even while engaging in debate with their proponents. Ricoeur's study of Freud has affected my understanding of philosophy almost as much as has Lonergan's *Insight*. Both thinkers have effected a transformation in the direction of 'greater concreteness on the side of the subject' (Lonergan 1992, 19), in the domain of 'the pulsing flow of life' (Ibid. 13). Moreover, while for Ricoeur this greater concreteness has meant that philosophy must become a hermeneutic and dialectic of symbols, for Lonergan it means that 'the very possibility of the old distinction between philosophy and theology vanishes.'[6] Starting from this twofold move, I wish to take one further step in the direction of greater concreteness. Beyond the conclusions of Ricoeur's dramatic engagement with psychoanalytic explorations and Lonergan's proposals to interrelate philosophy and theology on the basis of

-----

6. Lonergan 1988, 245 ('Dimensions of Meaning'). Note that Lonergan is speaking of the *old* distinction, not of all distinction.

the subject-as-subject even while preserving a difference in respective methods, I want to suggest the functional unity-in-difference of philosophy, theology, and depth psychology in the movement of self-appropriation. Converging contributions to this movement now stand ready to be joined in a single but differentiated process of foundational subjectivity. The key to this unity-in-difference is the understanding of self-appropriation as the elaboration of the semantics of human desire.

My attempt to move further in the direction of greater concreteness will eventually involve a more detailed study of the analytical psychology of Carl Jung than I am able to undertake in this work.[7] This future study will be conducted from a standpoint similar to that which governs Ricoeur's study of Freud, and with a similar question as to Jung's pertinence for a philosophy of self-appropriation. The differences in my study of Jung from Ricoeur's study of Freud will be at least twofold: my philosophical master is Lonergan, and my interest in Jung originates from analytic experience. The latter experience is at the basis of the proposal defended later in the present work that Jung's psychology may feature in our reflection as opening the subject upon the teleological movement of symbolism in much the same way as Freud's reveals its archeological dimensions. In the present work, I will review Riceour's reading of and debate with Freud and place my own reading of and debate with Jung within this already well-established context. My debate with Jung will be both epistemological and psychological. Kantian presuppositions prevented Jung from giving an adequate account of what he was about, of its relation to the concerns of the

---

7. 1993 note: my most complete engagement with Jung is recorded in chapter 10 of my book *Theology and the Dialectics of History*, 1990.

philosopher and the theologian, and of the ontological reference and import of his statements about the human psyche.
These difficulties I hope to correct in the present work. Furthermore, though, a phenomenology of the psyche would
show that Jung needlessly shortcircuits the teleology of the
psyche, by reason of his epistemological confusion, and so
ultimately traps psychic unfolding in an intrapsychic erotic
cul de sac, in an eternal return, in a perpetually recurring psychic stillbirth. The absence of a clear notion of cognitional
self-transcendence prevents Jung from vigorously accent-
ing the dynamism to self-transcendence immanent in the
psyche itself. There is a kind of love that is beyond the wholeness of the mandala. The psychology of Jung breaks down
when the process of individuation invites one to surrender to
such love. But so, perhaps, does all psychology unless psychic process is sublated into the movement of existential subjectivity to the authenticity of self-transcendence. It is
Lonergan's invitation to this movement, then, that provides
our total context.[8]

I hope I may be forgiven a brief account of the personal
quest for meaning which has brought me to the position here
offered. It has been a journey guided by a complex foundational question. The general contours of the question were
first framed by the slow growth of the persuasion that the
paths of thought opened up by Lonergan and by Martin
Heidegger were somehow of comparable foundational significance for authentic living, for genuine reflection on that

---

8. 1993 note: in the first edition I had in this paragraph some expressions about the negotiation of 'Father' through entering into the image of
the Crucified. While I think this may appropriately represent Christian
religious experience, I am not ready to claim for it a transcendental status,
and so I have dropped this type of expression here and elsewhere in this
revision.

living, and for theology in particular. For nearly a decade.[9] I
have been in search of a horizon which would allow these
two paths, seemingly so very different—the one mysterious,
poetic, and elusive, the other forged by a formidable and au-
thoritative intellect—their proper due. Such a horizon was
not to be achieved, I was convinced, by a theoretical dialectical interplay of the respective positions of Heidegger and
Lonergan. There is a sense in which this would be contrary
to the very nature of their thought, which in each case opens
upon a personal adventure of exploration and understanding.[10] The solution would have to be found in accepting the
invitations of both and in negotiating the corresponding conflict. And so I was in search of a horizon where my understanding could issue in an articulate utterance embodying
the meeting of these two paths of thought and their mutual
interest and qualification.

The quest was furthered by my study of Paul Ricoeur's
philosophy of symbol, by his understanding of the hermeneutic enterprise as an exploration demanded by the very
exigences of philosophic rigor. I came to suspect that perhaps here, in the realm of symbolic utterance, I would find
the key to unlocking a mystery of opposites; that the horizon
so carefully sought might be opened up by a symbolic
coniunctio of the archetypal significances of these two deli-

---

9. 1993 note: this was written in 1974-1975.

10. 1993 note: a dialectical study *would* disclose, I believe, that
Heidegger never reaches truth and being, but that he *does* disclose the
transcendental time structure of imagination; the problem is that he as-
sumes this time structure as the horizon for reaching being. Time is 'within'
being, not being 'within' time. The issue is to relate the structured imagination of Heidegger to the transcendental intending of Lonergan, acknowledging each and giving each its proper place in the process of self-appropriation.

cately forged ways of being human; that I would find these two procedures which I experienced within myself to be themselves archetypally compensatory and complementary to one another; that perhaps both Lonergan and Heidegger were themselves *figurae*, embodiments of the profoundest archetypal significance, and that the resolution of my question was to be found in the realm of symbolism.

Thus, in reading both Lonergan and Heidegger, the subject is plunged into struggles of archetypal significance. Lonergan's work to date is, I believe, a cumulative and ever more self-conscious retrieval of a path chosen in the West at some fateful moment in the past. In the reading of *Insight*, and especially, I believe, of its first thirteen chapters, one finds oneself engaged in the archetypal struggle of the desire to understand with the flight from understanding. This struggle provides the deepest archetypal meaning of the dramas of both Oedipus and Orestes. The flight from understanding, archetypally understood, is an unknowing betrayal or primal murder of intentionality and an undifferentiated incestuous relationship with the psyche, undifferentiated despite its protestations of wanting to know. The desire to know, the recognition and acceptance of *logos*, the acknowledgment of the intention of being, on the other hand, is—again in archetypal terms—a vindication of intentionality's primal authority and a resolute though expeditious slaying of the uroboric psyche, followed by the dreadful flight from the psychic powers at their darkest until one is finally vindicated by psyche as wisdom, by Athena, by Anima-Sophia, who has been set free by one's resolute choice to understand. She is the archetypal embodiment of the dynamism of the psyche itself toward self-transcendence. Neither Western civilization nor method has yet secured her blessing in any lasting fashion. We are Orestes without Athena, fleeing the Furies. Heidegger is in search of this blessing, but prematurely. We must first go the whole way with Lonergan in an appropriation and resolute defense of the Western option before exploring the road not taken. The way opens upon this new exploration by the extension of self-appropriation into the home of psyche, where science joins wisdom. It is this *coniunctio* that Lonergan is in search of in his late reflections on value, feeling, and the symbolic. His is not a premature search; the blessing should be given, the decision vindicated.

In a psychotherapeutic process that was basically Jungian, I then began to travel through the labyrinthine paths of the psyche, meeting some of the various figures of what, to adapt a phrase from Edmund Husserl, may be called the system of the concrete *a priori*. (Husserl 1960, par. 39). I found, first, that such an experience allows, in a singular way, the unfolding of a meaningful contingency (Ricoeur 1970, 381), the arrival of a 'passive genesis of meaning' and of its active appropriation (ibid. 380), the laying bare of the 'Cogito that founds in proportion as it lets be' (ibid. 278), the inching toward a post-critical immediacy in which the primal Word is simply heard and understood as the dream is lived forward, its *logos* enfleshed. I discovered, too, that depth psychology is no personalistic affair, that it is the discovery and delineation of the 'unity of the race of man, not only in its biology but also in its spiritual history,' that it is the archeological digging of 'the deep, very deep well of the past,' so as to lay bare the very foundations of a science of the human roots of revelation (Campbell 1970, v, 5, 7).

But I still did not have a unified horizon. I was still assembling its elements. A first, partial, and completely unexpected resolution of my question was given as I began what was initially to be a study unpacking the Heideggerian roots of Rudolf Bultmann's theological categories. My avenue into Heidegger this time was through *Kant und das Problem der Metaphysik* (Heidegger 1951). I came to believe that Heidegger's relentless retrieval of the lost imagination from the first edition of the *Critique of Pure Reason*, the transcendental *Einbildungskraft* as instituting primordial time, was the opening upon a unified field of understanding. For I knew then that there was a further dimension to the foundational domain of the existential subject than that which had been cleared by Lonergan, that this domain was time, the imaginally instituted horizon of the psychic dimension of interiority, and that, while its dimensions had been and were still being reconstituted in Heidegger's meditations, a sublation of the depth-psychological phenomenon into a foundational quest guided by Lonergan embodies these dimensions in the archeological-teleological unity-intension of a living symbolic process, thus providing an inner space correlated with primordial time. I then postulated that the process cosmology of Alfred North Whitehead might perhaps be reinterpreted as a cosmology of this inner space, of the imaginal, and that its relevance to external space could be determined only by the joint researches of those physicists and depth psychologists exploring the phenomenon of synchronicity, of the *unus mundus imaginalis et physica*.[11]

Finally, the coupling of my analytic experience with the making and directing of the Ignatian *Exercises* and my good fortune of associating and collaborating with Sebastian Moore as he molded a series of meditations from a similar coupling (Moore 1977) convinced me that the exploration of the imaginal based in large part on the principles of Jung may become an avenue to profound and genuine religious experience. From this discovery one may proceed to the establishment of the relationship of certain depth-psychological and theo-

---

11. See for example von Franz (1974). My proposed interpretation of Whitehead is still in the order of a postulate. It may turn out to be little more than a 'bright idea.'

logical categories and place the entire psychotherapeutic phenomenon into its ultimately most adequate context, that of spiritual discernment, thus providing proper limits for the otherwise limitless treadmill of self-analysis.[12] In Lonergan's words, 'Man can reach basic fulfillment, peace, joy, only by moving beyond the realms of common sense, theory *and interiority* into the realm in which God is known and loved' (Lonergan 1993, 84, emphasis added).

With reference to my original question, then, the *coniunctio oppositorum* is a matter of the fullness of appropriation, of the totality of the mediation of immediacy. Nor is this a matter of Hegelian overambition, for not only is this totality only asymptotically approached but also our question is not one of the mediation of totality but of the totality of the mediation of what in itself is always finite, in part imaginally constituted by the dimensions of time, namely, the immediacy of the subject as subject to the operations by which a world is mediated by meaning, constituted by meaning, motivated by value, and to the dispositional states attendant upon those operations.

Such is the overall vision. It cannot be explored in its completeness at this point. In fact, only a very few of its features are to be explicated in the following attempt to articulate the meeting of method and psyche. And it is all-important that we begin with method.

---

12. See Progoff (1973a) for a discussion of the significance of the work of Otto Rank in emphasizing the necessity of a 'soul beyond psychology.' A more profound treatment of Rank is offered by Becker (1973), a book which, if taken as seriously as it deserves to be, should mark the beginning of a new stage of psychological thought.

1 Logic, Method, and Psyche

1 A Contrast

In the Preface to the first edition of his *Wissenschaft der Logik*, Georg Wilhelm Friedrich Hegel tells us that the movement of *Geist* is the absolute method of knowing and at the same time the immanent soul of the content of knowledge (Hegel 1965, 17). For Hegel it is only along a path of the self-construction of *Geist* that philosophy can become objective and demonstrated knowledge. This path is the phenomenology of spirit. It is logic, however, which shows the schema of movement of concrete knowing in its pure essence. Through logic consciousness frees itself in self-reflection from immediacy and engrossment in externality and becomes pure knowing, the knowledge of the pure essence of the schema of movement of *Geist* in and for itself. Logic, beyond the exhibition of the movement of *Geist*, is *Geist* thinking its own essence.

In continuity with the thought of Lonergan rather than with the philosophy of Hegel, I prefer to speak not of logic but of method, not of *Geist* but of the human subject. Method is, first, the phenomenological exhibition of the movement of human subjectivity. Secondly, it is the knowing of the essence of the schema of this movement in and for itself. But as 'for itself,' it is, thirdly, the self-recovery of human subjectivity, its concrete because self-appropriated recovery. If human subjectivity is recovered with some approximation to its full concreteness, the concrete knowing which occurs in and as a result of this recovery becomes, albeit asymptotically, equal to itself.

Method, then, is not simply the movement of human subjectivity, nor even the knowledge of this movement in itself, but the appropriation of this movement for itself. As such, method is not the Cartesian device correctly deplored by Hans-Georg Gadamer, the 'universal procedure for any and every knowledge describable by fixed rules, controllable by set principles, and capable of sealing off the way of knowledge against prejudices and rash assumptions and in general against the unruliness of guesses and flashes of insight' (Lawrence 1972, 170). Nor is it, *a fortiori*, a procedure which excludes moral truth, believed truth, and the provisional from playing a role in human knowing. Finally, far down the line from Descartes, method is not what Lonergan curtly dismisses as 'a set of rules to be followed meticulously by a dolt' (Lonergan 1993, xi.), or as 'a set of recipes that can be observed by a blockhead yet lead infallibly to astounding discoveries' (Lonergan 1973, 48).

The notion of method arose for Lonergan in his pursuit of 'greater concreteness on the side of the subject' (Lonergan 1992, 19). He tells us at the very beginning of his philosophical treatise Insight:

> Besides the *noêma* or *intentio intenta* or *pensée pensée* ... there also is the *noêsis* or *intentio intendens* or *pensée pensante* that is constituted by the very activity of inquiring and reflecting, understanding and affirming, asking further questions and reaching further answers. Let us say that this noetic activity is engaged in a lower context when it is doing mathematics or following scientific method or exercising common sense. Then

it will be moving towards an upper context when it scruti-
nizes mathematics or science or common sense in order to grasp
the nature of noetic activity. And if it comes to understand
and affirm what understanding is and what affirming is, then
it has reached an upper context that logically is independent
of the scaffolding of mathematics, science, and common sense.
Moreover, if it can be shown that the upper context is invariant, that any attempt to revise it can be legitimate only if the
hypothetical reviser refutes his own attempt by invoking experience, understanding, and reflection in an already pre-
scribed manner, then it will appear that, while the *noêma* or
intentio intenta or *pensée pensée* may always be expressed with
greater accuracy and completeness, still the immanent and
recurrently operative structure of the *noêsis* or *intentio intendens*
or *pensée pensante* must always be one and the same (ibid. 19-20).

This invariant upper context, articulated by Lonergan in his
pursuit of greater concreteness on the side of the subject, is
what he calls transcendental method.[1]

I too am seeking greater concreteness on the side of the
subject, but with respect, not to the playground of our intelligence which is human conception, but to the playground of

---

1. In Lonergan's later work, to be precise, the invariant upper context is not limited to experience, understanding, and judgment or reflection, but includes decision, evaluation, or dialectic. Thus, 'the function of
method is to spell out for each discipline the implications of the transcendental precepts, Be attentive, Be intelligent, Be reasonable, Be responsible.' *Philosophy of God, and Theology* 48. Thus too, two of the functional
specialties of theology are called dialectic and foundations, and they are
correlated with the fourth level of intentional consciousness, with evaluation and decision. To understand the movement to the notion of the good
as a distinct notion from the intelligent and the reasonable is, in my esti-
mation, the key to any discussion of the 'later Lonergan.' In addition,
Lonergan's treatment of dialectic and foundations, joined of course with
his seminal insight of functional specialties, is the key to understanding
Method in Theology. The inclusion of evaluation in the invariant upper context of the movement of human subjectivity sublates cognitional analysis
into intentionality analysis.

our desires and fears which is human imagination.[2] So it is that I propose with the aid of Lonergan's intentionality analysis to further the task of disengaging the structure-in-process of human subjectivity by concentrating on the complex of imagination and disposition. This complex has been the subject of scientific investigation at least since the origins of psychoanalysis in the work of Sigmund Freud. I wish to suggest that a concrete disengagement of this structure-in-process would be a further contribution to the articulation of transcendental method. Transcendental method is the self-conscious articulation of the structure-in-process of the human subject as cognitional and existential. The latter dimension calls for a sublation of psychic analysis into intentionality analysis, and it is this sublation whose contours I wish to articulate in the present work. If intentionality analysis provides the basic context of a transcendental method, the analysis of the psychic dimensions of the existential subject provides a kind of transcendental aesthetic: the clarification of the moral and religious consciousness capable of sublating an intellectually self-appropriating consciousness.[3] Depth

---

2. See Lonergan, *Insight* 32: 'Just as imagination is the playground of our desires and our fears, so conception is the playground of our intelligence.'

3. 1993 note: in the first edition, I claimed at this point a Christian interpretation of the religious aesthetic. I am not prepared to defend that interpretation *as transcendental*, though it may articulate a transcendental dimension. Whatever is claimed to be transcendental must, if the claim is correct, be a constituent feature of the infrastructure of subjectivity which I will call immediacy. The function of transcendental method will be to articulate this infrastructure, to mediate it by meaning. The function of the aesthetic dimension of method will be to articulate the moral and religious dimensions of this infrastructure insofar as these affect the human psyche. The argument of the last chapter of *Insight* that the problem of evil is met only by an absolutely supernatural solution is valid. It is at this

psychology and the imaginative resources which it sets free can reveal to the already methodical consciousness a manifold of data which from the standpoint of intentionality analysis is purely coincidental. The critically informed appropriation and articulation of this manifold can provide the reflective thinker with a needed complement to the horizon afforded by Lonergan's disengagement of the intentionality of human consciousness.

My decision to utilize Lonergan's term 'method' rather than Hegel's term 'logic' to characterize the knowing of the schema of movement of the human subject is not arbitrary. It reflects a profound difference between Lonergan's position and my own, on the one hand, and what Hegel has bequeathed to us on the other. For, no matter how the term 'logic' has been used in the history of philosophy — and it has had several meanings, among which Hegel's appears unique

---

point that a Christian phenomenology of the psyche would diverge sharply from Jung's. For then, 'human perfection itself becomes a limit to be transcended' and 'the humanist viewpoint loses its primacy, not by some extrinsicist invasion, but by submitting to its own immanent necessities. For if the humanist is to stand by the exigences of his own unrestricted desire, if he is to yield to the demands for openness set by every further question, then he will discover the limitations that imply man's incapacity for sustained development, he will acknowledge and consent to the one solution that exists, and if that solution is supernatural, his very humanism will lead beyond itself.' Lonergan, *Insight* 749. In Ernest Becker's words, 'Absolution has to come from the absolute beyond.' *The Denial of Death* 173. Jungian psychology contains an attempt to integrate evil psychically in a manner quite parallel to Hegel's attempt to integrate it speculatively. As Kierkegaard provided one of the death blows to the absolute system, so the work of a man like Becker mercilessly destroys any claims to totalitarianism on the part of the psychotherapeutic profession.

Nonetheless, to argue for the constituent function of a particular religious figure, such as Christ crucified and risen, in the transcendental religious infrastructure of the psyche raises enormous questions with which I am not ready to deal.

—it refers to a movement other than that which will give us what we need. The key to the difference lies in the notion of the *control of meaning*. Logic either is, or functions in aid of, a movement on the part of thought which seeks a control of meaning in terms of system.[4] Logic is a constituent feature of

---

4. In *Philosophy of God, and Theology*, Lonergan makes the decisive contrast between logic and method one between a static and dynamic viewpoint. While the logic he refers to is a deductivist logic other than Hegel's logic, and while one certainly cannot call Hegel's viewpoint static, the positive relations Lonergan posits between logic and method are quite valid and must be brought into our present discussion. 'Like the mortician, the logician achieves a steady state only temporarily. The mortician prevents not the ultimate but only the immediate decomposition of the corpse. In similar fashion the logician brings about, not the clarity, the coherence, and the rigor that will last forever, but only the clarity, the coherence, and the rigor that will bring to light the inadequacy of current views and thereby give rise to the discovery of a more adequate position.

'The shift from the static to the dynamic viewpoint relativizes logic and emphasizes method. It relativizes logic. It recognizes to the fullest extent the value of the clarity, coherence, and rigor that logic brings about. But it does not consider logic's achievement to be permanent. On the contrary, it considers it to be recurrent. Human knowledge can be constantly advancing, and the function of logic is to hasten that advance by revealing clearly, coherently, and rigorously the deficiencies of current achievement.

'... It is method that shows the way from the logically clear, coherent, and rigorous position of today to the quite different but logically clear, coherent, and rigorous position of tomorrow' (47-48). Logic and method are said to enter into 'a higher functional unity' (ibid. 48). Lonergan lists four inadequacies of a position that takes its stand on logic and does not think of method, the last of which at least is applicable *mutatis mutandis* to a discussion of Hegel. 'For the man who knows his logic and does not think of method, the term "system" will have only one meaning. Systems are either true or false. True system is the realization of the deductivist ideal that happens to be true and, in each department of human knowledge, there is only one true system. But when method is added to the picture, three notions of system are distinguished. There is the mistaken notion of system that supposes that it comprehends the eternal verities. There is the empirical notion of system that regards systems as successive

the emergence of *logos* from *mythos*, of theoretically differentiated consciousness from the undifferentiated or, in psychoanalytic terms, from 'the unconscious.' The early struggles of this movement are represented in the pre-Socratic philosophers and its first secure triumph in the Socratic maieutic. Hegel achieved an understanding of this movement as essentially dialectical, claimed an identification of it with the dialectic of reality itself, and attempted an articulation of logic in relation to this dialectical process.

But a control of meaning in terms of system is precisely what we do not need, what we cannot any longer assimilate, what we would have to regard as relative, as of itself without proper grounding.[5] What is needed is the self-appropriating recovery of human interiority, and this is other than a control of meaning through system. It is, I believe, a second movement of historical Western mind, and our age marks its at times excruciatingly painful beginning. It is not the movement from *mythos* to *logos* but the movement from *logos* to *methodos*. Method in its fullness, I submit, is an interiorization of *both logos* and *mythos*. Its first step is the interiorization of *logos* through cognitional analysis. But the dynamism urging

---

expressions of an ever fuller understanding of the relevant data and that considers the currently accepted system as the best available scientific opinion. Finally, there is system in the third sense that results from the appropriation of one's own conscious and intentional operations.' Ibid. 49. The first notion of system may be said to seek a control of meaning in terms of system. The second at least implicitly takes its stand rather on method than on logic. The third regards the self-appropriating subject as maieutic.

5. I am not saying that we do not need system, but that we cannot accept a control of meaning in terms of system (except, of course, in terms of the third notion of system mentioned by Lonergan in the quotation in the previous footnote—but this notion of system is the fruit, not of logic, but of method).

such interiorization will move beyond cognition to evaluation and, in this move, to psyche, and can then release a cumulative and ever more universal progress to an appropriated second immediacy on the part of the subject. This immediacy entails both a methodical consciousness instructed
through intentionality analysis and a post-critical symbolic
consciousness, the self-articulated unfolding of which would
be a transcendental aesthetic. The transcendental aesthetic
is in a sense, the culmination rather than, as with Kant, the
beginning of reflective philosophy.[6] The progress to such an
immediacy would pass beyond the self-appropriation of the
cognitional subject to the self-appropriation of the existential subject. This latter movement in its fullness calls for psychic self-appropriation. The fulfilment of this movement for
each individual and for the cosmos would be eschatological,
the poetic enjoyment of the truth about humanity and God.
The movement to a transcendental aesthetic is a complement
to the movement initiated by heeding Lonergan's call to
method. For 'the key to method is … the subject as subject
… To do "method" calls … for a release from all logics, all
closed systems or language games, all concepts, all symbolic
constructs to allow an abiding at the level of the presence of
the subject to himself' (Lawrence 1972, 203).

Hegel came very close to, and yet remained qualitatively
removed from, assuming responsibility for the transition from
logos to *methodos*, the transition from a control of meaning in
terms of system to an interiorization of system and a progressive advance to the fullness of second immediacy. It is
his ambition of an absolute system that marks the end of this
movement of historical Western mind, the movement of the
emergence of *logos* from *mythos*. The frustration to which this

------

6. 1993 note: it would also be something quite different from what
Kant means by a transcendental aesthetic.

ambition was doomed, perhaps most keenly and certainly very quickly sensed by Kierkegaard, signalled the need for a transition to another movement of historical Western mind.

Nonetheless, because of psychological recapitulation of phylogenesis by ontogenesis, the emergence of *logos* from *mythos* must and will be repeated in individuals. So too may be the ambitioning of absolute knowledge and the recognition of the inevitable frustration of such an ambition. At this point, the individual reflective thinker will be prepared to make his or her own unique contribution to the new movement of historical Western mind—provided, of course, that the disappointment of one's frustrated ambition is not equated with a despair over truth. Perhaps no thinker can contribute to this new movement without having first experienced the suffering of the frustration of the former enterprise. The frustration will take the form of what Lonergan calls an inverse insight: the point is that there is no point. In this case, there is no point to the absolute knowledge anticipated by the ambitions of *logos*.

Why, then, do we say that Hegel came so close to realizing the transition from logic to method? The reason is that there is a very definite sense in which he affirmed the pivotal presupposition of the new movement: *authentic subjectivity is the source of objectivity*, the only source of objectivity.[7] That Hegel is qualitatively still so distant from the transition is due, however, to his understanding of subjectivity. 'Das Logische ist seine eigentümliche Natur selbst' (Hegel 1965, 21). Thus he could not but misinterpret objectivity. And a

---

7. 'Objectivity is the fruit of authentic subjectivity, of being attentive, intelligent, reasonable and responsible.' Lonergan, *Philosophy of God, and Theology* 49. 'Subjective doesn't mean anything distinct from objective; it's the source of objectivity' (ibid. 66).

misunderstanding of objectivity entails a counterposition on reality. 'Nur in seinem Begriffe hat etwas Wirklichkeit' (ibid. 46).

According to Jung, Hegel divined a fundamental psychological truth but did not understand it as psychological. This truth is at least roughly glimpsed in the following sentence from Jung: 'A wholeness, of which he (the individual ego) is a part, wants to be transformed from a latent state of unconsciousness into an appropriate consciousness of itself' (Jung 1967, 180). For Jung, Hegel was 'a psychologist in disguise who projected great truths out of the subjective sphere into a cosmos he himself had created' (Jung 1969, 169). It might be said that, if method mediates both *logos* and psyche, it mediates *both* Hegel's insistence on objectivity, missed by Jung because of the latter's psychological immanentism, because of his inability to appreciate the self-transcending movement of psyche itself from unconscious to conscious, darkness to light, *and* Jung's insistence on the psychological features of all philosophic thinking, overlooked by Hegel because of a concern not to fall into psychologism.[8]

But surely we cannot claim, can we, that the science of psychology is then to be adopted as the foundation of this new movement of historical Western mind? No, we cannot claim this. At least we cannot do so with reference to any existing psychology, for no current psychological doctrine or praxis is methodologically aware enough of its conditions, its foundations, and its term. No such doctrine or praxis has engaged in adequate philosophical reflection on its own procedures and knowledge. But I can and do claim that the foundation of the new movement of historical Western mind is in part psychological. There is an underlying unity-in-differentiation of philosophy, theology, and depth psychology, which

---

8. I am indebted to Matthew Lamb for this formulation.

is to be located in the transcendental infrastructure of the subject-as-subject. This infrastructure is immediacy. It is mediated in different ways: philosophically through intentionality analysis, psychologically in psychotherapy, theologically in an objectification of religious conversion. All three mediations feature in the theological functional specialty 'foundations.' The meaning of a reference to a new movement of historical Western mind is grounded in the functional unity-in-differentiation of these three mediations.

The cognitive foundations of this new movement of historical Western mind—a movement prepared by the anthropological shift in modern philosophy, by the development of modern scientific and scholarly methods, by Marxism and psychoanalysis, and by existential philosophy—are laid by Lonergan in *Insight* and *Method in Theology*. Lonergan's cognitional theory, coupled with his increasing later insistence on historicity and the constitutive function of meaning, afford a foundational key to the concrete mediation of theory and praxis and thus to an advance to an appropriated second immediacy. For Lonergan has opened up for us the fact that the foundations of reflective thought lie in the self-appropriation of the reflective thinker. It is self-appropriation that constitutes the emerging unity-in-differentiation of philosophy, depth psychology, and theology.

2 The Subject as Control of Meaning

2.1 *The Call for a New Maieutic*

The call for a new control of meaning was issued by Lonergan in his 1965 lecture 'Dimensions of Meaning' (Lonergan 1988), and the nature of the answer to this call as self-appropriation is specified in his 1968 lecture 'The Subject.' (Lonergan 1974). The former lecture begins with a distinction between immediacy and the world mediated by meaning. The distinction meets the objection of the uncritical realist that meaning is, after all, a quite secondary affair, that what counts is the reality that is meant. The objection would be quite weighty, Lonergan argues in effect, if the very stuff of human living were the reality encountered by the infant. But since we develop beyond infancy, such realism finds itself involved in something of an oversight.

> ... as the command and use of language develop, there comes a reversal of roles. For words denote not only what is present but also what is absent, not only what is near but also what is far, not only the past but also the future, not only the factual but also the possible, the ideal, the ought-to-be for which we keep on striving though we never attain. So we come to live, not as the infant in a world of immediate experience, but in a far vaster world that is brought to us through the memories of other men, through the common sense of the community, through the pages of literature, through the labors of scholars, through the investigations of scientists, through the experience of saints, through the meditations of philosophers and theologians (Lonergan 1988, 232-33).

Meaning as act, then, consists not merely in experiencing but also in understanding and usually in judging and evaluating. The larger world mediated by meaning is thus constituted by human acts of understanding, affirming or denying, and evaluating. And it is this larger world, constituted by meaning, that is the real world in which we live out our lives. Moreover, not only is it a world known through our acts of meaning; it is also made and transformed by means of these same acts, and the transformation is not restricted to nature but extends to ourselves.

> ... the difference produced by the education of individu-
> als is only a recapitulation of the longer process of the educa-
> tion of mankind, of the evolution of social institutions, and of
> the development of cultures. Religions and art forms, languages
> and literatures, sciences, philosophies, the writing of history,
> all had their rude beginnings, slowly developed, reached their
> peak, perhaps went into decline and later underwent a renais-
> sance in another milieu. And what is true of cultural achieve-
> ments, also, though less conspicuously, is true of social insti-
> tutions. The family, the state, the law, the economy, are not
> fixed and immutable entities. They adapt to changing circum-
> stance; they can be reconceived in the light of new ideas; they
> can be subjected to revolutionary change ... all such change is
> in its essence a change of meaning: a change of idea or con-
> cept, a change of judgment or evaluation, a change of the or-
> der or the request (ibid. 234).

It is where meaning is constitutive that our freedom and responsibility are greatest. It is precisely here that the existential subject emerges, the subject 'finding out for himself that he has to decide for himself what he is to make of himself' (ibid. 235). It is at this level of constitutive meaning, too, that 'individuals become alienated from community, that communities split into factions, that cultures flower and decline, that historical causality exerts its sway' (ibid.).

Lonergan then proposes the notion of the control of meaning. Just as changes in understood and accepted meanings are at the root of social and cultural changes, so 'changes in the control of meaning mark off the great epochs in human history' (ibid.). We find the classical expression of the effort to control meaning in Socrates' insistence on universal definitions that apply *omni et soli*. The Socratic maieutic makes plain that there are at least two levels to meaning, the primary and spontaneous level reflected in ordinary language and a secondary level in which a reflexive movement leads us to say what we mean by ordinary language. Moreover, says Lonergan, the movement of mind in fourth-century Ath-

ens represents a line of cleavage dividing two historical epochs. Cultures and civilizations without such a maieutic, no
matter what their achievements in the practical affairs of life,
are penetrated, surrounded, and dominated, in their routine
activities and in the profound and secret aspirations of the
heart, by myth and magic. This is 'a malady to which all men
are prone. Just as the earth, left to itself, can put forth creep-
ers and shrubs, bushes and trees, with such excessive abundance that there results an impenetrable jungle, so too the
human mind, led by imagination and affect and uncontrolled
by any reflexive technique, luxuriates in a world of myth with
its glories to be achieved and its evils banished by the charms
of magic.'9 The Socratic maieutic, then, represents an epochal
or axial shift in the control of meaning, a shift that gave rise
to classical culture. The features of classical culture are perhaps most clearly highlighted in the notion of science put
forth in Aristotle's *Posterior Analytics*. Science is 'true, certain
knowledge of causal necessity' (ibid. 238), and the fact that
there are many things in the world that are not necessary but
contingent means that the universe is split between necessity
and contingency, and the human mind between science and
opinion, theory and practice, wisdom and prudence.

> Insofar as the universe was necessary, it could be known
> scientifically; but insofar as it was contingent, it could be
> known only by opinion. Again, insofar as the universe was
> necessary, human operation could not change it; it could only
> contemplate it by theory; but insofar as the universe was con-
> tingent, there was a realm in which human operation could be
> effective; and that was the sphere of practice. Finally, insofar

----

9. Ibid. 237. The reflexive technique introduced by Socrates is an
insistence on *logos* in preference to *mythos*. It is a championing of the cause
of differentiated consciousness vis-à-vis what certain depth-psychological
systems have called the unconscious.

as the universe was necessary, it was possible for man to find ultimate and changeless foundations, and so philosophy was the pursuit of wisdom; but insofar as the universe was contingent, it was a realm of endless differences and variations that could not be subsumed under hard and fast rules; and to navigate on that chartless sea there was needed all the astuteness of prudence (ibid. 239).

The major points of this 1965 lecture are that the classical culture resulting from this Greek mediation of meaning has passed away; that the multiplicity and complexity of thought forms and techniques that have replaced it leave us bewildered, perplexed, and anxious; and that a new control of meaning is needed, a new maieutic. The change can be seen most clearly in the field of science. While the classical notion maintained science to be ture, certain knowledge of causal necessity,

> ... modern science is not true; it is only on the way towards truth. It is not certain; for its positive affirmations it claims no more than probability. It is not knowledge but hypothesis, theory, system, the best available scientific opinion of the day. Its object is not necessity but verified possibility ... not what cannot possibly be otherwise, but what in fact is so. Finally, while modern science speaks of causes, still it is not concerned with Aristotle's four causes of end, agent, matter, and form; its ultimate objective is to reach a complete explanation of all phenomena, and by such explanation is meant the determination of the terms and intelligible relationships that account for all data (ibid. 238-39).

Thus instead of contrasting science and opinion, we speak of scientific opinion. For the differentiation of theory and practice, we substitute a continuum from basic research to industrial activity. Rather than the notion of philosophy as the search for changeless ultimates, we find our philosophers concerned with such matters as the authenticity of the

existential subject and the hermeneutic of cultural phenomena. This extension of philosophy into concrete living 'cur-
tails the functions formerly attributed to prudence ... the old-
style prudent man, whom some cultural lag sends drifting
through the twentieth century, commonly is known as a
stuffed shirt' (ibid. 240).

Classically oriented human science, which focused on
the essential, necessary, and universal, has given way to an
interest in 'all the [people] of every time and place, all their
thoughts and words and deeds, the accidental as well as the
essential, the contingent as well as the necessary, the particular as well as the universal' (ibid. 241). Classical human
science is seen to be an arbitrary standardization obscuring
our nature, constricting our spontaneity, sapping our vitality, and limiting our freedom.

> To proclaim with Vico the priority of poetry is to pro-
> claim that the human spirit expresses itself in symbols before
> it knows, if ever it knows, what its symbols literally mean. It is
> to open the way to setting aside the classical definition of man
> as a rational animal and, instead, defining man with the cul-
> tural phenomenologists as a symbolic animal or with the per-
> sonalists as an incarnate spirit (ibid. 241-42).

Lonergan summarizes the modern rediscovery of myth in
depth psychology and of intersubjectivity and the body in
phenomenology, only to conclude that 'the psychologists and
phenomenologists and existentialists have revealed to us our
myriad potentialities without pointing out the tree of life,
without unraveling the secret of good and evil. And when we
turn from our mysterious interiority to the world about us
for instruction, we are confronted with a similar multiplicity,
an endless refinement, a great technical exactness, and an
ultimate inconclusiveness' (ibid. 243).

There is still the individual's moment of profound existential crisis, then, 'when we find out for ourselves that we

have to decide for ourselves what we by our own choices and decisions are to make of ourselves' (ibid.). Definitions and doctrines are qualified to the point of relativism and skepticism by our knowledge of their histories and their adventures of development and decline. Authorities too, are historical beings and so require commentary, interpretation, exegesis. The emerging modern mediation of meaning is one

> ... that interprets our dreams and our symbols, that thematizes our wan smiles and limp gestures, that analyzes our minds and charts our souls, that takes the whole of human history for its kingdom to compare and relate languages and literatures, art forms and religions, family arrangements and customary morals, political, legal, educational, economic systems, sciences, philosophies, theologies and histories (ibid. 244).

But while countless scholars and scientists devote themselves to this task of understanding meaning, the individual is on his or her own when it comes to judging meaning and to deciding. 'There is far too much to be learnt before he could begin to judge. Yet judge he must and decide he must if he is to exist, if he is to be a man' (ibid.).

The call for a new maieutic could not be issued more clearly and persuasively. It can be developed, Lonergan judges, only by those 'big enough to be at home in both the old and the new, painstaking enough to work out one by one the transitions to be made, strong enough to refuse half measures and insist on complete solutions even though [they] have to wait' (ibid. 245).

2.2 *The Cognitional Subject as Maieutic*

In his 1968 lecture 'The Subject,' Lonergan explores further the dimensions of the new maieutic and points to the contributions he has already made to its articulation. If in 'Dimensions of Meaning' he had stated that the crisis of our age is rooted in the immaturity of the modern culture that replaced classical culture, in 'The Subject' he roots that immaturity in the neglect of the subject and of the vast labor involved in knowing the subject. The subject is twofold: a knowing subject and an existential subject, a deciding, evaluating subject. Modern culture's knowledge of the knowing subject is restricted by philosophic issues that render the subject a neglected, truncated, and immanentist subject, and the remedy to this tragic state of affairs consists essentially in the affirmation of the correct positions on knowing, being, and objectivity, an affirmation rendered possible only by a personal philosophic experience of conversion.

Contemporary philosophy itself does not neglect the subject, of course. Rather, it emphasizes the subject. But the very emphasis points to and is a reaction against a previous neglect conditioned by at least three factors: a fascination with the objectivity of truth; Aristotelian and modern rationalist notions of science and pure reason; and the metaphysical doctrine of the soul.

Lonergan, to be sure, has no quarrel with the objectivity of truth, but here as throughout his work he impugns fascination with such objectivity. It is true that once truth is attained it can be contradicted only by falsity. But truth nonetheless resides only in the subject, in the self-transcendence achieved in true judgment.

> Intentionally it goes completely beyond the subject, yet it does so only because ontologically the subject is capable of an intentional self-transcendence, of going beyond what he feels, what he imagines, what he thinks, what seems to him, to something utterly different, to what is so. Moreover, before the subject can attain the self-transcendence of truth, there is the slow and laborious process of conception, gestation, par-

turition. But teaching and learning, investigating, coming to understand, marshalling and weighing the evidence, these are not independent of the subject, of times and places, of psychological, social, historical conditions. The fruit of truth must grow and mature on the tree of the subject, before it can be plucked and placed in its absolute realm.[10]

A fascination with the objectivity of truth would neglect this process of its emergence in the subject. In Catholic circles, such onesidedness marks the old catechetics and the old censorship as well as the theological embarrassment of manual theologies with their syllogistic demonstrations of the mysteries of faith.

> What God reveals is a truth in the mind of God and in the minds of believers, but it is not a truth in the minds of nonbelievers; and to conclude that the mysteries of faith are truths in the mind of God or in the minds of believers in no way suggests that the mysteries are demonstrable. But this simple way out seems to have been missed by the theologians. They seem to have thought of truth as so objective as to get along without minds (ibid. 71-72).

Secondly, in Aristotelian science and rationalism, conclusions are held to follow necessarily from self-evident premises. If this is the case, the road to truth would seem to be 'not straight and narrow but broad and easy. There is no need to be concerned with the subject. No matter who he is, no matter what his interests, almost no matter how cursory his attention, he can hardly fail to grasp what is self-evident and, having grasped it, he can hardly fail to draw conclusions that are necessary' (ibid. 72).

---

10. Lonergan, 'The Subject' 70-71. For some of the dynamics of the achievement of truth in judgment, see Lonergan, *Insight*, chapters 9 and 10.

Thirdly, in Thomist circles there has been defended a metaphysical account of the soul which applies one and the same method to the study of plants, animals, and humans, a method which moves back from objects to acts, from acts to potencies, from potencies to habits, and from habits to the essence of the soul. Human science remains the same whether one is awake or asleep, a saint or a sinner, a genius or an imbecile. But the study of the subject is not a study of the soul. Its concern is with consciousness, with the operations of consciousness, and with their center, not in the soul but in the self. The study of the subject 'discerns the different levels of consciousness, the consciousness of the dream, of the waking subject, of the intelligently inquiring subject, of the rationally reflecting subject, of the responsibly deliberating subject' (ibid. 73). The same distinction occurs in the 1964 paper '*Existenz* and *Aggiornamento*':

> Of the human substance it is true that human nature is always the same; a man is a man whether he is awake or asleep, young or old, sane or crazy, sober or drunk, a genius or a moron, a saint or a sinner. From the viewpoint of substance, those differences are merely accidental. But they are not accidental to the subject, for the subject is not an abstraction; he is a concrete reality, all of him, a being in the luminousness of being (Lonergan 1988, 223).

These three factors, then, have resulted in the philosophic neglect of the subject. But beyond the neglected subject, who does not know himself or herself, there is the truncated subject, who is unaware of one's ignorance of oneself and so concludes that what one does not know does not exist. The grossest philosophic reflections of such double ignorance, for Lonergan, are found in behaviorism, logical positivism, and pragmatism. More subtle is the procedure of conceptualism, a style of philosophic thought which cuts across many lines. Conceptualism results from the 'apparently reasonable rule of acknowledging what is certain and disregarding what is controverted.' Such a procedure fastens on the concept and overlooks the act of understanding with its 'triple role of responding to inquiry, grasping intelligible form in sensible representations, and grounding the formation of concepts' (Lonergan 1974, 74). Conceptualism is marred by an anti-historical immobilism which cannot account for the development of concepts; by an excessive abstractness that is more concerned with the abstraction of the universal from the particular than with the grasp of a unity or pattern in sense data, images, and symbols; and by an abstract concept of being, least in connotation and greatest in denotation, rather than by a concrete notion of being as the desire to know, which intends the unknown in questions, partially discovers it in answers, presses on to fuller knowledge in further questions.

> The neglected subject, then, leads to the truncated subject, to the subject that does not know himself and so unduly impoverishes his account of human knowledge. He condemns himself to an anti-historical immobilism, to an excessively jejune connection between abstract concepts and sensible presentations, and to ignorance of the proleptic and utterly concrete character of the notion of being.[11]

The subject who does not know one's own knowing does not know that one's knowing involves an intentional self-transcendence. Thus one may come to claim that one's knowing is merely immanent. At the root of this claim there lies an

---

11. Ibid. 75. 'By a conceptualist I mean a person that is a keen logician, that is extremely precise in his use of terms, and that never imagined that the meaning of terms varied with the acts of understanding that they expressed.' Lonergan, *Philosophy of God, and Theology* ix.

inadequate notion of objectivity for which the notions of 'object' and 'objective' are correlates of picture-thinking. An object is something one looks at, and objectivity is seeing all there is to be seen and nothing that is not to be seen. For such thinking, the intention of questioning and the understanding of intelligible unity as possibly relevant to data cannot themselves be looked at, and so they must be 'merely subjective.' The same holds for concepts and judgments, which proceed respectively from direct and reflective understanding. Picture-thinking thinks in visual images and 'visual images are incapable of representing or suggesting the normative exigences of intelligence and reasonableness and, much less, their power to effect the intentional self-transcendence of the subject' (Lonergan 1974, 77). Thus the Kantian position on knowing is ultimately rooted in the notion of 'object' as what one looks at in sensitive intuition, which alone is immediately related to objects and must mediate the relation to objects of understanding and judgment. The value of judgments for such a position is no more than the value of intuition, and since intuitions reveal not being but phenomena, judgments are confined to a merely phenomenal world. They are not knowledge of the real. The alternative to such a notion of the immanence of knowledge, however, can be discovered only by an appropriation of the exigences of human intelligence and human reasonableness which generate a process of knowledge moving from the experiential objectivity of data to the terminal objectivity of judgments with its sharp distinction between what we feel, imagine, or suppose, and what we know. This alternative is available only to a subject who knows himself or herself better than does the neglected or truncated subject, who knows oneself well enough 'to discover that human cognitional activities have as their object being, that the activity immediately related to this object is questioning, that other activities such as sense and consciousness, understanding and judgment, are related mediately to the object, being, inasmuch as they are the means of answering questions, of reaching the goal intended by questioning' (ibid. 78-79). The genesis of such self-knowledge, however, 'is not a matter of finding out and assenting to a number of true propositions ... it is a matter of conversion' (ibid. 79), of intellectual self-appropriation, achieved through the 'basic discipline' of cognitional analysis.[12]

2.3 The Existential Subject as Maieutic

I believe it would be correct to say that intellectual self-appropriation, the self-knowledge of the subject in his or her intention of being as a knower, is the first and indispensable step in the development of the new maieutic. It is the step I am assuming in the present work, the maieutic of the first thirteen chapters of *Insight*. For Lonergan as for myself, however, while this extraordinarily delicate and subtle procedure is necessary, it is not sufficient. For the subject is not only a knower but also a doer, an existential subject who deliberates, evaluates, decides, and acts, and by his or her actions

---

12. 'The basic discipline, I believe, is not metaphysics but cognitional theory. By cognitional theory is meant, not a faculty psychology that presupposes a metaphysics, but an intentionality analysis that presupposes the data of consciousness.' Lonergan, *Philosophy of God, and Theology* 33. 'Metaphysics is prior if you consider that what you're studying is fully known objects. In other words, it's dealing with objects. When you start out that way, you have no way of critically justifying your metaphysics. You can critically justify it if you derive it from a cognitional theory and an epistemology. And you can critically justify the cognitional theory by finding it in yourself: the terms of the theory are found in your own operations, of which you are conscious and which you are able to identify in your own experience, and the relations connecting the terms are to be found in the dynamism relating one operation to the other.' Ibid. 60.

changes not only the world of objects but also, and more important, oneself.

> ... human doing is free and responsible. Within it is contained the reality of morals, of building up or destroying character, of achieving personality or failing in that task. By his own acts the human subject makes himself what he is to be, and he does so freely and responsibly; indeed, he does so precisely because his acts are the free and responsible expressions of himself (Lonergan 1974, 79).

The self-constituting existential subject is not to be understood according to the older schemes of intellect and will, of speculative and practical intellect or pure and practical reason, and of theory and praxis. 'None of these distinctions adverts to the subject as such and, while the reflexive, self-constituting element in moral living has been known from ancient times, still it was not coupled with the notion of the subject to draw attention to him in his key role of making himself what he is to be' (ibid.). The new schema in which the existential subject can be understood is very well known to Lonergan students, but it is so basic both to Lonergan and to this present work that I quote in full the articulation given it in this 1968 lecture. It is a schema of distinct but related levels of consciousness, the highest level being that of the existential subject, of the subject as agent.

> ... we are subjects, as it were, by degrees. At the lowest level, when unconscious in dreamless sleep or in a coma, we are merely potentially subjects. Next, we have a minimal degree of consciousness and subjectivity when we are the helpless subjects of our dreams. Thirdly, we become experiential subjects when we awake, when we become the subjects of lucid perception, imaginative projects, emotional and conative impulses, and bodily action. Fourthly, the intelligent subject sublates the experiential, i.e., it retains, preserves, goes beyond, completes it, when we inquire about our experience,

investigate, grow in understanding, express our inventions and discoveries. Fifthly, the rational subject sublates the intelligent and experiential subject, when we question our own understanding, check our formulations and expressions, ask whether we have got things right, marshal the evidence *pro* and *con*, judge this to be so and that not to be so. Sixthly, finally, rational consciousness is sublated by rational self-consciousness, when we deliberate, evaluate, decide, act. Then there emerges human consciousness at its fullest. Then the existential subject exists and his character, his personal essence, is at stake.[13]

The metaphor of levels of consciousness denotes a relationship of sublation, according to which a lower level is retained but also transcended and completed by a higher. Lonergan speaks of the sublation of waking consciousness by intelligence, of experience and intelligence by judgment, and of experience, understanding, and judgment by deliberation and action. The key to our notion of psychic self-appropriation will involve extending this process of sublation so that the level of dreaming consciousness is sublated by experience, intelligence, judgment, and action. The notion of sublation enables Lonergan to speak of the distinction and functional interdependence of the levels of consciousness. A further unity is provided 'by the unfolding of a single transcendental intending of plural, interchangeable objectives' (Lonergan 1974, 81). These objectives are approximately identical with the scholastic transcendentals: *ens, unum, verum,* and *bonum.* Thus:

---

13. Ibid. 80. Ernest Becker in *The Denial of Death* has captured the terror sometimes experienced in the full emergence of the subject as existential. Of value to our discussion is that it is within such a context that Becker discusses psychotherapy.

What promotes the subject from experiential to intellectual consciousness is the desire to understand, the intention of
intelligibility. What next promotes him from intellectual to
rational consciousness, is a fuller unfolding of the same intention: for the desire to understand, once understanding is
reached, becomes the desire to understand correctly; in other
words, the intention of intelligibility, once an intelligible is
reached, becomes the intention of the right intelligible, of the
true and, through truth, of reality. Finally, the intention of the
intelligible, the true, the real, becomes also the intention of
the good, the question of value, of what is worth-while, when
the already acting subject confronts his world and adverts to
his own acting in it (ibid.).

The notion of value, which is this highest, existential
level of consciousness, intends something other than the particular good of the satisfaction of individual appetite and the
good of order which ensures for a given group of people the
regular recurrence of particular goods. 'It is by appealing to
value or values that we satisfy some appetites and do not
satisfy others, that we approve some systems for achieving
the good of order and disapprove of others, that we praise or
blame human persons as good or evil and their actions as
right or wrong' (ibid. 81-82). The notion of value is further
explained by comparing it with the notion of being:

> Just as the notion of being intends but, of itself, does not
> know being, so too the notion of value intends but, of itself,
> does not know value. Again, as the notion of being is the dy-
> namic principle that keeps us moving toward ever fuller knowl-
> edge of being, so the notion of value is the fuller flowering of
> the same dynamic principle that now keeps us moving toward
> ever fuller realization of the good, of what is worth while ...
> Just as the notion of being functions in one's knowing
> and it is by reflecting on that functioning that one comes to
> know what the notion of being is, so also the notion or inten-
> tion of the good functions within one's human acting and it is
> by reflection on that functioning that one comes to know what

the notion of good is. Again, just as the functioning of the notion of being brings about our limited knowledge of being, so too the functioning of the notion of the good brings about our limited achievement of the good. Finally, just as our knowledge of being is, not knowledge of essence, but only knowledge of this and that other beings, so too the only good to which we have first-hand access is found in instances of the good realized in themselves or produced beyond themselves by good men (ibid. 82-83).

The existential subject, then, not only freely and responsibly makes oneself what one is, but also makes oneself good or evil and one's actions right or wrong. The notion of value is a transcendental principle of appraisal and criticism giving rise to instances of the good in choices and actions. The determination of the good is 'the work of the free and responsible subject producing the first and only edition of himself' (ibid. 83). This is why ethical systems are also so vague about what it is to do good. We do better to turn to examples about us, to stories, to the praise and blame of others' conversations, and to our own sense, now of elation, now of shame, with respect to our own actions. However it may be that we come to know the good, Lonergan's concern is with the subject, and with the primacy of the subject as existential, as becoming good or evil. It is with respect to the existential subject that we may turn to reflection on the body, on image and feeling, on symbol and story, on intersubjectivity, companionship, collaboration, friendship, and love. It is also the existential subject who brings into being, maintains, and transforms the world mediated by meaning. This world objectifies the choices of existential subjects.

The primacy of the existential, finally, does not eliminate the pertinence of the questions concerning knowing, the real, and objectivity. On the contrary it reinforces their crucial importance in many ways, not least of all with respect to the question of God's existence, omnipotence, and goodness.

It is ... no accident that a theatre of the absurd, a literature of the absurd, and philosophies of the absurd flourish in
a culture in which there are theologians to proclaim that God
is dead. But that absurdity and that death have their roots in a
new neglect of the subject, a new truncation, a new
immanentism. In the name of phenomenology, of existential
selfunderstanding, of human encounter, of salvation history,
there are those that resentfully and disdainfully brush aside
the old questions of cognitional theory, epistemology, metaphysics. I have no doubt, I never did doubt, that the old answers were defective. But to reject the questions as well is to
refuse to know what one is doing when one is knowing; it is to
refuse to know why doing that is knowing; it is to refuse to set
up a basic semantics by concluding what one knows when
one does it. That threefold refusal is worse than mere neglect
of the subject, and it generates a far more radical truncation.
It is the truncation that we experience today not only without
but also within the Church, when we find that the conditions
of the possibility of significant dialogue are not grasped, when
the distinction between revealed religion and myth is blurred,
when the possibility of objective knowledge of God's existence and of his goodness is denied (ibid. 86).

Insofar as the doubt extends to objective knowledge of God's
existence, omnipotence, and goodness, it entails a skepticism
about the value of God's world. If we alone then are good,
we are alien to the rest of the world; and if one 'renounces
authentic living and drifts into the now seductive and now
harsh rhythms of his psyche and of nature, then man is alienated from himself' (ibid.).

The only alternative, however, to the neglected or truncated or immanentist or alienated subject lies in cognitional
and existential self-appropriation. Psychic self-appropriation
is obviously to take place within the context of existential
self-appropriation. The articulation of the dynamics of cognitional and existential self-appropriation constitutes the new
maieutic. More precisely, the self-appropriating subject *is* the
new maieutic, the only viable control of meaning in modern

culture. No finer instrument of cognitional self-appropriation has been provided than Lonergan's *Insight*. But, I believe, the dynamics of existential self-appropriation can be given further refinement. The context has been set by Lonergan, but it is toward the further refinement that the present work heads, under the rubric of an attempt to extend interiority analysis to the level of the psyche. One must first go all the way with Lonergan beyond the cognitional subject to the existential subject before asking the question of the contribution of depth psychology to the new maieutic. For it is Lonergan who has provided the context and essential structure of a viable control of meaning for our age.

3 The Existential Subject as Moral and Religious

A further concretion of the necessary and fundamental context of our problem is provided in Lonergan's treatment of moral and religious conversion in *Method in Theology*. These two conversions, along with the philosophic conversion of intellectual self-appropriation, provide the criteria for the discrimination of psychic process involved in the self-appropriation of the existential subject. Lonergan's discussion of these two conversions is the beginning of the further refinement referred to above and sets the immediate context for our discussion of the psyche.

3.1 The Problem of Ethics in Insight

Mention must be made of the treatment accorded ethics in *Insight*, both for the sake of highlighting the greater concreteness of the discussion of the existential subject in Lonergan's later writings, and in order to help us situate more fully the context of our present problematic. In '*Insight* Revisited,' Lonergan states a difference in his later work which accounts for its greater concreteness in the treatment of the moral subject.

> In *Insight* the good was the intelligent and reasonable. In *Method* the good is a distinct notion. It is intended in questions for deliberation: Is this worth while? Is it truly or only apparently good? It is aspired to in the intentional response of feeling to values. It is known in judgments of value made by a virtuous or authentic person with a good conscience. It is brought about by deciding and living up to one's decisions. Just as intelligence sublates sense, just as reasonableness sublates intelligence, so deliberation sublates and thereby unifies knowing and feeling.[14]

There is no contradiction between this later notion of the good and the earlier one, but there is, I believe, a very important development in the articulation of the good as a distinct notion from the intelligent and reasonable. What is highlighted is real self-transcendence in the making of being and constitution of the world as distinct from cognitional self-transcendence in the knowing of being. This distinction is far from absent in chapter 18 of *Insight*, but the emergence of the existential subject is now granted a primacy not fully accorded it in the earlier work. Furthermore, and of special concern to the present work, the positive function of feelings vis-à-vis the existential subject, their transcendental significance as the locus of the primordial apprehension of value, and the role of symbols as a way of certifying affective development or decline are all granted much greater explicit sig-

---

14. Bernard Lonergan, '*Insight* Revisited,' in *A Second Collection* 277.

nificance in *Method in Theology*. What is of lasting value from the discussion of ethics in *Insight* is preserved in this later discussion, but significant new features are introduced which further concretize our understanding of the emergence of the existential subject. The criterion of moral authenticity shifts from an emphasis on the intelligent and reasonable to an ascending scale of values certifying the extent of the subject's self-transcendence.

It seems important, nonetheless, to mention the context of ethical decision as this is presented in *Insight*. After the establishment of a method of ethics, of an ontology of the good, and of the fact of essential freedom and responsibility, there is a discussion of the problem of effective freedom. 'Is an ethics possible in the sense that it can be observed? Is man condemned to moral frustration? Is there a need for a moral liberation if human development is to escape the cycle of alternating progress and decline?' (Lonergan 1992, 618) What renders these questions so acute is the fact that certain conditions must be met if the dynamic structure that is our essential freedom is to find an operational range within which to exercise itself. These conditions are fourfold. First, there are limitations placed upon effective freedom by external constraint. 'Whatever one's external circumstances may be, they offer only a limited range of concretely possible alternatives and only limited resources for bringing about the enlargement of that range' (ibid. 645). Secondly, effective freedom is limited by one's psychoneural state in several ways: by inadequately developed sensitive skills and habits, and by the anxiety, obsessions, and other neurotic phenomena resulting from the scotosis responsible for a disproportion between intellectual and psychic development. Thirdly, 'the less the development of one's practical intelligence, the less the range of possible courses of action that here and now will occur to one' (ibid. 646). Finally, effective freedom is dependent on a particular quality of antecedent willingness, which alone keeps one open to various possible courses of action. As long as one's antecedent willingness defines only a more or less narrow pattern of routine, as long as one's dynamism to moral self-transcendence is less radical than the dynamism of the desire to know toward cognitional self-transcendence, one's effective freedom will suffer restriction.

> In brief, effective freedom itself has to be won. The key point is to reach a willingness to persuade oneself and to submit to the persuasion of others. For then one can be persuaded to a universal willingness; so one becomes antecedently willing to learn all there is to be learnt about willing and learning and about the enlargement of one's freedom from external constraints and psychoneural interferences. But to reach the universal willingness that matches the unrestricted desire to know is indeed a high achievement, for it consists not in the mere recognition of an ideal norm but in the adoption of an attitude towards the universe of being, not in the adoption of an affective attitude that would desire but not perform but in the adoption of an effective attitude in which performance matches aspiration.
>
> Finally, if effective freedom is to be won, it is not to be won easily. Just as the pure desire to know is the possibility but not in itself the attainment of the scientist's settled habit of constant inquiry, so the potency 'will' is the possibility but not in itself the attainment of the genuine person's complete openness to reflection and to rational persuasion. Clearly, this confronts us with a paradox. How is one to be persuaded to genuineness and openness, when one is not yet open to persuasion? (ibid. 647)

The incompleteness of our intellectual and volitional development is for Lonergan at this point the radical root of the restriction of effective freedom that he calls moral impotence. Moral impotence is measured by 'a gap between the proximate effective freedom he actually possesses and, on the other hand, the remote and hypothetical effective freedom that he would possess if certain conditions happened to be fulfilled' (ibid. 650). This moral impotence is neither grasped with perfect clarity nor totally unconscious.

> For if one were to represent a man's field of freedom as a circular area, then one would distinguish a luminous central region in which he was effectively free, a surrounding penumbra in which his uneasy conscience keeps suggesting that he could do better if only he would make up his mind, and finally an outer shadow to which he barely if ever adverts. Further, these areas are not fixed; as he develops, the penumbra penetrates into the shadow and the luminous area into the penumbra while, inversely, moral decline is a contraction of the luminous area and of the penumbra. Finally, this consciousness of moral impotence not only heightens the tension between limitation and transcendence but also can provide ambivalent materials for reflection; correctly interpreted, it brings home to man the fact that his living is a developing, that he is not to be discouraged by his failures, that rather he is to profit by them both as lessons on his personal weaknesses and as a stimulus to greater efforts; but the same data can also be regarded as evidence that there is no use trying, that moral codes ask the impossible, that one has to be content with oneself as one is (ibid.).

Not only does society both reflect and heighten this tension and ambivalence, but also there is a threefold bias to common sense leading us to expect 'that individual decisions will be likely to suffer from individual bias, that common decisions will be likely to suffer from the various types of group bias, and that all decisions will be likely to suffer from general bias.'[15] General bias opposes the detachment and dis-

---

15. Ibid. 651. 1993 note: one way of approaching the complement that I would add to Lonergan's analysis is through a discussion of the further variety of bias that he calls dramatic bias. Dramatic bias, which is discussed in *Insight* 214-31, makes psychoneural interference a more significant root of moral impotence than Lonergan seems prepared to admit in chapter 18 of *Insight*.

interestedness required for self-transcendence in knowing and doing.

> More or less automatically and unconsciously, each successive batch of possible and practical courses of action is screened to eliminate as unpractical whatever does not seem practical to an intelligence and a willingness that not only are developed imperfectly but also suffer from bias. But the social situation is the cumulative product of individual and group decisions, and as these decisions depart from the demands of intelligence and reasonableness, so the social situation becomes, like the complex number, a compound of the rational and irrational. Then if it is to be understood, it must be met by a parallel compound of direct and inverse insights, of direct insights that grasp its intelligibility and of inverse insights that grasp its lack of intelligibility. Nor is it enough to understand the situation; it must also be managed. Its intelligible components have to be encouraged towards fuller development; and its unintelligible components have to be hurried to their reversal (ibid. 651-52).

It is this social compound of the intelligible and the absurd that constitutes the materials for further practical insights, the conditions for further reflection, and the reality to be modified by further decisions. But:

> Just as there are philosophies that take their stand upon the positions and urge the development of the intelligible components in the situation and the reversal of the unintelligible components, so too there are counterphilosophies that take their stand upon the counterpositions, that welcome the unintelligible components in the situation as objective facts that provide the empirical proof of their views, that demand the further expansion of the objective surd, and that clamor for the complete elimination of the intelligible components that they regard as wicked survivals of antiquated attitudes. But philosophies and counterphilosophies are for the few. Like Mercutio, the average man imprecates a plague on both their houses. What he wants is peace and prosperity. By his own light he selects what he believes is the intelligent and reason-

able but practical course of action; and as that practicality is the root of the trouble, the civilization drifts through successive less comprehensive syntheses to the sterility of the objectively unintelligible situation and to the coercion of economic pressures, political forces, and psychological conditioning (ibid. 652).

There is a tension between limitation and transcendence inherent in all development. But as this tension is conscious in human beings, it is intensified to the point of desperation by the outer conditions and inner mentality prevalent in social decline. The intelligence, reasonableness, and willingness of human beings proceed from the unfolding of a single transcendental intending of truth and value to be realized by self-transcending cognitional and existential subjectivity. Nonetheless, while these potentialities for effective freedom can integrate psychic, organic, chemical, and physical manifolds, they also 'stand in opposition and tension with sensitive and intersubjective attachment, interest, and exclusiveness, and ... suffer from that tension a cumulative bias that increasingly distorts immanent development, its outward products, and the outer conditions under which the immanent development occurs' (ibid. 653). The root of the problem lies in our inherent incapacity for sustained development. This incapacity is radical, affecting every issue, for it is inherent in the very dynamic structure of cognitional, volitional, and social activity. It is permanent, for both development and tension pertain to our very nature. This incapacity does not lie in the physical, chemical, organic, and sensitive manifolds which can be integrated by intelligence, reasonableness, and willingness, but in the very dynamic structure of the integrating components. This incapacity is not radically social; rather, it results in the social surd and 'receives from the social surd its continuity, its aggravation, its cumulative character' (ibid. 654). This incapacity is not to be met by the discovery of a correct philosophy, ethics, or human science, nor a fortiori by a benevolent despotism that would enforce a correct philosophy, ethics, or human science. The problem of our incapacity for sustained development does not reside in some theoretical realm, but takes its dimensions from the very dimensions of human history. Its only solution can be a higher integration of human living even than that provided by our intelligence, reasonableness, and genuine willingness. This solution must begin with people as they are, it must acknowledge, respect, and utilize their intelligence, reasonableness, and freedom, but it must replace an incapacity for sustained development with a capacity for sustained development without eliminating the tension inherent in all development.

I shall return to the problem of this necessary higher integration of human living after discussion of Lonergan's treatment of moral and religious conversion in *Method in Theology*.

3.2 *Moral Conversion*

The development of the discussion of morality from *Insight* to *Method in Theology* lies principally, as we have seen, in the emergence of a distinct notion of the good. Parallel with this development is a consideration very important to our present discussion. When the good is the intelligent and reasonable, everything psychic is a lower manifold to be integrated by knowledge. When the good is a distinct notion, however, and when it is correlated with a fourth level of intentional consciousness, feelings and their symbolic constitution become at least under one aspect a coincidental manifold from the standpoint of intelligent and reasonable consciousness. Their integration and that of the psyche into the dynamism of conscious intentionality toward real self-transcendence becomes the function, not of knowing, but of deliberating. 'Just as intelligence sublates sense, just as reason-ableness sublates intelligence, so deliberation sublates and thereby unifies knowing and feeling.'[16]

Moral conversion, then, is a shift of the criterion of one's decisions and choices from satisfactions to values (Lonergan 1993, 240). Values and potential satisfactions are both appre-hended in feelings, particularly those feelings called inten-tional, those arising out of perceiving, imagining, or repre-senting particular objects. Such objects may be, on the one hand, agreeable or disagreeable, satisfying or dissatisfying, or on the other hand, truly worth while or not worth while. The two classifications do not coincide, for what is agreeable may not be worth my while and what is worth my while may be such that it can be pursued only at the cost of selfdenial. But the sufficient criterion of the difference lies not here, for what is agreeable may also be worth my while, and what is disagreeable may indeed be also worthless. The difference is located rather in the measure of self-transcendence toward which our response carries us. 'Response to value both car-ries us towards self-transcendence and selects an object for the sake of whom or of which we transcend ourselves. In contrast, response to the agreeable or disagreeable is ambigu-ous' (ibid. 31). The same criterion of self-transcendence en-ables the construction of an ascending scale of values: vital (health and strength, grace and vigor); social (the good of order, conditioning the vital values of the whole community); cultural (the discovery, expression, validation, criticism, cor-rection, development, and improvement of the meanings mediating our worlds and of the values motivating our per-formance); personal (the person in his or her self-transcen-dence, as loving and being loved, as originator of values in

---

16. Lonergan, '*Insight* Revisited' 277.

oneself and in one's milieu); and religious (the self-transcendence experienced in and flowing from religious conversion) (ibid. 31-32).

The movement from basic moral conversion to moral goodness entails discovering and rooting out one's biases, developing one's knowledge of human reality and potentiality—one's own and that of others—in concrete situations, continually scrutinizing one's intentional feeling responses to value and their implicit scales of preference, listening to criticism and protest and remaining ready to learn from others. This moral growth obviously entails the development of feelings, which may be reinforced by advertence and approval or curtailed by distraction and disapproval. Such action on one's feelings will modify one's spontaneous scale of preferences. Thus feelings are related not only to their objects and to one another but also to the subject as subject. 'They are the mass and momentum and power of his conscious living, the actuation of his affective capacities, dispositions, habits, the effective orientation of his being' (ibid. 65). This description is particularly apt for those feelings which are 'so deep and strong, especially when deliberately reinforced, that they channel attention, shape one's horizon, direct one's life'(ibid. 32).

The *transcendental significance of feelings* lies in the fact that they are the locus of the primordial apprehension of value. Lonergan thus discusses feelings as mediating consciousness at its fullest, the consciousness of the existential subject. We have already seen that value, as what I intend when I ask whether this or that object or possible course of action is truly or only apparently good, is part of the dynamism of conscious intentionality, just as much a part as the intelligible intended in questions for understanding and the truth intended by questions for reflection. The apprehension of possible value and of potential satisfaction in feelings initiates the process of questions for deliberation which promote the conscious subject from the rational to the existential level of consciousness, where the individual decides for oneself what one is going to make of oneself, where one takes a stand reflecting one's dynamic orientation to the authenticity of self-transcendence. This dynamic orientation as transcendental notion provides the criterion of one's performance as existential subject. A person who would consistently affirm and choose what is truly good would have achieved the self-transcendence which is the authentic realization of one's conscious intentionality. Obviously, such sustained authenticity demands that feelings be 'cultivated, enlightened, strengthened, refined, criticized and pruned of oddities' (ibid. 38). In this way, 'the development of knowledge and the development of moral feeling head to the existential discovery of oneself as a moral being, the realization that one not only chooses between courses of action but also thereby makes oneself an authentic human being or an unauthentic one. With that discovery, there emerges in consciousness the significance of personal value and the meaning of personal responsibility. One's judgments of value are revealed as the door to one's fulfilment or to one's loss' (ibid. 38-39). The apprehension of value in feelings initiates the process to these existentially significant judgments of value. The feelings in which potential satisfactions and values are apprehended range everywhere from 'the initial infantile bundle of needs and clamors and gratifications' to 'the deep-set joy and solid peace, the power and the vigor, of being in love with God.' In the measure that one has been brought to this summit, 'values are whatever one loves, and evils are whatever one hates ... then affectivity is of a single piece. Further developments only fill out previous achievement. Lapses from grace are rarer and more quickly amended' (ibid. 39).

Such moral self-transcendence is equated with what Abraham Maslow calls self-realization, which he finds in less than one percent of the adult population. Judgments of value occur, then, not only within a context of developing knowledge, refinement of feeling, and an ascending scale of preferences, but also within a context determined by neurotic need, by the refusal of change, by rationalization, bias, ideology, and by what Max Scheler calls *ressentiment*. 'So one may come to hate the truly good, and love the really evil. Nor is that calamity limited to individuals. It can happen to groups, to nations, to blocks of nations, to mankind. It can take different, opposed, belligerent forms to divide mankind and to menace civilization with destruction' (ibid. 40). The individual bias of the egoist, the group bias of the class, and the general bias of common sense, which demands that theoretical premises conform to and support supposed matters of fact, are all at the root of the neglect of the precepts demanding fidelity to the transcendental notions. Such neglect is the basic form of human alienation, while a doctrine justifying such alienation is the basic form of ideology. One is alienated to the extent that one disregards the dynamism of the human spirit with its imperatives, Be attentive, Be intelligent, Be reasonable, Be responsible, and consequently fails to promote oneself or allow oneself to be promoted to the authenticity of self-transcendence. One is the victim of the mystification of ideology to the extent that one justifies this inauthenticity.

Now, as it is within the context of the treatment of value that Lonergan discusses feelings, so it is within the same context that he mentions psychotherapy. The relation of feelings to the imperative of fidelity to the transcendental notions is such that 'to take cognizance of them makes it possible for one to know oneself, to uncover the inattention, obtuseness, silliness, irresponsibility that gave rise to the feeling one does not want, and to correct the aberrant attitude' (ibid. 33) — and, we might add, conversely, to uncover the feeling that gave rise to the inattention, obtuseness, silliness, irresponsibility one does not want. Not to take cognizance of one's feelings is to leave them in 'the twilight of what is conscious but not objectified' known in psychotherapy as the unconscious (ibid. 34). Then there results a misconception of what one spontaneously is, a conflict between the self as conscious and the self as objectified. Psychotherapy, then, is an appropriation of one's feelings analogous to the appropriation of one's attending, inquiring, understanding, conceiving, and affirming effected through the cognitional analysis of *Insight*, so much so as to be a second mediation of immediacy by meaning (ibid. 77). Furthermore, feeling becomes unified in one's advance toward moral self-transcendence, and at the summit, where God's love consolidates one's interiority, there is found an affectivity of a single piece, a psychic totality or wholeness.[17]

Now the same objects may invoke different feelings in different individuals. One of the ways of ascertaining individual uniqueness in affective response is through the symbolic images evoked by or evoking a feeling. A symbol for Lonergan is precisely 'an image of a real or imaginary object that evokes a feeling or is evoked by a feeling' (Lonergan 1993, 64). Affective development or aberration, then, is a process that may be ascertained or certified symbolically. It involves 'a transvaluation and transformation of symbols. What

---

17. It is important that we do not identify this unified affectivity with a state of complete harmony with the rhythms of the psyche. As we shall see, the psyche is ambiguous; its structure is dialectical. The psychic self-appropriation of the existential subject is an ongoing, never-ending task of integrating psychic energy into the dynamism of intentionality toward self-transcendence. The psyche cannot be given the upper hand in this process. The failure of Jung adequately to distinguish psychic energy and intentionality is, I fear, the basis of a potential psychic totalitarianism on the part of his followers.

before was moving no longer moves; what before did not move now is moving. So the symbols themselves change to express the new affective capacities and dispositions … Inversely, symbols that do not submit to transvaluation and transformation seem to point to a block in development' (ibid. 66).

The proper meaning of symbols is that they fulfil a need for internal communication on the part of the existential subject, a need which cannot be satisfied by logic, dialectic, or (we might add) cognitional analysis.

> Organic and psychic vitality have to reveal themselves to intentional consciousness and, inversely, intentional consciousness has to secure the collaboration of organism and psyche. Again, our apprehensions of values occur in intentional responses, in feelings: here too it is necessary for feelings to reveal their objects and, inversely, for objects to awaken feelings. It is through symbols that mind and body, mind and heart, heart and body communicate (ibid. 66-67).

Thus the understanding or explanation or interpretation of the symbol is effected by appealing to the context of this internal communication with its associated images and feelings, memories and tendencies. There are many different interpretive contexts displayed in the various psychotherapeutic techniques, and Lonergan judges that this multiplicity reflects the different ways in which development and deviation can occur.

I find Lonergan's treatment of these matters illuminating and quite precise, and I believe he provides better than many psychotherapists a key for the integration of feeling into the sweep of the self-appropriation of interiority through a conscious — attentive, intelligent, reasonable, and responsible — negotiation of the symbolic function. From what has already been exposed of Lonergan's treatment, it is not difficult to argue for the construction of a new psychotherapeutic model which would view affective immediacy as imaginally constructed, the aim of psychotherapy as the integration of this immediacy into the dynamism of conscious intentionality to self-transcendence, and the significance of psychotherapy as facilitating the sublation of intellectual by moral conversion through the symbolically charged transformation of the feelings in which values are apprehended. Psychic wholeness and the self-transcendence of authentic subjectivity can be correlative and mutually reinforcing. This is implicit in Lonergan's qualifications of the summit of moral self-transcendence in the love of God, where 'values are whatever one loves, and evils are whatever one hates' and where affectivity is of a single piece; in his discussion of psychotherapy within the context of authenticity; and in his qualification of affective development and aberration as symbolically certifiable. I conclude: if psychotherapy is a matter of the differentation and appropriation of feelings through the attentive, intelligent, reasonable, and responsible negotiation of the symbolic function; if this negotiation heals a rift between differentiated consciousness and the psyche at the root of contemporary individual and social ethical crises; if the feelings discovered and negotiated in psychotherapy are the locus of the apprehension of value; if our apprehension of value is crippled by the rift between differentiated consciousness and the symbolic function constitutive of feeling; and if psychotherapy, by healing this rift and promoting psychic wholeness in the interest of self-transcending subjectivity, reinstitues on a new level of conscious awareness the ethically necessary commerce of the existential subject with symbolically charged feeling: then psychotherapy can function in strengthening something bearing remarkable resemblances to what Lonergan describes as moral conversion.

3.3 Religious Conversion

The nature of the higher integration of human living acknowledged as a necessity at the end of chapter 18 of *Insight* is by now probably apparent from our references to religious values as the highest level of value in Lonergan's ascending scale of values, and from Lonergan's references in *Method in Theology* to the consolidating power of the gift of God's love. The higher integration of human living beyond that provided by intelligence, reasonableness, and responsibility, beyond one's intelligent, reasonable, and responsible efforts to integrate feelings and symbolic process into the dynamism of conscious intentionality toward the authenticity of self-transcendence, is the integration provided by the authentic religion that is the fruit of the gift of God's love. There is a further vector to the self-transcendence which constitutes human authenticity, a vector beyond the cognitional self-transcendence of the knowing subject faithful to the exigences of the desire to know and the real self-transcendence of the moral subject faithful to the orientation to value as the criterion of one's decisions, choices, and actions. This further vector we might call vertical self-transcendence.

3.3.1 The Question of God

Between the acknowledgement of the need for a higher integration of human living at the end of chapter 18 of *Insight* and the specification of that higher integration in chapter 20, there occurs a demonstration of the existence of God in chapter 19. Lonergan has since pointed to an incongruity, not in the very notion of the kind of philosophy of God he presents in this chapter, but in the context of the chapter as a whole. 'While my cognitional theory was based on a long and methodical appeal to experience, in contrast my account of God's existence and attributes made no appeal to religious experience' (Lonergan 1973, 12). Moreover, 'if *Method in Theology* may be taken as the direction in which *Insight* was moving, then that direction implies not only intellectual conversion but also moral and religious conversion. One might claim that *Insight* leaves room for moral and religious conversion, but one is less likely to assert that the room is very well furnished' (ibid.).

The problem is not with the idea of a proof of God's existence but with the horizon presupposed by the system within which such a proof would occur. A horizon is 'a differentiation of consciousness that has unfolded under the conditions and circumstances of a particular culture and a particular historical development' (ibid.). Chapter 19 of *Insight* 'made no effort to deal with the subject's religious horizon. It failed to acknowledge that the traditional viewpoint made sense only if one accepted first principles on the ground that they were intrinsically necessary and if one added the assumption that there is one right culture so that differences in subjectivity are irrelevant' (ibid. 13). If objectivity is the fruit of authentic subjectivity, a philosophy of God must take into account not only intellectual conversion, but also moral and religious conversion as well.

The origin of a philosophy of God lies, then, in religious conversion. 'Religious experience at its root is experience of an unconditioned and unrestricted being in love. But what we are in love with, remains something that we have to find out. When we find it out in the context of a philosophy, there results a philosophy of God' (ibid. 51). This philosophy deals with a series of questions on different levels. Lonergan distinguishes four forms of the question of God.

The basic form of the question of God consists in the questioning of our own questioning. A first form of this ques-

tioning relates to our questions for intelligence: what? why?
how? what for?

> Answers to such questions are reached when the desire
> to understand expressed in the question is met by the satisfac-
> tion of actually understanding. Still the desire to understand
> is not simply a desire for a subjective satisfaction. It wants
> more. It wants to understand the persons and things that make
> up one's milieu and environment. How is it, then, that the sub-
> jective satisfaction of an act of understanding can be the rev-
> elation of the nature of the persons and things in one's milieu
> and environment? Obviously, if intelligence can reveal them,
> they must be intelligible. But how can they be intelligible?
> Does not the intelligibility of the object presuppose an intelli-
> gent ground? Does not an intelligent ground for everything
> in the universe presuppose the existence of God?[18]

Besides questions for intelligence, there are questions
for reflection: Is it so? These questions are answered when
we reach a virtually unconditioned, a conditioned whose conditions happen to be fulfilled. No objects in the sensible universe can be known in any other way. 'Their existence is not
necessary but conditioned. They are contingent beings and
so they can be known to exist only when their existence has
been verified. But can everything be contingent? Must there
not exist necessary being, whose existence is unconditioned,

---

18. Ibid. 53. 'The possibility of inquiry on the side of the subject lies
in his intelligence, in his drive to know what, why, how, and in his ability
to reach intellectually satisfying answers. But why should the answers
that satisfy the intelligence of the subject yield anything more than a subjective satisfaction? Why should they be supposed to possess any relevance
to knowledge of the universe? Of course, we assume that they do. We can
point to the fact that our assumption is confirmed by its fruits. So implicitly we grant that the universe is intelligible and, once that is granted,
there arises the question whether the universe could be intelligible without having an intelligent ground. But that is the question about God'
(Lonergan 1993, 101).

to account for the existence of the beings whose existence is conditioned?'[19] Thus there arises a second form of the question of God.

The forms of the question of God arising from questioning our questions for intelligence and our questions for reflection are metaphysical. But besides questions for intelligence and questions for reflection, there are questions for deliberation. Questioning these questions results in a third form of the question of God.

> To deliberate is to ask whether this or that course of action is worthwhile. To deliberate about one's deliberating is to ask whether it is worthwhile ever to stop and ask whether one's course of action is worthwhile. No doubt, we are moral beings. No doubt, we are forever praising X and blaming Y. But the fundamental question is whether or not morality begins with the human race. If it does, then basically the universe is amoral; and if basically the universe is amoral, then are not man's aspirations to be moral doomed to failure? But if man is not the first instance of moral aspiration, if basically the universe is moral, then once more there arises the question of God. One asks whether the necessarily existing and intelligent ground of the universe also is a highly moral being.[20]

---

19. Lonergan 1973, 53-54. 'If we are to speak of a virtually unconditioned, we must first speak of an unconditioned. The virtually unconditioned has no unfulfilled conditions. The strictly unconditioned has no conditions whatever. In traditional terms, the former is a contingent being, and the latter is a necessary being. In more contemporary terms the former pertains to this world, to the world of possible experience, while the latter transcends this world in the sense that its reality is of a totally different order. But in either case we come to the question of God. Does a necessary being exist? Does there exist a reality that transcends the reality of this world?' (Lonergan 1993, 102)

20. Lonergan 1973, 54. 'To deliberate about x is to ask whether x is worth while. To deliberate about deliberating is to ask whether any deliberating is worth while. Has "worth while" any ultimate meaning? Is moral

Finally, the question of God arises when we question religious experience. Despite its many forms due to the variety of human culture and its many aberrations resulting from the precariousness of authenticity, 'underneath the many forms and prior to the many aberrations some have found that there exists an unrestricted being in love, a mystery of love and awe, a being grasped by ultimate concern, a happiness that has a determinate content but no intellectually apprehended object. Such people will ask, With whom are we in love? So in the fourth and final manner there arises the question of God.'[21]

---

enterprise consonant with this world? We praise the developing subject ever more capable of attention, insight, reasonableness, responsibility. We praise progress and denounce every manifestation of decline. But is the universe on our side, or are we just gamblers and, if we are gamblers, are we not perhaps fools, individually struggling for authenticity and collectively endeavoring to snatch progress from the ever mounting welter of decline? The questions arise and, clearly, our attitudes and our resoluteness may be profoundly affected by the answers. Does there or does there not necessarily exist a transcendent, intelligent ground of the universe? Is that ground or are we the primary instance of moral consciousness? Are cosmogenesis, biological evolution, historical process basically cognate to us as moral beings or are they indifferent and so alien to us?' (Lonergan 1993, 102-03)

21. Lonergan 1973, 54. 'To our apprehension of vital, social, cultural, and personal values, there is added an apprehension of transcendent value. This apprehension consists in the experienced fulfilment of our unrestricted thrust to self-transcendence, in our actuated orientation towards the mystery of love and awe. Since that thrust is of intelligence to the intelligible, of reasonableness to the true and the real, of freedom and responsibility to the truly good, the experienced fulfilment of that thrust in its unrestrictedness may be objectified as a clouded revelation of absolute intelligence and intelligibility, absolute truth and reality, absolute goodness and holiness. With that objectification there recurs the question of God in a new form. For now it is primarily a question of decision. Will I love him in return, or will I refuse? Will I live out the gift of his love, or

In each instance, the question of God 'rises out of our conscious intentionality, out of the *a priori* structured drive that promotes us from experiencing to the effort to understand, from understanding to the effort to judge truly, from judging to the effort to choose rightly' (Lonergan 1993, 103). It arises by questioning the pure question that the subject-as-subject *is*. This pure question, as one, unifies the four levels on which the question of God arises and renders the four forms of the question of God cumulative. 'The question of God is epistemological, when we ask how the universe can be intelligible. It is philosophic when we ask why we should bow to the principle of sufficient reason, when there is no sufficient reason for the existence of contingent things. It is moral when we ask whether the universe has a moral ground and so a moral goal. It finally is religious when we ask whether there is anyone for us to love with all our heart and all our soul and all our mind and all our strength' (Lonergan 1973, 54-55).

Furthermore, while the basic form of the question of God is discovered by questioning our questioning, the basic question itself of God is the religious question. 'The vast majority of mankind have been religious. One cannot claim that their religion has been based on some philosophy of God. One can easily argue that their religious concern arose out of their religious experience. In that case the basic question of God is the fourth question that arises out of religious experience. It is only in the climate of a philosophically differentiated culture that there occurs reflection on our questions for

---

will I hold back, turn away, withdraw? Only secondarily do there arise the questions of God's existence and nature, and they are the questions of the lover seeking to know him or of the unbeliever seeking to escape him. Such is the basic option of the existential subject once called by God' (Lonergan 1993, 115-16).

intelligence, our questions for reflection, and our questions for deliberation' (ibid. 55).

3.3.2 Religious Experience

What is this experience which gives rise to the basic question of God? Lonergan employs various phrases, some borrowed from other authors, to describe religious conversion. With Paul Tillich, he speaks of 'being grasped by ultimate concern' (ibid. 240). With St Paul, he speaks of 'God's love flooding our hearts through the Holy Spirit given to us' (ibid. 241). In terms of the theoretical stage of meaning represented incipiently by Augustine and more fully by Aquinas, religious conversion is operative grace as distinct from cooperative grace. But these are now described in scriptural imagery. 'Operative grace is the replacement of the heart of stone by a heart of flesh, a replacement beyond the horizon of the heart of stone. Cooperative grace is the heart of flesh becoming effective in good works through human freedom' (ibid.). In his own terminology, suited more to the stage of meaning when the world of interiority becomes the ground of theory, religious conversion is 'other-worldly falling in love. It is total and permanent self-surrender without conditions, qualifications, reservations' (ibid. 240). As such it is 'being in love with God,' which is 'the basic fulfilment of our conscious intentionality. That fulfilment brings a deep-set joy that can remain despite humiliation, failure, privation, pain, betrayal, desertion. That fulfilment brings a radical peace, the peace that the world cannot give. That fulfilment bears fruit in a love of one's neighbor that strives mightily to bring about the kingdom of God on this earth' (ibid. 105).

The experience of this love is that of 'being in love in an unrestricted fashion' and as such is the proper fulfilment of the capacity for self-transcendence revealed in our unre-

stricted questioning. But it is not the product of our knowledge and choice. 'On the contrary, it dismantles and abol-
ishes the horizon in which our knowing and choosing went
on and it sets up a new horizon in which the love of God will
transvalue our values and the eyes of that love will transform
our knowing' (ibid. 106). As conscious but not known, the
experience of this love is an experience of mystery, of the
holy. It belongs to the level of consciousness where deliberation, judgment of value, decision, and free and responsible
activity take place.

> But it is this consciousness as brought to a fulfilment, as
> having undergone a conversion, as possessing a basis that may
> be broadened and deepened and heightened and enriched but
> not superseded, as ready to deliberate and judge and decide
> and act with the easy freedom of those that do all good be-
> cause they are in love. So the gift of God's love occupies the
> ground and root of the fourth and highest level of man's inten-
> tional consciousness. It takes over the peak of the soul, the
> *apex animae* (ibid. 107).

There is a twofold expression of religious conversion.
Spontaneously it is manifested in changed attitudes, for which
Galatians 5.22-23 provides something of a descriptive enumeration: 'The fruit of the Spirit is love, joy, peace, patience,
kindness, goodness, faithfulness, gentleness, self-control.' But
another kind of expression is concerned with the base and
focus of this experience, the *mysterium tremendum et fascinans*
itself. There is an enormous variation to be discovered in the
investigation of such expression, and Lonergan correlates this
variety with the predominant stages of meaning operative in
one's self-understanding and in one's spontaneously assumed
stance toward reality—i.e., with the manner in which one's
world is mediated by meaning. He constructs a series of stages
of meaning based on a cumulative differentiation of consciousness. These stages correspond to the three epochs of histori-

cal Western mind of which we spoke early in this chapter. In the Western tradition there have been three stages of meaning, and they can be ontogenetically reproduced in the life history of a contemporary individual.

The first stage of meaning is governed by a commonsense differentiation of consciousness, or, what amounts to the same thing, by a consciousness which is undifferentiated with respect to theory and interiority. The second stage of meaning is familiar also with theory, system, logic, and science, but is troubled because the difference of these from common sense, while obvious, is not adequately thematized. The third stage is prepared by all those modern philosophies governed by the turn to the subject, which thus take their stand on human interiority. Here consciousness is adequately differentiated into the various realms of meaning—common sense, theory, interiority, transcendence, scholarship, and art—and these realms are consciously related to one another. One consciously moves from one to the other by consciously changing one's procedures.

In all three stages, meaning fulfils four functions. First, it is cognitive in that it mediates the real world in which we live out our lives. Secondly, it is efficient in that it governs our intention of what we do. Thirdly, it is constitutive in that it is an intrinsic component of human cultures and social institutions. And fourthly, it is communicative in that, through its various carriers—spontaneous intersubjectivity, art, symbol, language, and incarnation in the lives and deeds of persons—individual meaning becomes common meaning, and, through the transmission of training and education, generates history. But in the first stage these functions are not clearly recognized and accurately articulated. So the blend of the cognitive and constitutive functions, for example, brings about not only the constitution of cultures and institutions but also the story of the world's origins in myth. And just as the constitutive function of meaning pretends to speculative capacities beyond its genuine range, so the efficient function of meaning pretends to practical powers which a more differentiated consciousness denominates as magic. Religious expression at this stage is a result of the projective association or identification of religious experience with its outward occasion. The focus is on what we would call the spatial, the specific, the external, the human, as contrasted with the temporal, the generic, the internal, the divine. What is indeed temporal, generic, internal, divine is associated with or projected upon what is spatial, specific, external, human, and so there result the gods of the moment, the god of this or that place, of this or that person, of Abraham or Laban, of this or that group, of the Canaanites, the Philistines, the Israelites.

A primitive language has little difficulty in expressing all that can be pointed out or directly perceived or directly represented. But the generic cannot be directly pointed out or perceived or represented. So in Homer there were words for such specific activities as glancing, peering, staring, but no generic word for seeing. Again, in various American languages of the aborigines one cannot simply say that the man is sick; one also has to retail whether he is near or far, whether he can or cannot be seen; and often the form of the sentence will also reveal his place, position, and posture. Again, the temporal cannot be pointed out or directly perceived or represented. Time involves a synthesis of all events in a single continuum of earlier and later. So an early language may have an abundance of tenses but they are found to mean, not a synthesis of temporal relationships, but different kinds of action. Thirdly, the subject and his inner experience lie not on the side of the perceived but on the side of the perceiving. One can point to the whole man or to some part of him, but one cannot point out the pointer. So possessive pronouns develop before personal pronouns, for what one possesses can be pointed out, but oneself as a subject is another story. Again, inner processes of thinking or deliberating are represented in Homer, not as inner processes, but as personalized interchanges. The

Homeric heroes do not think or deliberate; they converse with
a god or goddess, with their horse or with a river, with some
part of themselves such as their heart or their temper. Finally,
the divine is the objective of questioning our questioning. It
cannot be perceived or imagined. But it can be associated with
the object or event, the ritual or the recitation that occasion
religious experience, and so there arise the hierophanies (ibid. 2).

The key to the movement from the first stage of meaning to the second and to the religious development consequent upon this movement is to be located, however, not in
the shift from exteriority, space, the specific, and the human,
to interiority, time, the generic, and the divine, but in the
differentiation of the functions of meaning. The advance of
technique will enable the association of the efficient function
with *poiêsis* and *praxis* and reveal the inefficacy of magic. But
far more important in its implications will be the differentiation of the cognitive function of meaning from the other three
functions. As the key to the religious expression of an undifferentiated consciousness lies in insight into sensible presen-
tations and representations, so the limitations of such consciousness to the spatial, the specific, the external, and the
human will recede to the extent that the sensible presenta-
tions and representations are provided by language itself
(Lonergan 1993, 92). This does not mean, however, that a
self-conscious transposition to interiroity, time, the generic,
and the divine occurs. This must await the emergence of the
third stage of meaning.

The second stage of meaning, then, is characterized by
a twofold mediation of the world by meaning: in the realm of
common sense and in that of theory. This split is troubling. It
was interpreted by Plato in such a way that, at a certain stage
in his thought, there seem to be two really distinct worlds,
the transcendent world of eternal Forms and the transient
world of appearance. In Aristotle, as we have seen, it led to

the distinction, not between theory and common sense, but between necessity and contingence. The basic concepts of science — i.e., universal and necessary knowledge — were metaphysical, and so the sciences were conceived as continuous with philosophy.

The introduction of the theoretical capacity into religious living is represented in the dogmas, theology, and juridical structures of Western religion. But just as the two tables of Eddington — 'the bulky, solid, colored desk at which he worked, and the manifold of colorless "wavicles" so minute that the desk was mostly empty space '(ibid. 84) — reveal the presence of a conflict between common sense and science, so in the realm of religion 'the God of Abraham, Isaac, and Jacob is set against the God of the philosophers and theologians. Honoring the Trinity and feeling compunction are set against learned discourse on the Trinity and against defining compunction. Nor can this contrast be understood or the tension removed within the realms of common sense and of theory' (ibid. 115). So there is demanded a movement to a third stage of meaning, the stage of the differentiation of consciousness through the appropriation of human interiority.

The sciences then come to be regarded, not as prolongations of philosophy, but as autonomous, ongoing processes; not as the demonstration of universal and necessary truths but as hypothetical and ever better approximations to truth through an ever more exact and comprehensive understanding of data. Philosophy is no longer a theory in the manner of science but the self-appropriation of intentional consciousness and the consequent distinguishing, relating, and grounding of the various realms of meaning, the grounding of the methods of the sciences, and the ongoing promotion of their unification. Theology then becomes, in large part, the understanding of the diversity of religious utterance on the basis of the differentiaton and interrelation of the realms of common sense, theory, interiority, and transcendence. Religious experience is understood as correlated with this fourth realm of meaning, the realm of transcendence.

> What I have referred to as the gift of God's love, spontaneously reveals itself in love, joy, peace, patience, kindness, goodness, fidelity, gentleness, and self-control. In undifferentiated consciousness it will express its reference to the transcendent both through sacred objects, places, times and actions, and through the sacred offices of the shaman, the prophet, the lawgiver, the apostle, the priest, the preacher, the monk, the teacher. As consciousness differentiates into the two realms of common sense and theory, it will give rise to special theoretical questions concerning divinity, the order of the universe, the destiny of mankind, and the lot of each individual. When these three realms of common sense, theory, and interiority are differentiated, the self-appropriation of the subject leads not only to the objectification of experiencing, understanding, judging, and deciding, but also of religious experience.

> Quite distinct from these objectifications of the gift of God's love in the realms of common sense and of theory and from the realm of interiority, is the emergence of the gift as itself a differentiated realm. It is this emergence that is cultivated by a life of prayer and self-denial and, when it occurs, it has the twofold effect, first, of withdrawing the subject from the realm of common sense, theory, and other interiority into a 'cloud of unknowing' and then of intensifying, purifying, clarifying, the objectifications referring to the transcendent whether in the realm of common sense, or of theory, or of other interiority (ibid. 266).

3.3.3 Religion as Higher Integration

In *Philosophy of God, and Theology*, religion is called 'the major factor in the integration and development of the person' (Lonergan 1973, 59). Parallel to this claim is the analysis of authentic religion, in the last chapter of *Insight*, as the higher integration of human living acknowledged as necessary at the end of the chapter on ethics. This higher integration is demanded because of the existence of a problem of evil rooted in our inherent incapacity for sustained development, in a moral impotence which is part and parcel of the dynamic structure of human intelligence, reflection, and deliberation. For the sake of completeness, it seems important that we present a summary account of Lonergan's treatment of authentic religion in *Insight*.

Within the context of religious experience, the problem of evil becomes a question of what God is or has been doing about the fact of evil. Within this same context, the evil rooted in the moral impotence of our incapacity for sustained development becomes sin. 'The hopeless tangle of the social surd, of the impotence of common sense, of the endlessly multiplied philosophies, is not merely a *cul-de-sac* for human progress; it is also a reign of sin, a despotism of darkness; and men are its slaves' (Lonergan 1992, 714). The reign of sin is a twofold expectation of sin.

> On a primary level, it is the priority of living to learning how to live, to acquiring the willingness to live rightly, to developing the adaptation that makes right living habitual. On a second level, it is man's awareness of his plight and his self-surrender to it; on each occasion, he could reflect and through reflection avoid sinning; but he cannot bear the burden of perpetual reflection; and long before that burden has mounted to the limit of physical impossibility, he chooses the easy way out. On both the primary and the second levels, there is the transposition of the inner issue into the outer social milieu; concrete situations become infected with the social surd; they are intractable without dialectical analysis; and the intractability is taken as evidence that only in an increasingly limited fashion can intelligence and reasonableness and good will have any real bearing upon the conduct of human affairs. Finally, dialectical analysis can transpose the issue, but it cannot do so effectively. It goes beyond common sense to a critical human science that supposes a correct and accepted philosophy; but

a correct philosophy will be but one of many philosophies,
and precisely because it is correct it will be too complicated to
be commonly accessible and too alien to sinful man to be widely
accepted (ibid. 715).

If the answers to the various forms of the question of
God which arise from questioning our questioning lead to
the affirmation of the existence of an omniscient, omnipotent, completely good God, then this affirmation provides a
further intelligibility to be grasped beyond the intelligibility
of the possibilities of intelligent, reasonable, and good courses
of action, beyond the statistical intelligibility of their frequency, beyond the direct intelligibility of actual good choices
and the inverse intelligibility that grasps that unintelligent,
unreasonable, and sinful courses of acton are unintelligible.
'Because God is omniscient, he knows man's plight. Because
he is omnipotent, he can remedy it. Because he is good, he
wills to do so. The fact of evil is not the whole story' (ibid.
716).

The divine solution to the problem of evil will be one,
universally accessible and permanent, a harmonious continuation of the actual order of this universe (ibid. 718). Since the
problem of evil is a human problem, the solution will be a
solution for human beings, and it will involve the introduction of new habits in our intelligence, willing, and sensitivity
(ibid.). These habits will reverse the priority of our living to
our intellect, will, and sensitivity, by being operative throughout our living (ibid. 719). According to a later formulation,

> It used to be said, *Nihil amatum nisi praecognitum,* Knowl-
> edge precedes love. The truth of this tag is the fact that ordi-
> narily operations on the fourth level of intentional conscious-
> ness presuppose and complement corresponding operations
> on the other three. There is a minor exception to this rule in-
> asmuch as people do fall in love, and that falling in love is
> something disproportionate to its causes, conditions, occasions,

antecedents. For falling in love is a new beginning, an exercise of vertical liberty in which one's world undergoes a new organization. But the major exception to the Latin tag is God's gift of his love flooding our hearts. Then we are in the dynamic state of being in love. But who it is we love, is neither given nor as yet understood. Our capacity for moral self-transcendence has found a fulfilment that brings deep joy and profound peace. Our love reveals to us values we had not appreciated, values of prayer and worship, or repentance and belief. But if we would know what is going on within us, if we would learn to integrate it with the rest of our living, we have to inquire, investigate, seek counsel. So it is that in religious matters love precedes knowledge and, as that love is God's gift, the very beginning of faith is due to God's grace (Lonergan 1993, 122-23).

So it is that the new habits introduced are in some sense transcendent or supernatural. 'They are not the result of accumulated insights, for such accumulation takes time, and the problem arises because man has to live during the interval in which insights are being accumulated' (Lonergan 1992, 719).

The new habits, nonetheless, are a harmonious continuation of a universe so ordered that successive higher integrations emerge to systematize otherwise coincidental manifolds on lower levels. In this way, the new habits constitute a new and higher integration of human living, unifying and consolidating otherwise coincidental elements (ibid.). The universe into which these habits are introduced develops from the lower static systems known by physics and chemistry to the higher dynamic systems known in biology, sensitive psychology, and cognitional theory or intentionality analysis, and so these new habits pertain not to static system but to system on the move. They 'have to meet a problem that varies as man develops and declines, and so they too must be capable of some development and adaptation' (ibid.).

All higher integrations within the actual order of the universe leave intact the laws of the underlying manifolds which they integrate. Consequently, the new habits or forms introduced into human subjectivity to meet the problem of evil 'will come to men through their apprehension and with their consent' (ibid. 720). The intelligibility of the emergence of the solution to the problem of evil and the intelligibility of its propagation, furthermore, will be statistical intelligibilities, and the relevant probabilities to be understood are those 'that regard the occurrence of man's intelligent and rational apprehension of the solution and his free and responsible consent to it' (ibid.). Thus a distinction must be drawn between 'the realization of the full solution and, on the other hand, the emergent trend in which the full solution becomes effectively probable' (ibid.).

According to the formulation of *Insight*, with which Lonergan's later appeal to Romans 5.5 is in complete continuity, the solution to the problem is further determined by stating that 'the appropriate willingness will be some type or species of charity'(ibid.); a 'love of God that is prompted not by a hope of one's own advantage but simply by God's goodness' (ibid.); a love of God that reaches for harmony with the order of the universe which, apart from the surd of sin, is in love with God (ibid. 721); a love that wills every other good because of the order of the universe, the order of the universe because of the love of God (ibid.), and the good of all persons in the universe because of the love of God (ibid.); a love that adopts the dialectical attitude of meeting evil with good, of loving one's enemies, of praying for those who persecute and calumniate one, and so makes of the social surd a potential good through a self-sacrificing love that matches the dialectical method of intelligence grasping the absurdity of evil and refusing to systematize and perpetuate it by treating it as intelligible (ibid. 721-22); a love that repents of former blindness and involvement in individual, group, and general bias, of past flights from selfknowledge, rationalizations of wrong, surrender to evil and commitment to error, and that repents not by feelings of guilt but by acts of will informed by understanding and reasonableness (ibid. 722); a love whose repentance, then, takes the form of sorrow flowing from a personal relation to the one with whom one is in love (ibid.); a love, finally, which, while repentant over the past and self-sacrificing as it looks to the future, is at one with the universe in its love of God and so joyfully shares a 'dynamic resilience and expectancy' which rises above past achievement, urges generic potential forward to specific perfection, meets evil with good, wills with the dynamic joy and zeal of the order of the universe (ibid.).

Besides this love which makes one's willing good, the solution to the problem of evil will involve the introduction of a hope through which one's willing makes one's intelligence good by a deliberate decision to overrule the competition of attached and interested sensitive and intersubjective desire with the intention of being and truth which is the pure desire to know. The objective of the desire to know is the knowledge of God, and the deliberate decision to take issue with conflicting tendencies will be a decision against both 'the hopelessness that allows man's spirit to surrender the legitimate aspirations of the unrestricted desire and to seek comfort in the all too human ambitions of the Kantian and the positivist' (ibid. 723), and the presumption which would locate the conditions for the achievement of the objective of the pure desire to know, not in God but in ourselves. The hope introduced by being in love with God is confident that 'God will bring man's intellect to a knowledge, participation, possession of the unrestricted act of understanding' (ibid. 724).

Nonetheless, hope's assurance and love's motivation rest also on present knowledge. The solution to the problem of evil calls, then, for a present, 'universally accessible and permanently effective manner of pulling men's minds out of the counterpositions, of fixing them in the positions, of securing for them certitude that God exists and that he has provided a solution which they are to acknowledge and to accept' (ibid.). This knowledge, though, has no probability of being immanently generated because the root of the problem of evil lies in the very structure of human intentionality. But there may be an attainment of truth both possible and probable through the communication of reliable knowledge and its reception in belief (ibid. 725).

What, then, is believing? Belief is the reception of reliably communicated knowledge. The general context of belief is 'the collaboration of mankind in the advancement and the dissemination of knowledge' (ibid.), a collaboration in which men contribute to a common fund of knowledge in virtue of their own experience, understanding, and judgment, but also receive from this fund in a manner other than that which informs their contribution. Collaboration in the advancement and dissemination of knowledge is inevitable.

> Our senses are limited to an extremely narrow strip of space-time, and unless we are ready to rely on the senses of others, we must leave blank all other places and times or, as is more likely, fill them with our conjectures and then explain our conjectures with myths. Again, the personal contribution of any individual to the advance of human understanding is never large. We may be astounded by men of genius; but the way for their discoveries was prepared by many others in a long succession; and if they took enormous strides, commonly it was because the logic of their circumstances left them no opportunity to take shorter ones. But without collaboration each successive generation, instead of beginning where its predecessor left off, would have to begin at the very beginning and so could never advance beyond the most rudimentary of primitive levels (ibid. 726).

Collaboration, moreover, is not only inevitable but also cumulative. As a result, 'the mentality of any individual becomes a composite product in which it is impossible to separate immanently generated knowledge and belief' (ibid. 727). In fact there are not many items of immanently generated knowledge totally independent of beliefs. 'One does not simply know that England is an island. Neither does one merely believe it. Perhaps no one has immanently generated knowledge that general relativity is more accurate than Newtonian theory on the perihelion of Mercury. But it does not follow that for everyone it is purely a matter of belief.'[22] While the consequence of collaboration in the pursuit of truth is a symbiosis of knowledge and belief, its alternative is a necessarily primitive ignorance.

> The development of the human mind is by the self-correcting process of learning, and in that process personal knowledge and belief practice an unrelenting symbiosis. The broadening of individual experience includes hearing the opinions and convictions of others. The deepening of individual understanding includes the exploration of many viewpoints. The formation of individual judgment is a process of differentiation, clarification, and revision, in which the shock of contradictory judgments is as relevant as one's own observation and memory, one's own intelligent inquiry and critical reflection. So each of us advances from the nescience of infancy to the fixed mentality of old age, and however large and determinate the contributions of belief to the shaping of our minds, still every belief and all its implications have been submitted to the endlessly repeated, if unnoticed, test of fresh experiences, of further questions and new insights, of clarifying and qualifying revisions of judgment (ibid.).

There are five stages to the typical process of true belief: '(1) preliminary judgments on the value of belief in gen-

---

22. Ibid. 728. 1993 note: The reference to England is an allusion to Newman's example, but, as the editorial note in the 1992 edition of *Insight* states, Newman was more accurate: Great Britain, not England, is an island.

eral, on the reliability of the source for this belief, and on the accuracy of the communication from the source, (2) a reflective act of understanding that, in virtue of the preliminary judgments, grasps as virtually unconditioned the value of deciding to believe some particular proposition, (3) the consequent judgment of value, (4) the consequent decision of the will, and (5) the assent that is the act of believing' (ibid. 729-30).

Nonetheless, any belief is only as intelligent and reasonable as is human collaboration in the advancement and dissemination of knowledge. There are not only intelligent and reasonable beliefs, but also mistaken beliefs, and they are rooted in 'the scotosis of the dramatic subject, in the individual, group, and general bias of the practical subject, in the counterpositions of philosophy, and in their ethical implications and consequences' (ibid. 735). They are conditioned by the proximity of their relevant fields of data to the very stuff of human living.

> In belief as in personal thought and judgment, men go wrong when they have to understand and to judge either themselves or other things in relation to themselves. The serenity and surefootedness of the mathematician, the physicist, the chemist, are not independent of the remoteness of these fields from human living ... On the other hand, when it comes to the study of life, of the psychological depths, of human institutions, of the history of nations, cultures, and religions, then diversity multiplies, differences become irreconcilable, and the name of science can be invoked with plausibility only by introducing methodological conventions that exclude from scientific consideration the heart of the matter. The life of man on earth lies under the shadow of a problem of evil; the evil invades his mind; and as it diverts his immanently generated knowledge, so also it distorts his beliefs (ibid. 735-36).

As important, then, as an analysis of the process of belief is an understanding of what is involved in a critique of mistaken beliefs.

> ... learning one's errors is but a particular case of learning. It takes as its starting point and clue the discovery of some precise issue on which undoubtedly one was mistaken. It advances by inquiring into the sources that may have contributed to that error and, perhaps, contributed to other errors as well. It asks about the motives and the supporting judgments that, as they once confirmed one in that error, may still be holding one in others. It investigates the consequences of the view one now rejects, and it seeks to determine whether or not they too are to be rejected. The process is cumulative. The discovery of one error is exploited to lead to the discovery of others; and the discovery of the others provides a still larger base to proceed to the discovery of still more. Moreover, this cumulative process not only takes advantage of the mind's native process of learning, in which one insight leads on to other insights that open the way to still further insights, but it also exploits the insistence of rational consciousness on consistency; for just as our love of consistency, once we hae made one mistake, leads us to make others, so the same love of consistency leads us to reject other mistakes when one is rejected, and at the same time it provides us with abundant clues for finding the others that are to be rejected (ibid. 736).

There is nothing unintelligent or unreasonable or irresponsible, then, about believing, nor is the correction of mistaken beliefs to be regarded as either impossible or as evidence for the futility of all belief. There is, then, no contradiction with the actual order of the universe implied in affirming that the knowledge underlying hope's assurance and love's motivation in the divine solution to the problem of evil will be some kind of belief. Furthermore, the solution as cognitively informed by belief will involve 'a new and higher collaboration of men in the pursuit of truth ... because the solution is a harmonious continuation of the actual order, it too will be a collaboration that involves belief, truthfulness, accuracy, and immanently generated knowledge. Again, because the solution is a higher integration, it will be a new and higher collaboration. Finally, because the solution meets a problem of error and sin, the new and higher collaboration in the pursuit of truth will provide an antidote to the errors to which man is inclined' (ibid. 740-41).

This new and higher collaboration will not simply be one of people with one another but fundamentally a collaboration of human beings with God in working out the solution to our problem of evil. One's entrance into this higher collaboration and one's participation in its fruits will be through faith, through a transcendent belief which 'makes a man a participant in the new and higher collaboration in which God is the initiator and the principal agent.' (ibid. 741). This faith will be 'an assent of intellect to truths transmitted through the collaboration, and it will be motivated by man's reliance on the truthfulness of God' (ibid. 742). It will include 'an affirmation of man's spiritual nature, of his freedom, responsibility, and sinfulness, of God's existence and nature, and of the transcendent solution God provides for man's problem of evil' (ibid.). Intelligent and reasonable participation in the new and higher collaboration will entail an acknowledgment of the problem of evil; of our inability to cope with this problem; of God's ability to provide a solution and God's goodness in exercising that ability; of an emergent trend and a full realization in human history of a solution to the problem of evil; of the value of assenting to the new and higher collaboration; and of the wisdom of deciding to join that collaboration, by making known to others the good news of the solution, by seeing that it is transmitted from one generation to the next, by helping to recast the expression of the solution so that it can be understood by people of different places, times, classes, and cultures, or by attempting to conceive and express the solution in terms of the transcendental infrastructure of human subjectivity, or by announcing in concrete and successive situations of individuals, classes, nations, and the world the relevance and effectiveness of the divinely initiated solution to the problem of evil (ibid. 743).

As the divinely originated solution to the problem of evil leaves our freedom intact, even our collaboration in its execution will be marked by deficiencies and failures of human origin. But these aberrations will not eliminate the solution, for the solution is the work not of ourselves but of God (ibid. 743-44).

As the humanity for which evil is a problem is not only capable of intelligence and willing but also endowed with a consciousness which, in the main, flows in dramatic and practical patterns of experience, the solution to the problem of evil not only will involve the introduction of faith and hope and love into our intelligence, reasonableness, and willing, but also must penetrate to human sensitivity and inter-subjectivity through images and symbols.

> … inasmuch as intelligence and reasonableness and will issue into human words matched with deeds, they need at their disposal images so charged with affects that they succeed both in guiding and in propelling action. Again, besides the image that is a sign of intelligible and rational contents and the image that is a psychic force, there is the image that symbolizes man's orientation into the known unknown; and since faith gives more truth than understanding comprehends, since hope reinforces the detached, disinterested, unrestricted desire to know, man's sensitivity needs symbols that unlock its transforming dynamism and bring it into harmony with the vast but impalpable pressures of the pure desire, of hope, and of self-sacrificing charity (ibid. 744).

The newness of God's solution to the problem of evil will thus be that of 'a mystery that is at once symbol of the uncomprehended and sign of what is grasped and psychic force that sweeps living human bodies, linked in charity, to the joyful, courageous, wholehearted, yet intelligently controlled performance of the tasks set by a world order in which the problem of evil is not suppressed but transcended' (ibid. 745). The mystery that is demanded must be a matter, not of fiction but of fact, not of story but of history, for the problem of evil is a fact to be found in our living within the actual order of the universe. But it will also have a nature and content and meaning and power of its own, for it will introduce a new level on which human living develops and rejoices (ibid.). While every solution which introduces a new and higher integration into human living may be called transcendent, while every solution which is constituted by a faith and hope and love that look primarily to God will be religious, to the extent that the solution goes beyond these minimal demands, it will reveal to faith 'truths that man never could discover for himself nor, even when he assented to them, could he understand them in an adequate fashion' (ibid. 746). If the solution to the problem of evil is one, finally, whose sole ground and measure is God, if consequently faith includes objects inaccessible to any finite understanding, if hope is for a vision of God that exhausts our unrestricted desire to know, if love is 'the transport, the ecstasy and unbounded intimacy that result from the communication of the absolute love that is God himself and alone can respond to the vision of God' (ibid. 747), then the divinely originated solution to our problem of evil is to be understood not simply as in some sense transcendent, but as absolutely supernatural, as absolutely disproportionate to the capacities of human nature, human reason, human good will, human esteem. If that is the case, the tension which always accompanies the integration of otherwise coincidental manifolds by some higher order will be in this instance significantly heightened.

> ... the supernatural solution involves a transcendence of
> humanism, and the imperfect realization of the supernatural
> solution is apt to oscillate between an emphasis on the super-
> natural and an emphasis on the solution. Imperfect faith can
> insist on believing to the neglect of the understanding that
> makes faith an effective factor in human living and human
> history; and an even less perfect faith can endanger the gen-
> eral collaboration in its hurry to show forth its social and cul-
> tural fruits. Imperfect hope can so expect the New Jerusalem
> as to oppose any foretaste of intellectual bliss and union in
> this life; and an even less perfect hope can forget that a super-
> natural solution involves a real displacement of the center of
> human concerns. Imperfect charity lacks the resources needed
> to combine both true loving and the true transformation of
> loving. It can be absorbed in the union of the family, in the
> intersubjectivity of comrades in work and in adventure, in the
> common cause of fellows in nationality and in citizenship, in
> the common aspiration of associates in scientific, cultural, and
> humanitarian pursuits. On the other hand, it can withdraw
> from home and country, from human cares and human ambi-
> tions, from the clamor of the senses and the entanglement of
> the social surd, to fix its gaze upon the unseen ultimate, to
> respond to an impalpable presence, to grow inwardly to the
> stature of eternity. But imperfect charity, inasmuch as it is
> imperfect, will not realize at once the opposed facets of its
> perfection; if it is in the world, it ever risks being of the world;
> and if it withdraws from the world, the human basis of its
> ascent to God risks a contraction and an atrophy (ibid. 748-49).

This heightened tension will find its objectification in the dialectical succession of human situations:

> ... there will be a humanism in revolt against the prof-
> fered supernatural solution. It will ignore the problem of evil;
> it will contest the fact of a solution; it will condemn mystery as
> myth; it will demand reason and exclude faith; it will repudi-
> ate hope and labor passionately to build the city of man with
> the hands of man; it will be ready to love God in song and
> dance, in human feasting and human sorrow, with human in-
> telligence and human good will, but only so. For a time, it
> may base its case upon the shortcomings of those that profess

the solution but live it imperfectly or intermittently or not at all. But this incidental argument sooner or later will give place to its real basis. For it rests on man's proud content to be just a man, and its tragedy is that, on the present supposition of a supernatural solution, to be just a man is what man cannot be. If he would be truly a man, he would submit to the unrestricted desire and discover the problem of evil and affirm the existence of a solution and accept the solution that exists. But if he would be only a man, he has to be less. He has to forsake the openness of the pure desire; he has to take refuge in the counterpositions; he has to develop what counterphilosophies he can to save his dwindling humanism from further losses; and there will not be lacking men clear-sighted enough to grasp that the issue is between God and man, logical enough to grant that intelligence and reason are orientated towards God, ruthless enough to summon to their aid the dark forces of passion and of violence (ibid. 749-50).

4 The Existential Subject as Psychic

I have already called attention to a significant transposition in Lonergan's location of the psyche within the transcendental infrastructure of human subjectivity. In *Insight*, the psyche 'reaches the wealth and fulness of its apprehensions and responses under the higher integration of human intelligence' (ibid. 747). In *Method in Theology*, both human intelligence and the psyche are sublated and unified by the deliberations of the authentic existential subject. The key to this change, as I have emphasized, is the emergence of the good as a distinct notion from the intelligent and reasonable. Mediating between judgments of fact and judgments concerning what is good and worth while is the apprehension of potential values and satisfactions in feelings. And feelings are said to be symbolically certifiable. The psyche, then, is a constituent feature of the deciding, deliberating, evaluating existential subject. The wealth and fullness of its apprehensions and responses are reached, not under the higher integration of human intelligence, but in the free and responsible decisions of the authentic existential subject.

The stage has been set, then, for arguing that the self-appropriation of intentional consciousness in method can be complemented by and include psychic self-appropriation, and that this psychic self-appropriation is a further refinement of the self-knowledge of the existential subject. In addition to the mediation of immediacy by meaning which occurs when one objectifies cognitional process, there is that which occurs when one discovers, identifies, accepts one's submerged feelings in psychotherapy (Lonergan 1993, 77). Self-appropriation and the mediation of immediacy or of the transcendental infrastructure of human subjectivity are one and the same process. Cognitional self-appropriation satisfies a critical-methodological exigence awakened by the scientific revolution and by the anthropological turn in modern philosophy. Psychic self-appropriation satisfies a further and complementary exigence, a therapeutic exigence, awakened by the crises of personal and political living that are reflected in psychoanalysis, Marxism, and existentialism. Furthermore, as Lonergan has developed the structure of method based on the mediation of intentionality, so I wish to begin to detail the potential methodological complement afforded by the mediation of psyche within the context provided by Lonergan. It will be my contention that intentionality analysis, as articulated in a pattern of judgments concerning cognitional fact, moral being, and religious experience, can be complemented by a psychic conversion which can critically ground one's moral and religious living in an expanding concrete pattern of judgments of value and one's sublation of an intellectually converted critical consciousness by moral and religious consciousness. Through this greater concreteness on the side of the subject, theology can come closer to accepting the possibilities which now, perhaps for the first time in its history as a systematic discipline, are available to it. For in our age not only are we confronted with the relativity of systematic conceptual schemes of all kinds, in every area, but also, precisely because of this seemingly very uncertain and ambivalent state of affairs, the individual is given

> ... the (often desperate, yet maximally human) opportunity to interpret life and experiencing directly. The historical crossroads of such a time is: either the reimposition of certain set values and schemes, or a task never before attempted: to learn how, in a rational way, to relate concepts to direct experiencing; to investigate the way in which symbolizing affects and is affected by felt experiencing; to devise a social and scientific vocabulary that can interact with experiencing, so that communication about it becomes possible, so that schemes can be considered in relation to experiential meanings, and so that an objective science can be related to and guided by experiencing (Gendlin 1962, 4).

What Eugene Gendlin here envisions for 'objective science' and particularly for human science can also be the goal of theology and is, in fact, the impetus to all contemporary creative theological endeavor, including the revolution in theological foundations proposed by Lonergan. For, according to the dynamic operative in Lonergan's articulation of theological foundations, as we shall see, the foundational reality of all theological endeavor is the subjectivity of the theologian. Lonergan has articulated foundational reality in terms of religious, moral, and intellectual conversion. Our articulation would develop and refine still further this formulation: theological foundations lie in the objectification of cognitive, psychic, moral, and religious subjectivity in a patterned set of judgments of cognitional fact and of value cumulatively heading toward the full position on the human subject.

It is my contention that our age marks the begining of a qualitative mutation in the evolution of human consciousness, one sign of which is that we can now, for the first time in history, speak of such an evolution in more than purely descriptive terms. More specifically, I would say we are moving into the third major epoch in the history of human consciousness. We have already seen that Lonergan presents us with a very illuminating understanding of this evolution in terms of stages of meaning. A complementary understanding of psychic evolution in terms of the relations between intentionality and the psyche can also be developed, and I shall try to present here some few of its features. I will find these two accounts parallel and complementary. Each is an explanation and at the same time a self-conscious foundation of the understanding of further human development. It is in terms of this evolution that the emerging relations between philosophy, depth psychology, and theology are to be understood. I fully accept Lonergan's statement that, 'once philosophy becomes existential and historical, once it asks about man, not in the abstract, not as he would be in some state of pure nature, but as in fact he is here and now in all the concreteness of his living and dying, the very possibility of the old distinction between philosophy and theology vanishes' (Lonergan 1988, 245). This distinction was characteristic of the second stage in human conscious evolution, that of the emergence of *logos* from *mythos*, and will vanish from the scene as we move more and more into the third, that of the emergence of method from logic. In addition, however, this same movement to a third stage of meaning, founded as it is in the self-appropriation of human interiority, calls for a self-conscious return to mythopoetic imagination through depth psychology. For the self-appropriation of human interiority is not coincident with the self-appropriation of cognitional process. This is especially obvious from the primacy of the existential in the writings of the 'later Lonergan.' Method itself, then, in the person of the self-appropriating subject, can participate in the depth-psychological effort at disengaging the symbolic constitutive structure-in-process of human experience. The objectification of the movement of human interiority in a patterned set of judgments of cognitional fact and of value will provide theological foundations and foundations of human science in the third epoch of human conscious evolution. These foundations will serve not only for systematic theology but also for a more all-embracing dialectically informed discipline which we might call an evaluative cultural hermeneutic. This discipline would derive its data from everything that enters or has entered into the consciousness or the life of human beings. Aside from this, there are no data. This unified, though variegated, field of data, insofar as it serves as the material for the objectification of the self-appropriation of human interiority, is what leads me to encourage and perhaps to try to hasten a bit the emerging unity-indifferentiation of philosophy, depth psychology, and theology. A methodically exigent consciousness can now engage in the differentiation and appropriation of the psychic bases of human experience. It is from such a perspective that the present work is undertaken. What happens when self-appropriating subjectivity, carefully tutored by Lonergan's intentionality analysis, becomes psychically self-appropriating subjectivity? What effect does it have for theology and for human science when one attentively, intelligently, reasonably, and responsibly extends the self-appropriation of human interiority and thus of the unified field of data for thoughtful reflection? These questions are primary in the pages which follow. At this point, I am able to treat them only methodologically. I am not yet prepared to write a phenomenology of the psyche, and it may be that each person has to write his or her own. Nonetheless, by pointing to the emerging unity-indifferentiation of philosophy, depth psychology, and theology through the objectification of the transcendental infrastructure of human subjectivity, I wish also to signal the future sublation into method of the psychotherapeutic phenomenon in a new constitution and control of meaning through a self-conscious and critically retrieved transcendental aesthetic. Psychotherapy as we have known it is clearly a transitional stage, not only in the lives of individuals but also in the evolution of Western culture. It must be relativized, not only by method, but also by the 'soul beyond psychology,' the soul in dialogue and concert with the God of love, the soul that is the life to which both method in its entirety and psychotherapy in particular point and which both method and psychotherapy mediate in a new way. Depth psychology leads beyond itself. It is an intermediary between the ages; it can lead to a creative life that can be lived only beyond itself; it initiates a process of self-knowledge which will continue to feed this life, but the life itself will turn from the 'treadmill of self-conscious analysis' (Progoff 1973a, 258) to the arenas of love and strife that are the human habitat. It achieves its fulfilment only beyond itself in the existential subjectivity of self-transcending men and women in love with the earth and with its origin and destiny.

The theologian Ernst Fuchs has said that what the essential word or authentic language does is to announce what it is time for. It cannot give a direct guarantee of itself, that it is essential or authentic. It can only determine the situation anew by calling a new world into being, the world waiting to be born (see Funk 1966, 55). From such a perspective, nobody has contributed to the essential word for our age with greater precision and finality than Lonergan. I find the poetic description of Heidegger applicable: 'The thought of being guards the Word and fulfills its function in such guardianship, namely care for the use of language. Out of long guarded speechlessness and the careful clarification of the field thus cleared, comes the utterance of the thinker.'[23] In announcing the exigence of our time as the exigence for the differentiation and appropriation of human interiority, Lonergan has announced what it is time for. The only guarantee of the authenticity of his word has come from heeding his invitation. Such acceptance has slowly, so slowly, made his essential word public, a ground of unity for a gradually growing community.

Only against this background can I speak of the potential complementary effect of depth psychology with respect to intentionality analysis. John Dunne speaks of climbing a mountain in order to discover a vantage point, a fastness of autonomy. The most complete autonomy comes, he says, from the knowledge, not of external things, but of knowledge itself.

> A knowing of knowing would be like a view from a mountaintop. By knowing all about knowing itself one would know in some manner everything there is to know. It would be like seeing everything from a great height. One would see everything near and far, all the way to the horizon, but there would be some loss of detail on account of the distances. The knowing of knowing would mean being in possession of all the various methods of knowing. It would mean knowing how an artist thinks, putting a thing together; knowing how a scientist thinks, taking a thing apart; knowing how a practical man thinks, sizing up a situation; knowing how a man of understanding thinks, grasping the principle of a thing; knowing how a man of wisdom thinks, reflecting upon human experience ...
>
> At the top of the mountain, as we have been describing it, there is a kind of madness—not the madness that consists in having lost one's reason, but a madness that consists in hav-

---

23. Ibid., quoting from Heidegger's 'What is Metaphysics?'

ing lost everything except one's reason. The knowing of knowing, to be sure, seems worthy of God and worthy of man. The only thing wrong is that man at the top of the mountain, by escaping from love and war, will have lost everything else. He will have withdrawn into that element of his nature which is most characteristic of him and sets him apart from other animals. It is the thing in him which is most human. Perhaps he will never realize what it is to be human unless he does attempt this withdrawal. Even so, the realization that he has lost everything except his reason, that he has found pure humanity but not full humanity, changes his wisdom from a knowledge of knowledge into a knowledge of ignorance. He realizes that he has something yet to learn, something that he cannot learn at the top of the mountain but only at the bottom of the valley (Dunne 1972, 17-19).

While Dunne's description would seem far more applicable to Hegel than to Lonergan, nonetheless nobody familiar with Lonergan can read these words without thinking of one of the most daring claims any thinker has ever offered for one's own work, true as it is: 'Thoroughly understand what it is to understand, and not only will you understand the broad lines of all there is to be understood but also you will possess a fixed base, an invariant pattern, opening upon all further developements of understanding' (Lonergan 1992, 22). There is too, however, a difference, in that the understanding of understanding is not the same thing as the knowing of knowing. Understanding is much more tied to imagination than knowing. One can understand without knowing, without understanding correctly, without achieving cognitional self-transcendence. While the true understanding of understanding would be a knowing of knowing, the thorough understanding of understanding would not entail the kind of 'madness' of which Dunne speaks, for it would also include an understanding of the essential dynamics of the flight from understanding, of the desire not to know, of life at the bottom of the valley.

Still, to allow one's knowledge of knowledge to be changed into a knowledge of ignorance may well involve the realization that there are many things in heaven and on earth that are not *dreamed* of in one's philosophy. It may then lead to the grasp that much of this life in the valley enters into one's life without being consciously objectified and appropriated, without providing data for one's knowing of knowing, without formally coming to light in even the most thoroughgoing intentionality analysis. One may discover a dark yet potentially creative and beneficial power at work in the valley and expend one's efforts by means of a different kind of withdrawal or introversion—into a forest or desert, in imitation of Gotama or Jesus, rather than up to a mountaintop—at appropriating, befriending, and to a certain extent transforming this dark power of nature so that it is not only creative of life but also originative of value. If one succeeds in this very risky adventure, one will have undergone a profound conversion.

The relocation of the psychic in Lonergan's recent explorations of value marks, if you will, a return from the mountaintop of cognitional analysis to the valley in which the existential subject decides for oneself what one is to make of oneself. And our task is that of articulating the integration of psychic energy into the thrust of conscious intentionality toward the love of God. There is a psychic energy manifested in the pure question of the transcendental infrastructure of the subject-as-subject. The articulation of its integration into the thrust of intentionality toward authentic religious living is a problem of mammoth proportions. That the articulation is possible is suggested by the many references of Jung to the God archetype or God image in the psyche. That Jung achieved a successful articulation of the relationship between psyche and intentionality is questionable. The problem lay, not in his knowledge of the psyche but in his understanding of intentionality. It is that problem alone which I hope to rectify in the present work, by presenting what I believe is a more adequate methodological framework for such depth-psychological articulation. The actual articulation of the integration of psyche into method must be done in another work.

The principal methodological contribution I intend in this work speaks of psychic conversion. Conversion is the central theme in Lonergan's recasting of the foundations of theology. While Lonergan speaks of intellectual, moral, and religious conversion, what I will propose is something different from these. Essentially it is the gaining of a critically and methodically mediated capacity attentively, intelligently, reasonably, and responsibly to disengage the symbolic constitution of the feelings in which values are apprehended and to live from that disengagement. As I shall argue in chapter 6, it figures in theological foundations as facilitating the sublation of intellectual conversion by moral and religious conversion.

I share the conviction of Dunne that something like a new religion is coming, must come, into being, and with Dunne I think of its genesis as largely a process of imaginative 'passing over' from one's own culture to others, from one's way of life to others, from one's own religion to others, and as a matter of coming back to one's own culture, one's own way of life, one's own religion, with new insight and creativity (Dunne 1972, ix). It seems to me that this adventure is happening by reason of something like a psychic law. But I believe that the contemporary age is in need of criteria for evaluating these experiments with truth, and that the criteria are to be discovered in method as the mediation of the transcendental infrastructure of human intentionality. The conversion I call psychic, when integrated into intentionality analysis, might further enable the subject to set forth on other adventures and to articulate the truth one discovers. It might free the subject, in a phrase Dunne appropriates from Goethe, to turn poetry into truth and truth into poetry. The latter poetry would feature in the theology appropriate to our age. The symbolic consciousness mediated by the psychic self-appropriation of the existential subject will render possible the critical use of poetic categories in systematic theology. Though poetic, these categories would be—perhaps contrary to the expectations of method untempered by the psychic journey—explanatory, because generated by heeding the exigence for the appropriation of interiority.

I have been convinced for quite some time that practically all of the criticism levelled at Lonergan's work, at least as reflected in *Insight*, results from a failure to realize and accept what Lonergan himself articulated concerning *Insight* at the 1970 International Congress on his work: 'My purpose was not a study of human life but a study of human understanding' (Lonergan 1972b, 310). More recently, however, I have wondered whether some of the enthusiasm inspired by this philosophical monument may not suffer from the same oversight. As the prolific and provocative Jungian analyst James Hillman has said in a completely different context and with no reference to Lonergan: 'The discrimination of spirit is not at all of the same order as the cultivation of soul. If the first is active mind in its broadest sense, the second is the realm of the imaginal, equally embracing, but very different' (Hillman 1973, 116). This distinction escapes too much of the current comment on Lonergan, I fear, whether this comment be favorable or adverse.

If the appropriation of cognitional process is not coextensive with the mediation of the transcendental infrastructure of human subjectivity in method, new vistas are opened for those who have already accepted Lonergan's invitation and found it rewarding. The reward is not without its price, but it is important that this price not be one exacted by an oversight of the cultivation of the imaginal, especially if this latter cultivation can be brought to figure in the self-appropriation of the existential subject.

We may, I believe, characterize the intellectual journey guided by Lonergan as an appropriation of the *logos* principle. We might perhaps understand it archetypally in Jungian terms as an appropriation of *animus*, thus correcting what I believe to be a mistaken assumption that *animus* is to be thought of only in contrasexual terms. If some Jungians are now abandoning the notion of *anima* as exclusively contrasexual,[24] the same revision of a mistaken assumption will probably follow in due time with respect to *animus*. Archetypally, *animus* is masculine, *anima* feminine: from this it by no means follows that they are to be understood only contrasexually. Hillman already seems to suggest as much: 'Animus refers to spirit, to logos, word, idea, intellect, principle, abstraction, meaning, *ratio, nous*' (ibid. 116). If this is the case, Lonergan's invitation is clearly to the discrimination and appropriation of *animus*.

On the other hand, Hillman redefines *anima* as 'archetype of psyche' (ibid. 120). Then it would be the case that those who have gone the route of intentionality analysis might be able to demonstrate that the appropriation of *animus* is a very good beginning of the appropriation of interiority. Like any beginning, it must at the right moment give way to the next steps, while not repudiating the beginning. It is from this perspective that I offer my suggestion that the appropriation of psyche will aid the emergence of the authentic existential subject in Lonergan's sense. The eventual outcome would be something like a unity of opposites, of *animus* and *anima*, a *coniunctio* of the basic principles of being human, of

---

24. This is one of the central points in Hillman's article.

the archetypal masculine and the archetypal feminine, of *logos* and psyche or *mythos*. As *animus* needs *anima*, so intentionality analysis needs psychic analysis. The discrimination of spirit must be complemented by the cultivaton of soul and finally by the surrender of both spirit and soul in authentic religion. In the final moment of surrender, too little understood in psychotherapeutic circles, one finds the soul beyond psychology in the return to life from the treadmill of self-conscious analysis.

Gilbert Durand has stated that at some fateful moment 'Western man' made a radical option not to remain feminine (Durand 1971, 94). Archetypally, this was an option for *animus* rather than for *anima*, for spirit, *logos*, word, idea, intellect, principle, abstraction, meaning, *ratio*, *nous*, rather than for psyche, *mythos*, image, symbol, atmosphere, feeling, relation, earth, nature, rhythm. This option has given rise to what we have come to know as Western civilization. The archetypal significance of Lonergan's achievement, then, would be that, for the first time in the history of the unfolding of this radical option, the very structure of the option itself is laid bare and rendered capable of appropriation by those who have succeeded its makers. But today there would seem to be a cultural exigence, manifested throughout the Western world, to retrieve the option not taken at our origins. In most instances, this exigence is being responded to blindly, on the basis of a repudiation of the option that is our heritage. The cultural significance of Lonergan's achievement, then, at least from this archetypal point of view, is that the appropriation to which he invites us also renders possible a heeding of this new cultural exigence for the retrieval of *anima*, a heeding that is not blind, that does not involve a repudiation of our archtypally masculine heritage, that is attentive, intelligent, reasonable, and responsibly discriminating. Might it not be that this is the meaning of the recent shift in the writings of

Lonergan to an atmosphere more permeated by an acknowledgement of feeling, symbol, love, the heart? And then, furthermore, the meaning of Lonergan's achievement for psychotherapy becomes clear. For the psychotherapeutic movement has been in the vanguard of this retrieval of psyche, but without, in many instances, an adequate appropriation of *animus*, without a satisfactory appreciation of intentionality, without a correct cognitional theory, and thus without a consistent account of the relationship between psychotherapy and human knowledge, morality, and religion. Psychic exploration without method can lead to the romantic agony; but method needs to be complemented by psyche. The twofold appropriation of intentionality and psyche is what can enable the coming-to-pass of a fully awake naivete of the twice-born adult which Paul Ricoeur calls a second, post-critical naiveté (Ricoeur 1970, 496). The articulate utterance of such an adult would constitute, in part, a transcendental aesthetic, a poetics of the will, a 'transformation of intentionality into kerygma, manifestation, proclamation' (ibid.).

What follows, then, is a methodological argument for reestablishing what Gilbert Durand has called 'the scandal of spiritual concretism' (Durand 1971, 87). To the present, our most reliable source of data and locus of verification for the argument is depth psychology, and, with qualifications, in particular that inspired by Jung. But this psychology becomes a source of data and locus of verification, not when it is merely studied as another theory, but only when it is heeded as a personal invitation to travel paths just as labyrinthine as those along which Lonergan guides us, as an invitation into the forest or desert after the ascent of the mountain but on the way back to the homeland of one's own life. With specific reference to theology, we might say that, just as Lonergan could frame his new context for theology only after having come to understand what it is to understand, so the signifi-

cance of depth psychology for theology is progressively discovered only as one learns to cultivate soul with its aid and
to surrender both spirit and soul in an embrace of the earth
which is simultaneously the prayerful acknowledgment of
one's creaturehood and the agreement to return to the homeland and live among one's fellows once again.

2 Second Immediacy

In the following four chapters, I wish to articulate appropriate methodological categories for understanding the process of psychic self-appropriation within the context of Lonergan's analysis of the existential subject. I begin, then, with a discussion of immediacy.

1 Primordial Immediacy and Second Immediacy

The key to method is the subject-as-subject. Method, as we have seen, calls for "a release from all logics, all closed systems or language games, all concepts, all symbolic constructs to allow an abiding at the level of the presence of the subject to himself' (Lawrence 1972, 203). Method is the objectification of the transcendental infrastructure of the subject-as-subject. Let us call this infrastructure the *primordial immediacy* of the human subject.

The fact that an adult's world is mediated by meaning renders that world different from the infant's world of immediacy. But the adult for all that is not deprived of an immediacy to the operations by which this world is mediated by meaning. If we were so deprived, the statement of Lonergan's which I have chosen as crucial to my present analysis would lose all significance: 'Besides the immediate world of the infant and the adult's world mediated by meaning, there is the mediation of immediacy by meaning when one objectifies cognitional process in transcendental method and when one discovers, identifies, accepts one's submerged feelings in psychotherapy' (Lonergan 1993, 77). Surely neither the immediacy mediated by cognitional theory nor that brought to articulate utterance in psychotherapy is that of the infant. In either case we are dealing with the immediacy of one for whom the world is mediated by acts of understanding, affirmation or denial, and evaluation, with the primordial immediacy of a human subject to precisely those operations, with the infrastructure of human subjectivity. This primordial immediacy is coextensive with consciousness, with the experience of self which is immanent in all attending, inquiring, understanding, reflecting, judging, deliberating, deciding, and acting. The basic structure of this primordial immediacy of ourselves to ourselves is disengaged in Lonergan's intentionality analysis, in his articulation of the dynamic structure of conscious intentionality. This articulation is method. Method, then, is more than the objectification of cognitional process, for the subject is not only a knowing subject but also an existential subject.

The emergence of a distinct notion of the good in *Method in Theology* locates for us the point of insertion of the second mediation of immediacy—that which occurs in psychotherapy—within the total context provided by method.[1] For the primordial apprehension of the good occurs in feelings,

---

1. This is not to assert that all in search of psychotherapy are methodologists! Rather, method is what enables us to understand what psychotherapy is all about.

and feelings are symbolically certifiable. Thus we may understand the process of psychic self-appropriation as facilitating the emergence of a capacity on the part of the existential subject to disengage the symbolic constitution of the feelings in which both values and satisfactions are apprehended, and from this disengagement to gauge the measure of self-transcendence operative in one's affective orientation as Being-in-the-world. Method thus includes psychic self-appropriation; it provides room for a critically mediated symbolic consciousness. To borrow a metaphor from Lonergan, in his own writings the room may not yet be very well furnished. But it is there, and it is my intention to phrase a methodological understanding of the process of furnishing it. The details of the arrangement of the furniture and the appointments of the room can be provided only in a phenomenology of the psyche. But the understanding of the process as a constituent feature of method is possible without going into the business of interior decorating.

The subject-as-subject is one. His or her unity is a function of the transcendental infrastructure of human subjectivity which I have called primordial immediacy. It is the unity that in the eleventh chapter of *Insight* is called 'the unity of consciousness' and that there is dealt with in relation to knowing.

> Conscious acts are not so many isolated, random atoms of knowing, but many acts coalesce into a single knowing. Not only is there a similarity between my seeing and your hearing, inasmuch as both acts are conscious; there also is an identity involved when my seeing and my hearing or your seeing and your hearing are compared. Moreover, this identity extends all along the line. Not only is the percept inquired about, understood, formulated, reflected on, grasped as unconditioned, and affirmed, but also there is an identity involved in perceiving, inquiring, understanding, formulating, reflecting, grasping the unconditioned, and affirming. Indeed, consciousness is much more obviously of this unity in diverse acts

than of the diverse acts, for it is within the unity that the acts
are found and distinguished, and it is to the unity that we appeal when we talk about a single field of consciousness and
draw a distinction between conscious acts occurring within
the field and unconscious acts occurring outside it (Lonergan
1992, 349).

This unity is not a postulate but a given (ibid. 350-
52). With the emergence of a distinct notion of the good, it is
made a more embracing unity, the unity of 'a single transcendental intending of plural, interchangeable objectives'
(Lonergan 1974, 81) including the intelligible, the true, and
the good. The unity is provided by a process of sublation
which retains lower levels but completes them by higher levels in a relationship of functional interdependence. Primordial immediacy, as identical with the transcendental infrastructure of the subject-as-subject, is thus unified, and this
unity not only is what enables Lonergan to speak of distinct
but related levels of consciousness, but is also what will shortly
enable us to ground a differentiation of primordial immediacy into its cognitive and dispositional aspects without sepa-
rating these dimensions from one another. That both knowing and feeling are sublated in the intention of value indicates that they join in a functional unity-in-differentiation.

In addition to this primordial immediacy, I wish to speak
of *second immediacy*. The term is suggested by Paul Ricoeur's
study of Sigmund Freud, where there is mention of a second
naiveté. But my meaning, while inclusive of Ricoeur's meaning, is, I believe, more far-reaching. Second immediacy is the
result of method's objectification of primordial immediacy. It
is the self-possession of the subject-as-subject achieved as a
result of the mediation of the transcendental infrastructure
of human subjectivity, and so of the objectification of the
single transcendental intending of the intelligible, the true,
and the good, the self-appropriation of the cognitional and

existential subject which is the fulfilment of the *anthropologische Wendung* of modern philosophy.[2] Second immediacy is the probably always asymptotic recovery of primordial immediacy through method.

Ricoeur's notion of second naiveté, however, is not alien to my notion of second immediacy. In Ricoeur's philosophy, second naiveté is a particular quality of awareness and speech, a quality intended in Ricoeur's entire philosophical project, a hoped-for conclusion of the quest for wisdom, a desired unity of intentionality and psychic energy in kerygmatic listening and speaking. Thus it has to do with what I am calling a transcendental aesthetic, with Ricoeur's poetics of the will, with a 'transformation of intentionality into kerygma, manifestation, proclamation' (Ricoeur 1970, 30). Ricoeur's notion of second naiveté is directly relevant to the psychic complement to the self-appropriation of the existential subject which I am here proposing. But the second naiveté of critical (or postcritical) symbolic consciousness is a portion of the second immediacy that is the fruit of the mediation of primordial immediacy in transcendental method, and it is the latter that provides us with a correct apprehension of the point of insertion of the former in the self-appropriation of the existential subject. We shall devote considerable space to Ricoeur in the next chapter. For the moment, I wish simply to indicate that I have no quarrel whatsoever with his notion of second naiveté, but that I understand it within the context of a more inclusive notion of second immediacy.

---

2. 'Philosophy finds its proper data in intentional consciousness. Its primary function is to promote the self-appropriation that cuts to the root of philosophic differences and incomprehensions. It has further, secondary functions in distinguishing, relating, grounding the several realms of meaning and, no less, in grounding the methods of the sciences and so promoting their unification' (Lonergan 1993, 95).

I have a suspicion, moreover, that what I am calling primordial immediacy is what Martin Heidegger calls *Dasein*. I cannot verify this suspicion at this point through a textual analysis of Heidegger's many and difficult writings. Let it suffice, then, to indicate that in *Being and Time* Heidegger speaks of two interlocking and equiprimordial constitutive ways of being the 'there': *Verstehen* and *Befindlichkeit* (Heidegger 1962, 171-72). Let us link this assertion with Lonergan's statement that 'there is the mediation of immediacy by meaning when one objectifies cognitional process in transcendental method and when one discovers, identifies, accepts one's submerged feelings in psychotherapy' (Lonergan 1993, 77). From the suspicion, the link, and the understanding of Lonergan articulated in my first chapter, I am led to claim that the primordial immediacy that is *Dasein* is mediated in two manners: through intentionality analysis and through psychic analysis.

The result of the full mediation would be a second immediacy, achieved in self-appropriation, through which the interlocking constitutive features of primordial immediacy are mediated to the subject in search of authenticity in his or her knowing, doing, and religion. Intentionality analysis or method provides the overall context, for it is concerned with the totality of the subject as knowing and doing. The subject as knowing is mediated, to my satisfaction at least, by Lonergan. The mediation of the subject as doing, as existential subject, however, could profit from further refinement. I do not question the structure already provided by Lonergan. But to a large extent, psychic self-appropriation is what will furnish the room, through the emergence of a consciousness familar with the symbols and images which evoke and are evoked by the feelings in which the existential subject experiences the primordial apprehension of possible values. Method as intentionality analysis articulates the overall dynamic: the appropriation or recovery of primordial immediacy. Psychotherapy, then, will be one of the ways of appropriating the dispositional aspect of primordial immediacy. It can aid the emergence of the existential subject by mediating a capacity to disengage the symbolic or imaginal constitution of the feelings in which values are apprehended. Primordial immediacy is the pure question which is the transcendental infrastructure of the subject-as-subject. This pure question is variously differentiated, and one of these variants, the one granted primacy in Lonergan's later writings, is the question which makes the subject an existential subject. The primordial apprehensions which generate the emergence of the question-as-existential occur in feelings. Feelings are symbolically certifiable. The psychic, then, is a constitutive feature of the subject as existential, as moral and religious. Perhaps the finality of the psychotherapeutic movement, then, will some day come to be understood as the fuller emergence of the subject as originative value, as free and responsible constitutive agent of the human world.

2 Dispositional Immediacy

Lonergan's statement about the two mediations of immediacy and Heidegger's assertion of two equiprimordial constitutive ways of being the 'there'—*Verstehen* and *Befindlichkeit*—lead me to suggest that primordial immediacy can be differentiated into cognitional and dispositional aspects. I focus on its dispositional aspect, for it is primarily this that is brought to objectification in the psychic moment of method which is my concern.

Eugene Gendlin, in his very clearly written book *Experiencing and the Creation of Meaning*, refers to this dispositional

aspect of immediacy as 'experiencing' and describes it as follows:

> It is something so simple, so easily available to every per-
> son, that at first its very simplicity makes it hard to point to.
> Another term for it is 'felt meaning,' or 'feeling.' However,
> 'feeling' is a word usually used for specific contents—for this
> or that feeling, emotion, or tone, for feeling good, or bad, or
> blue, or pretty fair. But regardless of the many changes in
> *what* we feel—that is to say, really, *how* we feel—there always
> is the concretely present flow of feeling. At any moment we
> can individually and privately direct our attention inward, and
> when we do that, there it is. Of course we have this or that
> specific idea, wish, emotion, perception, word, or thought, but
> we *always* have concrete feeling, an inward sensing whose
> nature is broader. It is a concrete mass in the sense that it is
> 'there' for us. It is not at all vague in its being there. It may be
> vague only in that we may not know what it is. We can put
> only a few aspects of it into words. The mass itself is always
> something there, no matter what we say it 'is.' Our defini-
> tions, our knowing 'what it is,' are symbols that specify as-
> pects of it, 'parts' of it, as we say. Whether we name it, divide
> it, or not, there it is (Gendlin 1962, 11).

Its importance is further highlighted in a manner more
appropriate to a discussion of the existential subject:

> For the sake of (this or that aspect of) experiencing man-
> kind can do all they do in a lifespan. Within experiencing lie
> the mysteries of all that we are. For the sake of our experien-
> tial sense of what we observe, we react as we do. From out of
> it we create what we create. And, because of its puzzles, and
> for the desperation of some of its puzzles, we overthrow good
> sense, obviousness, and reality, if need be … If our direct touch
> with our own personally important experiencing becomes too
> clouded, narrowed, or lost, we go to any length to regain it;
> we go to a friend, to a therapist, or to the desert. For nothing
> is as debilitating as a confused or distant functioning of expe-
> riencing. And the chief malaise of our society is perhaps that
> it allows so little pause and gives so little specifying response

and interpersonal communion to our experiencing, so that we must much of the time pretend that we are only what we seem externally, and that our meanings are only the objective references and the logical meanings of our words (ibid. 15-16).

We are concerned, then, with this ever-present flow of mood, now quiet, now turbulent, now easily designated, now undifferentiated, which accompanies every act of attending, seeing, tasting, hearing, conversing, questioning, understanding, reflecting, affirming, denying, deliberating, deciding, being attracted or repelled, meditating, praying, fleeing meditation, seeking distraction, drifting creatively, drifting in dissipation, falling in love, falling out of love, being active, being passive. If we attend sufficiently to the function of this flow of feeling, however, we shall discover that it not only accompanies these acts, but qualifies them, gives them a style, renders them aesthetically meaningful or gross, and even determines whether they take place or not. Thus, for example, the various biases discussed by Lonergan (Lonergan 1992, chapters 6 and 7), which interfere with intelligent and reasonable inquiry and short-circuit it, are not simply a matter of a deficiency of understanding, but are radically associated with the dynamics of the flow of mood. Moreover, the inner flow of feeling accompanies, qualifies, and organizes in a specific way not only our perception and dealings with the outer data of sense, but also and more radically our awareness of ourselves, our presence to the data of consciousness, and especially our constitution of ourselves as subjects through whose capacity for meaning and language the world is both mediated and constituted.

Psychotherapeutic investigations have sharpened our sensitivity to the centrality of the flow of feeling in the constitution of human life. What psychotherapists have all too frequently declined to admit, however, is that the domain of their discovery has also been dealt with and addressed profoundly and with deep respect and awe since time immemorial by such figures as Lao-Tzu, Gotama, and Jesus. Psychotherapy needs humbly to admit the continuity of its concern with the scriptures of the great world religions, or else the resources discovered by psychological investigations will not be integrated into the spiritual quest for wisdom and truth which is, I believe, the genuine finality of psychotherapeutic insight. The propriety and worth of this integration pertain also to what I am here proposing and to what I wish to study in depth in further work on Jung. Not only were the original discoveries of Freudian analysis accompanied by a number of questionable theories, but the potential spiritual finality of these discoveries has yet to be consistently defended against the temptations of an egalitarian professionalism perhaps best understood in terms of group bias.[3] I believe one very plau-

------

3. The refusal to deal with the possibility of such an integration is the most serious shortcoming in James Hillman's otherwise very good book *The Myth of Analysis*. The book is probably the most consistent and honest endeavor at professional self-relativization to date within the Jungian circle. Hillman's concern is to articulate the appropriate myth according to which psychoanalysts, at least of the Jungian variety, can understand themselves. The myth of Psyche and Amor, a myth of 'soul-making,' is found by Hillman to be appropriate. With all of this, I have no quarrel; far from it, I believe the profession of analytic work needs this sort of relativizing treatment. Where I would differ from Hillman is over his insistence that soul-making and spiritual direction are two quite separate processes. Thus he finds the images of both healing and enlightenment unsatisfactory as articulations of the analyst's self-understanding. '... our tradition is only partly represented by the medical pattern of our forebears—Galen, Mesmer, Pinel, Charcot ... So, too, the spiritual-director models of guru, rabbi, of Ignatius or Fenelon, of Zen master, are only substitutions on which we lean for want of surety about the true model for psychology. Because the psyche is hidden in illness or in ignorance, it must be healed or taught. So one is played by these other roles, based on other models. But one is played by the opus itself into these other roles for the purpose of reaching that fun-

sible dialectical interpretation of the career of Carl Jung, for example, could be delivered by viewing his cumulative researches and reflections as a kind of reparation for the extravagances of the initial enthusiasm which limited the horizon within which he viewed the human significance of the psychoanalytic revolution—even as a kind of sustained reaching, ever ambivalent, for the religious significance of the breakthrough. This significance might be stated very succinctly by postulating that the unappropriated functioning of the ever-present flow of mood is the root, not only of the neurotic guilt and neurotic anxiety which render so difficult even the first steps in psychic self-appropriation, but also of the less neurotic but thus also perhaps *more necessary* fears and desires,—e.g., the fear of living and the fear of dying—which present the emergence into spiritual freedom counseled by Lao-Tzu, Gotama, Confucius, and Jesus.

I choose to speak of dispositional immediacy, or with Heidegger of *Befindlichkeit*, as a way of referring to that which

---

damental aim, which is neither healing nor teaching but the awakening or engendering of soul' (ibid. 21).

Surely I do not wish to propose an undifferentiated unity of role for the analyst and the spiritual director. But I *do* maintain that method enables a unity-in-differentiation. Both psychotherapy and spiritual direction have to do with the appropriation of dispositional immediacy and with the advance to second immediacy. While I have long been convinced that spiritual direction ought to profit from the best insights of depth psychology, my experience at the C. G. Jung Institute in Zürich has convinced me also that Jungian analysis not informed by and related to the insights of the spiritual traditions of the various world religions is proceeding blindly and headlong for the romantic agony. We may understand the romantic agony, I believe, as a capitulation of intentionality to the rhythms and processes of the psyche. Its clearest expression is in the attempt to integrate evil psychically in a manner analogous to Hegel's attempt to integrate it speculatively. Some current variants of Jungian analysis are not immune to this charge.

is recovered in the second mediation of immediacy by meaning. In the remainder of this work, I shall use this term, rather than 'feeling,' as my central referent. My main reason for this choice is that the principal psychologist whose work I am interested in is Jung, and Jung has a very definite meaning for the word 'feeling,' a meaning which by no means covers all that is dealt with in this mediation, but refers rather to a particular function of personality, dominant in some people, recessive in others (see Jung 1971). But I believe it is fair to say that Jungian psychotherapy, as all psychotherapy, is concerned primarily with the mediation of the dispositional aspect of primordial immediacy.

In itself, then, dispositional immediacy is something very easy to designate. It is a matter of one's mood. It is what we inquire about when we sincerely ask another, 'How are you?' This heuristic definition is, I believe, quite clear. In such a question we are not usually inquiring about another's latest ideas or insights, the progress or hesitation of his or her on-going project, or even about the state of his or her physical health. Any or all of these may be somehow connected with the answer, but the question intends something else, a peculiar quality of being, of being here and now, of being the person one is. 'How do you find yourself?'

Now, no matter what type of personality one is—and typologies are legion and, Jung's included, purely descriptive and not explanatory—no matter whether one is, in Jung's scheme, a sensation type, an intuitive type, a feeling type, a thinking type, an extravert or an introvert, this question, when one finds oneself addressed by it, may be the most baffling of all questions. One may indeed find or suspect that he or she is completely incapable of answering it. Generally, anything but this puzzlement is what is reflected in one's answer, which is apt to be something as banal as 'Fine.' If one has adverted to the puzzlement, however, one is a step ahead of an *unknow-*

ingly banal answer. Such advertence can be the first step in leading one to seek help. It is the awareness that one is, in one's self-conscious being, out of touch with something rather important and, for all its seeming simplicity, very deep and mysterious. For reasons I will explain later, I prefer to describe this with Lonergan as an incommensurability of objectified and differentiated consciousness with the undifferentiated or nonobjectified, of the self as objectified with the self as conscious, rather than as a split between consciousness and the 'unconscious' (Lonergan 1993, 34). The latter term has been used in very misleading ways. At any rate, what one is out of touch with is the dispositional aspect of one's primordial immediacy. One does not know how one is, but has at least begun to advert to the fact of one's unknowing and secretly to admit it to oneself. The process of the mediation of dispositional immediacy by meaning in psychotherapy begins with this secret admission of confusion, of being out of touch, of not knowing how one is, who one is.

The notion of an appropriated dispositional immediacy, on the other hand—a notion central to Ricoeur's study and critique of Freud—defines in a rather precise manner the achievement of the mediation of the dispositional aspect of immediacy by meaning which is our present concern. We shall later have to examine in some detail Ricoeur's understanding of this appropriation. At the moment, I wish only to indicate that I share Ricoeur's problematic of attempting to pave the way for an intelligent mediation of dispositional immediacy on the part of the person of modernity, of the person who has been concerned with the modes of the mediation of immediacy and with their interrelations, but perhaps at the expense of a certain fullness of immediacy. The critical mentality of post-Kantain philosophy, the introduction of various critical techniques into every area of sustained inquiry, have rendered us 'sicklied o'er with the pale cast of thought.' Is there a way for us to return, not simply in spite of, but through the instruction of, the critique of naive consciousness, to the fullness of speech simply heard and understood? This is Ricoeur's question and it is also mine.[4] What would be the structure of such a recovery, of such a restoration?

Our first chapter has, I trust, made clear that I regard the crucial critique of naive consciousness to be that of Lonergan. This critique can be employed in understanding the mediation of dispositional immediacy which occurs in psychotherapy. It can also be used to help us sublate this mediation into the movement of method. Appropriated dispositional immediacy is not dependent on an appropriated cognitional immediacy, on the affirmation of the correct positions on knowing, being, and objectivity, for successful psychotherapy obviously occurs independently of whether the analysand or the analyst have read *Insight*! But the appropriation of dispositional immediacy also can figure as a part of method, as a feature in the existential subject's self-appro-

---

4. Ricoeur shares a concern with the 'new hermeneutic' of Gerhard Ebeling and Ernst Fuchs, in that he confronts the question of hermeneutic from the standpoint, first, of hearing the language anew in which meaning was first expressed. But he has significantly advanced the hermeneutic discussion, I believe, by correlating interpretation with symbolic or double-meaning linguistic expressions, with language which is overdetermined. For such a correlation, coupled with the internal variance within the hermeneutic field between the hermeneutic of recovery and that of suspicion, is explanatory of the contemporary failure of the language of faith bemoaned by the adherents of the new hermeneutic. Precisely because of this correlation, hermeneutic has become dialectical. The restoration of a post-critical man or woman to a fullness of immediacy occurs only through a resolution of this dialectic. We shall in the next chapter present a more detailed analysis of Ricoeur's notions of symbol and hermeneutic, while introducing our own qualifications on the therapeutic nature of the dialectic involved in the process Ricoeur proposes.

priation as heeding the methodical exigence. It is not achieved by attaining the correct positions on knowing, being, and objectivity, nor even, it would seem, by remaining consistently faithful to these positions. But these positions are indispensable in understanding it correctly. Intentionality analysis can even aid its effectiveness, in that the appropriation of dispositional immediacy stands the best chance of being successful if it is self-consciously attentive, intelligent, reasonable, and responsible. While the appropriation is *of* the hitherto undifferentiated, its agent is consciousness, and the better differentiated the agent, the more accurate and complete is its agency.

Perhaps we may say, then, that a mediation of primordial immediacy in its fullness involves (1) appropriating oneself as a question for intelligibility and truth by raising and answering what we may call the critical questions: What am I doing when I am knowing? Why is doing that knowing? What do I know when I do that?; (2) appropriating oneself as a question for value by attending to one's constitutive responsibility for the human world; and (3) appropriating the playground of one's desires and fears which is one's own imagination. There is obviously successful psychotherapy within a less comprehensive context. There is also authentic moral and religious subjectivity without psychotherapy. Authentic religion, moreover, surely has something to do with an exhortation of Jesus to men and women who were far from post-critical: 'Therefore do not be anxious about tomorrow, for tomorrow will be anxious for itself. Let the day's own evil be sufficient for the day' (Matthew 6.34). But the mediation of primordial immediacy in its fullness involves the discrimination of spirit or intentionality, the cultivation of soul or psyche, and the surrender of both spirit and soul to the action of God's love in the world. Second immediacy would be enjoyed by one who has labored to achieve a self-conscious integration of intentionality and psyche or who has learned to live attentively, intelligently, reasonably, responsibly, lovingly, with their customary tension. For perhaps their full integration occurs only in the 'mediated return to immediacy in the mating of lovers and in the prayerful mystic's cloud of unknowing' Lonergan 1993, 77).

3 Symbols

Any human subject whose world is mediated and constituted by meaning is primordially in a condition of cognitional and dispositional immediacy to the operations by which that world is mediated and to the states of mind that accompany those operations. Second immediacy is the recovery of this infrastructure in method. One way of recovering the dispositional aspect of primordial immediacy is through psychotherapy. This dimension of immediacy is accessible to conscious intentionality by the latter's focusing on the ever-present flow of mood which is constitutive of one's concomitant awareness of oneself in all of one's intentional operations. 'In every case Dasein always has some mood (Heidegger 1962, 173). Primordial immediacy is immediacy to oneself. Its dispositional mode is an immediacy of feeling, of mood, of 'how one is,' of how one finds oneself. It is what we intend when we ask another, 'How are you?' 'The mood has already disclosed, in every case, Being-in-the world as a whole, and makes it possible first of all to direct oneself towards something' (ibid. 176). We are concerned, then, with a state of immediacy to feeling or mood, and with its mediation. The mediation occurs in the objectification which takes place in psychotherapy.

1 Disposition and Symbol

In chapter 1, we saw the connection established by Lonergan between dispositional immediacy and the symbol. To repeat, a symbol is 'an image of a real or imaginary object that evokes a feeling or is evoked by a feeling' (Lonergan 1993, 64). These symbolic images provide one of the ways of ascertaining both individual uniqueness in dispositional response to objects and individual affective development or aberration and deviation. Symbols function in aid of internal communication on the part of the existential subject; they provide a disclosure of organic and psychic vitality to intentional consciousness and an instrument whereby the latter can secure the collaboration of organism and psyche in the existential subject's participation in the constitution of the human world.

In dependence on Lonergan's analysis, then, I wish to suggest that the dispositional aspect of immediacy is imaginally constructed, symbolically constituted. Our dispositions are structured by imagination, by the playground of our desires and fears. Thus the subject in his or her immediacy can be understood by disengaging one's symbol system.

But this imaginal constitution or symbolic determination is often not accessible to conscious intentionality in the same way as is the disposition itself. It often cannot be discovered simply by a heightened attentiveness to the ever-present flow of mood, but must be disengaged by specific techniques of psychological analysis. When one is out of touch with dispositional immediacy, these techniques of symbolic disengagement may be needed to enable one's dispositional immediacy to be objectified, appropriated, known. When so disengaged, symbols not only reveal 'how it stands' between the explicit articulate self-understanding of the existential subject and a larger totality, between the self as objectified and the self as conscious, but also enable one's selfunderstanding to approximate one's reality. If one is out of touch with how one is, with who one is, one needs to disengage the imaginal constitution of this larger totality. One cannot tell the story of one's own being as existential subject, but the story inevitably goes forward all the same. Psychic self-appropriation is a matter of gaining the capacity to articulate this story correctly and to guide it responsibly. It frequently involves a reversal of a cumulative misinterpretation of experience. Everyone tells his or her own story, but not all can tell it as it is.

I hazard that the most effective techniques yet developed for disengaging the story of felt meaning are the Jungian procedures of dream interpretation and active imagination and an associated process developed by Ira Progoff known as 'twilight imaging.'[1] In this chapter, though, rather than detailing these techniques, I wish to call attention to the realm or dimension of human subjectivity whose articulation and appropriation constitute in large part the mediation of dispositional immediacy. This dimension is referred to by Paul Ricoeur as the 'mytho-poetic core of imagination' (Ricoeur 1970, 35), which gives rise to the spontaneous elemental symbols which in fact constitute and reflect for each individual the structure of *Befindlichkeit*.

---

1. On twilight imaging, see Progoff 1973; on active imagination, see Weaver 1973.

While I believe that the finest philosophical study of symbolism to date is probably that of Ricoeur,[2] I have serious reservations as to whether philosophical reflection as understood by Ricoeur can sufficiently penetrate to the creative spontaneity which renders possible individual uniqueness in symbolic response, and thus as to whether Ricoeur does not overvalue the capacity of reflective philosophy to achieve, on the basis of its own resources, an appropriation of the symbolic dimension. Ricoeur is quite insistent that philosophy, in the interests of the selfappropriaton of the depths of the reflective subject, must become a hermeneutic of the symbolic contingencies of cultures. More radically, I will maintain that there is an individual core of spontaneous elemental imagination which is to be recovered by intelligent, reasonable, existential subjectivity in the interests of self-appropriation, and that this recovery is not achieved in a philosophical hermeneutic of cultural objectifications but in an existential, evaluative, dialectical hermeneutic of one's dreams, of one's own most radical individual spontaneity. It is this recovery which both moves psyche into the thrust of intentionality and provides one with the symbolic foundations for engaging in a hermeneutic of culture and religion.

Nonetheless, for four reasons I feel justified in detailing at some length Ricoeur's achievement in his study of Freud. First, Ricoeur has displayed the need of self-appropriation to have recourse to the interpretation of concrete symbols. Secondly, I find myself ever more impressed with the suggestiveness of his analysis of the dialectical structure of sym-

---

2. I have yet to do a detailed study of Ernst Cassirer's philosophy of symbol. For Ricoeur, Cassirer makes the notion of symbol too extensive, so much so that it includes expressions which are not overdetermined, whose meaning is both obvious and univocal. This is certainly what would be expected in one whose inspiration is a Kantian-based conceptualism.

bolic process. Thirdly, through Ricoeur's analysis we are introduced in superb fashion to Freud, whose work must figure in our understanding of the psychic self-appropriation of the existential subject. Fourthly, I can most expeditiously present my own philosophy of the symbol by indicating where I agree with Ricoeur and where I wish greater precison.

2 The Tension of the Symbol

2.1 *The Hermeneutic Conflict*

Ricoeur's philosophical project is surely among the most ambitious and sophisticated intellectual endeavors of our century. His treatment of cultural and religious symbolism figures as a part of a vast philosophical undertaking concerned with delineating the essential structure, limits, and possibilities of human existence. Ricoeur has moved from the structural phenomenological analysis of his earlier works (Ricoeur 1965 and 1966) to a concrete hermeneutic phenomenology of symbols[3] because of a conviction that the self which it is

---

3. The beginnings of this turn are reflected in Ricoeur (1969). *Freedom and Nature* is the first volume of a projected three-volume philosophy of the will. The second volume is to contain three parts, the first two of which are *Fallible Man* and *The Symbolism of Evil*. *Freedom and Nature* is referred to by Ricoeur as an eidetics of the will, employing the method of pure description in order to reveal in the abstract our fundamental possibilities. Two important factors are omitted from the eidetics, fault and transcendence. *Fallible Man* and *The Symbolism of Evil* consider the domain of fault, the first from the standpoint of investigating that which permits fault to arise, the second by investigating hermeneutically the 'language of avowal,' in which we confess our fault. The projected third part of this second volume would deal with transcendence, and the third volume is a

philosophy's task to recover is not a datum for naive immediacy but can be retrieved only by a detour through the non-
self. The *Sum* of the *Cogito* 'has to be "mediated" by the ideas,
actions, works, institutions,and monuments that objectify it'
(Ricoeur 1970, 43). 'I must recover something which has first
been lost; I make "proper to me" what has ceased being mine.
I make "mine" what I am separated from by space or time,
by distraction or "diversion," or because of some culpable
forgetfulness ... I do not at first possess what I am' (ibid. 45).
Philosophical reflection is to recover the *I am* through reflection on the works of men and women. The *I am* as such is not
given as an immediate datum of experience. Knowledge of it
occurs only through a displacement of the home of meaning
away from immediate consciousness, a displacement which
for Ricoeur means an understanding of our objectifications
in knowledge, action, and culture. Phenomenology becomes
herme„neutic when it becomes a matter of understanding
our *experience* by understanding our *expressions*.

The meaning of these objectifications or works, however, is neither immediately evident nor univocal. Our self-
expressions are capable of being variously interpreted. A
privileged instance of this susceptibility to different interpretations is found in language. Ricoeur designates the realm of
equivocal or plurivocal linguistic expressions as the domain
of symbolism and at this stage of his thought correlates its
exploration with the task of hermeneutic or interpretation. 'I
have decided to define, i.e., limit, the notions of symbol and
interpretation through one another. Thus a symbol is a
double-meaning linguistic expression that requires an inter-

---

projected poetics of the will. *Freud and Philosophy*, while not part of the
philosophy of the will, sharpens the hermeneutic tools first employed in
The Symbolism of Evil. See Kelbley's 'Translator's Introduction,' *Fallible Man*
ix-xv, and Ihde 1971, 181.

pretation, and interpretation is a work of understanding that aims at deciphering symbols.'[4]

The symbolic function consists in the designation of something other than what is said, through what is said.[5] 'Symbols occur when language produces signs of composite degree in which the meaning, not satisfied with designating some one thing, designates another meaning attainable only in and through the first intentionality' (ibid. 16). Symbolism is peculiar to and dependent upon language. Its power may be rooted in the expressiveness of the cosmos, in the *vouloir-dire* of human desire, and in human imagination, yet, for Ricoeur, it appears as such in language. 'There is no symbolism prior to man who speaks' (ibid.). It is the perhaps interminable task of interpretation to reveal the richness and overdetermination of symbols and to demonstrate that symbols have a role to play in human discourse.

The manifest meaning of a symbol, according to one style of interpretation, points beyond itself to a second, latent meaning or to a series of such meanings, by a type of analogy which cannot be dominated intellectually. The symbol is rather a movement which we can follow, a movement of the primary meaning intentionally assimilating us to the symbolized (ibid. 17).

Such is the operative notion of symbol in the phenomenology of religion. The symbols of any of the great religions of the world enable the historian to be drawn toward that religion's conception of the sacred and its relation to humanity. Much of the work of a scholar such as Mircea Eliade is a matter of moving with the symbols and being drawn by them

---

4. Ibid. 9. 1993 note: In Ricoeur's later hermeneutic thought, the task of interpretation is broadened beyond the realm of the symbolic.

5. 'To mean something other than what is said—this is the symbolic function' (Ibid. 12).

to a universe structured in a particular way and to a god or
gods relating in a certain manner to our world as we experience it. Thus, for example, the predominance of certain symbolic indications enables Eliade to distinguish religions of the
'eternal return' from religions of historically oriented faith
(Eliade 1959, chapter 4). The process of assimilation by which
the primary meaning moves us, draws us on, to a latent, symbolized meaning, is identified by Ricoeur as 'intentional analogy.' Symbols are 'the manifestation in the sensible — in imagination, gestures, and feelings — of a further reality, the expression of a depth which both shows and hides itself (Ricoeur
1970, 7).

But such intentional analogy is not the only kind of relationship that can exist between manifest and latent meaning. The manifest meaning may indeed be a pointer toward
an analogous second meaning, but it may also be a cunning
distortion of latent meaning. In either case, however, '... a
symbol exists ... where linguistic expression lends itself by
its double or multiple meanings to a work of interpretation.'
There are no symbols without the beginnings of interpretation. 'Where one man dreams, prophecies, or poetizes, another rises up to interpret. Interpretation organically belongs
to symbolic thought and its double meaning' (ibid. 18-19).

The opposition of these two relationships between manifest and latent meaning gives rise to the problem of conflicting hermeneutical styles. Ricoeur dramatizes the conflict by
highlighting the differences between the phenomenology of
religion and the psychoanalysis of Sigmund Freud. For the
latter, dreams, works of art, linguistic expressions, and cultural objectifications are the dissimulation of basic desire
rather than manifestations of a further reality beyond themselves. They conceal an unsurpassable instinct, and thus their
interpretation takes the form of the reduction of the illusion
effected in consciousness by their manifest meaning. These

two different styles of interpretation, the hermeneutic of recovery and the hermeneutic of suspicion, while not constituting a complete enumeration of hermeneutical styles, represent the polar extremes in contemporary hermeneutic, and point to the key difficulty of hermeneutic, the absence of a universal canon of interpretation. The hermeneutic field is 'internally at variance with itself' (ibid. 27). For the suspicious pole, hermeneutic is a demystification, a reduction of illusion. For the hermeneutic of recovery, the task is a restoration of meaning addressed to me as a message, a proclamation, a kerygma. We oscillate for the most part betwen demystification and recovery because we are the victims of a crisis of language peculiar to our age. Is the conflict of suspicion and recovery definitive, or is it provisional? Can we achieve a standpoint beyond it? The crisis gives rise to dialectic.

In *The Symbolism of Evil*, where Ricoeur begins his attempt to read human experience by interpreting human symbolic expressions, the task is still phenomenological. The hermeneutic war is not yet the problem. But hermeneutic phenomenology is nonetheless a departure from what we might call structural phenomenology in that it involves a wager which shatters the descriptive neutrality of most phenomenological work. 'I wager that I shall have a better understanding of man and the bond between the being of man and the being of all beings if I follow the *indication* of symbolic thought' (Ricoeur 1969, 355). In *Freud and Philosophy*, the same wager is seen to qualify the phenomenology of religion, which is animated by an intention, a series of philosophical decisions which lie hidden even within its apparent neutrality, a rational faith which employs a phenomenological hermeneutic as an instrument of achieving the restoration of meaning. The implicit intention of hermeneutic phenomenology is 'an expectancy of a new Word, of a new tidings of the

Word' (Ricoeur 1970, 31). Such interpretation, then, does not attempt to reach behind the symbols for underlying instinctual determinants but rather attempts to follow them forward, to follow their indications. 'Symbols alone give what they say' (ibid.).

Nevertheless hermeneutic phenomenology is not a matter of naive immediacy. To interpret symbols phenomenologically is to reenact them in sympathetic imagination, not through an immediate belief but through the recovery of implicit intentionality. One would reenact a myth through an immediate belief if one were to accept it, with its original adherents, as explanatory or etiological. To reenact it by sympathetically immersing oneself in its intentionality and following its indications, however, is to accept it as exploratory of ourselves, our place in the cosmos, our destiny. The cosmic significance which the symbol intends is not actually *given* in the symbol. If it were, the latter would cease to be a symbol. Symbols are intentions without fulfilments.

The phenomenology of religion may proceed either by analyzing the inherent structures of symbols and myths, or by relating them to one another in an evolutionary perspective or by relations of transposition, of opposition and identity of intentionality. In either case, says Ricoeur, three philosophical decisions are featured.

First, the decision is made to accent the *object* of the phenomenological investigation. A hermeneutic of recovery is a rational faith characterized by care for the object. This care is inherited from a more neutral phenomenology, which wishes to describe and not to reduce. Thus the phenomenology of religion intends to disengage the implicit object in myth, ritual, and belief rather than to focus upon subjective or sociological motivations and determinants of behavior. The task of the phenomenology of religion is 'to disimplicate (the sacred) from the various intentions of behavior, discourse, and emotion' (ibid. 29). Behind such concern, as we shall see, is the expectation of being addressed by the sacred and the placing of an intrinsic confidence in human discourse, 'the belief that language, which bears symbols, is not so much spoken by men as spoken to men, that men are born into language, into the light of the logos "who enlightens every man who comes into the world"'(ibid. 29-30).

Second, the hermeneutic of recovery is pervaded by a concern for the truth or fullness of symbols. In symbols we meet the fullness of language in the overdetermination of meaning. Here again the supposed neutrality of phenomenological research is broken, for one is placed within a kind of hermeneutic circle of faith and understanding.

> I admit that what deeply motivates the interest in full language, in bound language, is this inversion of the movement of thought which now addresses itself to me and makes me a subject spoken to. And this inversion is produced in analogy. How? How does that which binds meaning to meaning bind me? The movement that draws me toward the second meaning assimilates me to what is said, makes me participate in what is announced to me. The similitude in which the force of symbols resides and from which they draw their revealing power is not an objective likeness, which I may look upon like a relation laid out before me; it is an existential assimilation, according to the movement of analogy, of my being to being (ibid. 31).

Thirdly, then, the intention of such phenomenology is that one may 'finally greet the revealing power of the primal word' (ibid. 32). The hermeneutic of recovery is characterized by something like the Platonic theme of participation and reminiscence. 'After the silence and forgetfulness made widespread by the manipulation of empty signs and the construction of formalized languages, the modern concern for symbols expresses a new desire to be addressed' (ibid. 31).

The phenomenology of religion functions as a propaedeutic to the revelation of meaning (ibid. 32).

The opposed character of the hermeneutic of suspicion can be understood in terms of these three decisions. This conflicting style of interpretation reverses the three decisons made by the phenomenologist of religion. The hermeneutic task, moreover, cannot remain at a phenomenological level because of the mighty invasion of the hermeneutic of suspicion into modern thought. First, then, the focus of concern is not the object of investigation itself, the expression, but the underlying determinants of such expression. Secondly, the latent meaning of symbolic expression is not to be discovered by trusting in the fullness of language and thus following it forward, but by moving back to the realm of unsurpassable instinctual desire lying behind and determining the mendacious deliverances of consciousness. Thirdly, the intention of the phenomenology of religion to be spoken to anew by the primal Word is reversed when religion is described with Freud as the universal obsessional neurosis of humankind. While this description is Freud's and Freud is but one representative of the hermeneutic of suspicion, Ricoeur finds a common intention in all of its representatives, 'the decision to look upon the whole of consciousness primarily as "false" consciousness. They thereby take up again … the problem of the Cartesian doubt, to carry it to the very heart of the Cartesian stronghold … After the doubt about things, we have started to doubt consciousness' (ibid. 33). This doubt is the core of the hermeneutic of suspicion, the essence of the stamp it has imprinted, perhaps indelibly, on modernity.

2.2 *The Dialectic of the Symbol*

In psychology, such doubt of naive consciousness is reflected not only in the psychoanalysis of Freud but also in the very different analytical psychology of Jung. And in philosophy not only does it animate the thought of a Nietzsche but it is also central to Ricoeur's notion of philosophical reflection. Thus perhaps, despite its radical contrariety to any phenomenology of the sacred or to any hermeneutic understood nondialectically as the recollection of meaning, its ultimate significance may be quite other, even with regard to religion, than would appear from Freud or Nietzsche. The doubt of naive consciousness is carried to quite different religious conclusions by Jung and Ricoeur. And the same doubt permeates Lonergan's clearing of a previously undifferentiated structure of intentional consciousness in direct opposition to the philosophy he calls naive realism. So perhaps the philosopher's task is that of the dialectical resolution of the hermeneutic conflict. This is the task attempted by Ricoeur. In the course of executing it, he uncovers a notion of the symbol which should be operative in the mediation of psyche which we are here proposing and which was in fact operative in Jung's writings, though — as unfortunately is the case with most of Jung — it was never articulated with sufficient philosophic rigor.

Ricoeur judges that a long-term dialectical view of this radical doubt of immediate consciousness would find it salvific for authentic religious belief. It has cleared the horizon for a more authentic word, 'a new reign of Truth' (ibid.), the deidolization of religion. The way is open, too, for a mediate science of meaning, irreducible to the immediate consciousness of meaning (ibid. 33-34). Thus the hermeneutic of suspicion is, in the last analysis, no more a detractor of consciousness than is Ricoeur himself, or, we might add, Jung or Lonergan. Rather it aims at extending consciousness. Freud, for example, aims 'to substitute for an immediate and dissimulating consciousness a mediate consciousness taught by the reality principle' (ibid. 35). Nonetheless—as is dramatically evident in the differences between Freud and Jung— the controversy itself involves the fate of the 'mytho-poetic core of imagination,' the very condition of possibility for 'the upsurge of the possible,' for newness and creativity, and thus for the revelation of the primal Word. 'Does not this discipline of the real, this ascesis of the necessary, lack the grace of imagination? ... And does not the grace of imagination have something to do with the word as Revelation?'(ibid. 35-36).

Thus the importance of the conflict cannot be minimized. If, in fact, the hermeneutic war cannot be mediated, the thinker—whether philosopher, theologian, or psychologist— is left with a seemingly arbitrary option between these two styles, an option in its arbitrariness perhaps itself determined not by the exigences of evidence and disinterested inquiry but by the instinctual determinants of one's own psychic makeup. If the war cannot be mediated, the odds would seem to lie with the hermeneutic of suspicion, since either option in itself would appear arbitrary and thus itself an expression of unsurpassable instinct. The thinker's task would then be iconoclastic, purely and simply. One would proceed to 'purify discourse of its excrescences, liquidate the idols, go from drunkenness to sobriety, realize our state of poverty once and for all' (ibid. 27).

If the conflict can be mediated, though, the hermeneutic of suspicion would remain, but this iconoclastic form of interpretation would be taken up into the task of recovery, which would then become, not a parallel task, exclusive of and opposed to that of demystification, but inclusive of the latter. The thinker would then 'use the most "nihilistic," destructive, iconoclastic movement so as to *let speak* what once, what each time, was *said*, when meaning appeared anew, when meaning was at its fullest' (ibid.). The recovery of meaning would occur, not through a mere phenomenology of symbol, as in the phenomenology of religion, but by philosophical reflection in its fullest sense and in reliance upon a process of rigorous dialectic which would include extreme iconoclasm as a moment in the restoration of meaning.

Ricoeur favors the possibility of such a philosophic resolution of the hermeneutic conflict. The conflict can and must be moved onto the level of philosophical reflection, which Ricoeur understands as 'the appropriation of our effort to exist and of our desire to be, through the works which bear witness to that effort and desire' (ibid. 46). As against Descartes, the *Cogito ergo sum* 'remains as abstract and empty as it is invincible' (ibid. 43), and as against Kant, epistemology is only a part of the foundational concern of philosophy to recover the act of existing, the *Sum* of the *Cogito*, in all the density of its works. Philosophical reflection thus becomes the task of making my concrete experience equal to the positing of the 'I am.'[6] The emergence of our effort to exist or our desire to be — the *Sum* of the *Cogito* — is, then, delivered to reflection only through works whose meaning remains doubtful and revocable, and through symbolic utterance in particular. Symbols and myths, while prephilosophical, are instructive and nourishing for philosodphical reflection. They can be treated by a philosophical exegesis which regards them as exploratory pointers opening upon a world of meaning. Symbols call for philosophical reflection because through them attempts are made 'to generalize human experience on

---

6. Ibid. 45. This task is identical to what we have called the mediation of primordial immediacy through method.

the level of a universal concept or paradigm in which we can read our condition and history' (ibid. 38-39). It is their paradigmatic quality which invites philosophical reflection. In myths, symbols confer 'universality, temporality, and ontological import upon our self-understanding' (ibid. 39), for the myth is a second-order symbol which adds to primary symbols the temporal characteristics of narrative (Ricoeur 1969, 18). But, because the issue is one of conflict, of the concrete, the dynamic, and the contradictory, the reflection adequate to meeting it is neither phenomenological nor hermeneutical but dialectical. And as such it must resolve not only differences in standpoint and correlative content but also differences in underlying decisions in which one chooses one's standpoint, and it must prepare the subject for a further decision in which one chooses a more inclusive standpoint.7 Whereas reflection must have recourse to hermeneutic, the hermeneutic conflict must be arbitrated by a return to an expanded, dialectical, reflective critique of interpretations, which, although expanded, is also more concrete, penetrating as it does more profoundly into the effort to exist and the desire to be which reflection must appropriate through human expressions. 'To destroy the idols, to listen to symbols — are not these ... one and the same enterprise? Indeed, the profound unity of the demystifying and remythicizing of discourse can be seen only at the end of an ascesis of reflection,' in which 'the disposession of consciousness to the profit of another home of meaning' is 'the first gesture of reappropriation.' (Ricoeur 1970, 54-55).

And so Ricoeur moves to the task of integrating the discourse of Freudian psychoanalysis, a leading instance of

---

7. This articulation of the dynamic of dialectic is Lonergan's, but it surely expresses what Ricoeur is driving at. See Lonergan 1993, 128-30.

demystifying hermeneutic, into philosophical reflection, into the reappropriation of the *Sum* of the *Cogito*. Freudian psychoanalysis provides Ricoeur with an *archeology of the subject*. Thus the level on which Ricoeur proceeds with his investigation is the same level as that on which we are encouraging the appropriation of psyche as a complement to the appropriation of *logos* effectd by Lonergan in method. My insistence that intentionality analysis sublate psychic analysis is parallel to Ricoeur's insistence that philosophical reflection must become in part a hermeneutic and dialectic of symbols. The basic level for both Ricoeur and myself is the level of transcendental reflection, of the 'movement of self-appropriation by self which constitutes reflective activity' (ibid. 52). Ricoeur has correctly argued, I believe, that this movement is not exhausted by its cognitional moment, which for Ricoeur is represented by Kant, and for me by Lonergan. Symbols play an *a priori* role in this movement of self-appropriation because of the connection between reflection on the *Sum* of the *Cogito* and 'the signs scattered in the various cultures by that act of existing' (ibid.). Ricoeur goes so far as to say that this connection 'opens up a new field of experience, objectivity, and reality' (ibid.) — the field I shall later qualify as a genuine sphere of being and call *the imaginal*. To this field a transcendental logic of double meaning is said to pertain; this logic is disengaged by Ricoeur, at least in part, and it will be operative in the appropriation of psyche to which the psychotherapeutic movement gives rise and must give way.

2.3 *The Archeology of the Subject*

On Ricoeur's analysis, then, Freudian psychology is motivated by an intention to provide a critique of immediate consciousness, a decentering of the home of significations, a displacement of the birth of meaning. Freud's psychological topography and economics make me completely homeless, forcing me to admit the inadequacy of immediate consciousness despite the apodictic and irrefutable character of the *Cogito ergo sum*. A twofold movement permeates Freudian discourse: a displacement of meaning away from consciousness toward unconscious process and a recapturing of meaning in interpretation. Even the apodictic, though empty, character of the *Cogito ergo sum* never figures as such in Freud's systematization; the ego functions only as an economic variable. Nevertheless, the movement of interpretation is a first step toward becoming conscious, in the sense of becoming equal to the authentic *Cogito*. This movement of interpretation is possible only because instincts, however unknowable and unapproachable, are designated in the psyche by ideas and affects that represent them. Thus there is a certain homogeneity between unconscious process and consciousness. The reality of the psychical representatives of instinct exists *only* for interpretation. 'The reality of the unconscious ... is relative to the operations that give it meaning' (ibid. 436).

Philosophical reflection as self-appropriation, then, can speak of the emergence of desire, of the *Sum* at the heart of the *Cogito*, as giving rise to an archeology of the subject. To do so, it examines the Freudian economics, which becomes for philosophical interpretation not simply a model but a total view of things and of human beings in the world of things, a revelation of the archaic, a manifestation of the ever prior.

Thus, dreams and neuroses reveal 'the unconscious' to be timeless in character and desire to be 'unsurpassable.' Such an archeology climaxes in the theory of narcissism, 'the original form of desire to which one always returns' (ibid. 445). Since ideals and illusions are the analogues of dreams and neuroses, the psychoanalytic interpretation of culture is also archeological. This archeology culminates in Freud's critique of religion, 'the universal obsessional neurosis of mankind' (ibid. 447). The ethical world, too, and the superego which accounts for it, are seen to have distinctively archaic features, and the death instinct is the archaic index of all the instincts and of the pleasure principle itself. We are drawn backwards, by a detemporalizing agency, to a destiny in reverse.

Can such an archeology be understood within a philosophy of the subject? To answer this question, says Ricoeur, we must first ask about the ultimate meaning of Freud's economic point of view. There is a point within the economic perspective where the fate of the affective representatives of instinct no longer coincides with that of the ideational representatives. At this point, psychoanalysis becomes the borderline knowledge of that which, in representation, does not pass into ideas—i.e., desire qua desire, 'the mute, the nonspoken and non-speaking, the unnameable at the origin of speech' (ibid. 454). Only the energy metaphors of the economics can speak this muteness. This regressive movement of psychoanalysis designates, from the border, the *Sum* of the *Cogito*. 'Just as the "relinquishing" of consciousness in a topography is intelligible only because of a "recapture" in the act of becoming conscious, so too a pure economics of desire is intelligible only as the possibility of recognizing the emergence of desire in the series of its derivatives, in the density and at the borderline of the signifying' (ibid.). Thus, drawing upon Leibniz, Ricoeur states: '… as standing for objects or things, representation is pretension to truth; but it is also the expression of life, expression of effort or appetite' (ibid. 456). 'Desire is both the nonspoken and the wish-to-speak, the unnameable and the potency to speak' (ibid. 457).

What does such an archeology tell us, then, about human existence? Our representations must be studied, not only by an epistemology which views them as intentional relations ruled by objects, but also by an exegesis of the desires that lie hidden in that intentionality. Thus human knowledge is not autonomous but rooted in existence, desire, and effort. Epistemology is but one part of reflective philosophy. Life and desire, which alone are unsurpassable, tend to interfere with the intentionality which is the concern of epistemology. Truth becomes, in such an analysis, not a given, but a task. The movement of reflective philosophy to the sublation of the psyche makes of that philosophy a semantics of human desire.

The dependence of the knowing subject on the emergence of desire cannot be grasped in immediate experience. It can only be interpreted, deciphered through dreams, fantasies, and myths, 'the indirect discourse of [the] mute darkness' of desire (ibid. 458). Reflective consciousness must move with Ricoeur beyond structural phenomenology and the phenomenology of perception to hermeneutic phenomenology, for only hermeneutic can understand this rootedness of knowledge in life. The hermeneutic turn proves to be justified in terms of the very interest and project of philosophical reflection.

2.4 Archeology and Teleology

For the sake of concreteness, says Ricoeur, an archeology of the subject must be placed in a relationship of dialectical tension with a teleology of the subject. Only through such a relationship can self-appropriation become concrete. A second dispossession of immediate consciousness is required, precisely for the sake of becoming conscious, i.e., of attaining to the true being of the subject. This process of appropriating the meaning of one's existence is mediated through figures which give a *goal* to the process. The goal is expanded or heightened consciousness. The figures which mediate the process serially constitute what Hegel calls *Geist*.

They determine a new decentering of meaning away from immediate consciousness. Heuristically, we may say that, for Ricoeur, to understand the relation between these two dispossessions of consciousness is to understand that the hermeneutic conflict can be resolved. The dialectic of archeology and teleology is 'the true philosophical basis for understanding the complementarity of opposed hermeneutics in relation to the mytho-poetic formations of culture' (ibid. 460).

Freudianism itself is far more dialectical in nature than Freud admitted. It may be an explicit and thematized archeology, but it relates in and of itself to an implicit and unthematized teleology, much as Hegel's *Phenomenology* is an explicit teleological account of the achieving of consciousness, but emerging out of the substrate of life and desire, and thus an implicit archeology.[8]

Hegel presents a phenomenology of figures, categories, and symbols which guide the developmental process along the lines of a progressive synthesis. We become adult by assuming the new forms of master-slave, stoic thought, skepticism, the unhappy consciousness, service of the devoted mind, etc., which serially constitute *Geist*. A given consciousness must encounter and appropriate those spheres of meaning if it is to reflect itself as a self, a human, adult, conscious self. Consciousness is the internalization of this movement, which must be captured in the objective structures of institutions, monuments, works of art, and culture. Consciousness becomes self-consciousness only through this mediation, thus

---

8. 'I do not confuse Hegel with Freud, but I seek to find in Freud an inverted image of Hegel, in order to discern, with the help of this schema, certain dialectical features which, though obviously operative in analytic practice, have not found in the theory a complete systematic elaboration' (ibid. 461-62).

only by allowing a shift of the center of meaning away from itself just as much as in psychoanalysis.

Ricoeur takes two facets of Hegelian phenomenology[9] as guides in the development of a Freudian dialectic: its form and its content. The form of Hegelian dialectic is that of a progressive synthesis in which each figure receives its meaning from the *subsequent* one. As regards content, what is at stake in the progressive synthesis is the production of the self of self-consciousness. The form contrasts with the analytic and regressive character of psychoanalysis. The self that is at stake cannot figure in a topography or an economics. The 'education' of the self is not understood economically as a return to narcissism from object libido. The self *in itself* will know itself only in reflection, where the self is finally *for itself*. The way is open for creativity, since each moment includes in its certainty an element of the not known that all the later moments mediate and make explicit. In contrast, Freudianism appears to be a strange and profound philosophy of fate. Whereas *Geist* has its meaning in later forms or figures, 'the unconscious' in psychoanalysis means that intelligibility always proceeds from earlier figures. 'Spirit [*Geist*] is history and the unconscious is fate (Ricoeur 1970, 468).

Nevertheless, the Freudian problematic also appears within Hegelian phenomenology. The emergence of desire is central to the spiritual process of the reduplication of consciousness; the satisfaction of desire is inherent in the self-recognition of achieved self-consciousness. The education of the self proceeds on and arises from the substrate of life and desire, which has a teleological dimension to its dynamism. Life is the obscure density which self-consciousness, in its advance, reveals behind itself as the source of the synthetic

---

9. On the importance of Hegel for Ricoeur, see Ihde 1971, 15.

movement. Life and desire are both surpassed, in the sense of being progressively mediated, and unsurpassable, in the sense of being originary.

Conversely, the Hegelian problematic is within Freudianism. Ricoeur finds that three areas of Freudianism reveal an implicit teleology: the theory's operative concepts, the notion of identification, and the question of sublimation.

By 'operative concepts' Ricoeur means concepts that Freud uses but does not thematize. Principal among these is the intersubjective nature of the analytic situation, which contrasts with the solipsism of the topography of the psyche. Because of this intersubjectivity, the analytic relation between patient and analyst can be understood as 'a dialectic of consciousness, rising from life to self-consciousness, from the satisfaction of desire to the recognition of the other consciousness' (ibid. 474). By the attainment of the equality of the two consciousnesses, the patient is no longer alienated, no longer primarily another, but has become a self. Even more important, the therapeutic relation serves as a 'mirror image in reviving a whole series of situations all of which were already intersubjective ... All the dramas psychoanalysis discovers are located on the path that leads from "satisfaction" to "recognition"'(ibid.).

The genesis of the superego in Freudian theory also relates to an unthematized teleological dialectic by reason of the concept of identification. Because of the external nature of authority, an acquired differentiation of desire takes place, along with a semantics of ideals. Again, this differentiation is homologous to the Hegelian reduplication of consciousness. The desire in question here, one which precedes the Oedipus complex and is strengthened by its dissolution, is the *desire to be like*. This process of consciousness-to-consciousness can be understood only by an interpretation other than the Freudian metapsychology. It is a process which founds affectionate trends of feeling and cultural objectifications. As such, it eludes the economics. Freud's writings can thus be reread from the standpoint of the emergence of self-consciosness (ibid. 477-83).

Finally, there is the question of sublimation, which is *only* a question in Freud's theory. The more Freud distinguishes sublimation from other mechanisms, and in particular from repression and reaction formation, the more its own mechanism remains unexplained. Sublimation is a displacement of energy, but not a repression of it. It precedes and embraces all of the formations derived by way of aesthetic transfer of sensual pleasure from erotogenic zones or by way of desexualization of the libido during the dissolution of the Oedipus complex. Ultimately, the task of becoming I, the finality of analysis, a task set within the economics of desire, is in principle irreducible to the economics (ibid. 483-93).

2.5 *The Concrete Symbol*

For Ricoeur, the dialectic of archeology and teleology is the first step leading from abstract reflection to concrete reflection. To understand that symbols are the area of identity between progression and regression, though, is fully to enter into concrete reflection and to demonstrate most dramatically that self-appropriation needs to have recourse to symbols. The dialectic of opposed hermeneutics is rooted in a dialectic within the symbol itself. While the key to the solution of the hermeneutic conflict lies in the dialectic between archeology and teleology, these are found together in the concrete mixed texture of the symbol. These two lines of interpretation find their point of intersection in the meaningful texture of symbols. Symbols are thus the concrete, though not immediate, moment of the dialectic. After thought, after the ascesis of reflection, after the decentering of the origin of

meaning away from naive consciousess—and only after—
may one return to the simple attitude of listening to symbols,
the 'second naivete.' 'In order to think in accord with symbols one must subject them to a dialectic; only then is it possible to set the dialectic within interpretation itself and come
back to living speech' (ibid. 495). This is the transition to
concrete reflection. 'In returning to the attitude of listening
to language, reflection passes into the fullness of speech simply heard and understood' (ibid. 496).

> Let us not be mistaken about the meaning of this last
> stage: this return to the immediate is not a return to silence,
> but rather to the spoken word, to the fullness of language.
> Nor is it a return to the dense enigma of initial, immediate
> speech, but to speech that has been instructed by the whole
> process of meaning. Hence this concrete reflection does not
> imply any concession to irrationality or effusiveness. In its
> return to the spoken word, reflection continues to be reflec-
> tion, that is, the understanding of meaning; reflection becomes
> hermeneutic; this is the only way in which it can become con-
> crete and still remain reflection. The second naivete is not the
> first naivete; it is postcritical and not precritical; it is an in-
> formed naivete (ibid.).

Ricoeur's thesis is formulated as follows:

> … what psychoanalysis calls overdetermination cannot
> be understood apart from a dialectic between two functions
> which are thought to be opposed to one another but which
> symbols coordinate in a concrete unity. Thus the ambiguity of
> symbolism is not a lack of univocity but is rather the possibil-
> ity of carrying and engendering opposed interpretations, each
> of which is self-consistent (ibid.).

Symbols carry two vectors—repetition of our childhood (individually, culturally, racially, and species-wise) and exploration of our adult life. But these two functions are not external to one another; they constitute the overdetermination of

authentic symbols. Authentic symbols are truly regressive-progressive; remembrance gives rise to anticipation, archaism to prophecy.

The intentional structure of symbols may be described in terms of the unity of concealing and showing. At this point, Ricoeur becomes, I believe, very similar to Heidegger in the latter's notions of truth and language. True symbols both disguise and reveal. While they conceal the aims of our instincts, they disclose the process of self-consciousness. 'Disguise, reveal; conceal, show; these two functions are no longer external to one another; they express the two sides of a single symbolic function ... Advancement of meaning occurs only in the sphere of the projections of desire, of the derivatives of the unconscious, of the revivals of archaism ... The opposed hermeneutics disjoin and decompose what concrete reflection recomposes through a return to speech simply heard and understood' (ibid. 497).

Freud's inadequate theory of symbolism and language leads Ricoeur to suggest that we distinguish various levels of creativity within the symbolic realm. At the lowest level we come upon 'sedimented symbolism,' symbols so encrusted with age and worn with use that they have nothing but a past. Such, says Ricoeur, are the symbols of dreams, fairy tales, and legends. At a higher level are symbols that function, often without our knowing it, in ordinary human commerce. Interestingly enough, Ricoeur states that these are the symbols appropriate for study by structural anthropology. Finally, there is the level of prospective symbols, creations of meaning which take up the traditional symbols with their multiple significations and serve as the vehicles of new meanings. The task of one concerned with the future symbolic capabilities of humanity, says Ricoeur, is to grasp symbols in this creative moment, not when they arrive at the end of their course and are revived in dreams (ibid. 504-07).

3 A Further Radicalization

I accept from Ricoeur the archeological-teleological unity-in-tension of the concrete symbol. But I differ from him on several counts. My qualifications of his analysis are not in the interests of returning to naive consciousness untutored by criticism. The mediation of immediacy is a matter of the appropriation and articulation of what is otherwise undifferentiated and nonobjectified. In both its cognitive and dispositional dimensions, it effects a displacement of the home of meaning away from naive consciousness. But I start with the displacement effected, not by Kantian epistemology or Husserlian phenomenology but by Lonergan's cognitional analysis. The latter effects a mediation of cognitive immediacy or *Verstehen* by enabling one to answer correctly three questions: what am I doing when I am knowing? why is doing that knowing? what do I know when I do that? The displacement of the home or core of meaning away fron naive awareness is achieved in the startling strangeness of the combination of judgments which affirm that knowing is knowing being, but that being is not a subdivision of the 'already out there now,' but is rather whatever can be intelligently grasped and reasonably affirmed (Lonergan 1992, chapter 12).

First, then, I wish to radicalize the significance of the dialectical overdetermination of symbols. While it is true that reflective philosophy must move through a concrete hermeneutical turn to the dialectic of the symbol, the issue is not so much one of understanding human experience by understanding human expressions as it is one of understanding human expressions by a more radical and concrete understanding of human experience, by a mediation of dispositional immediacy through the disengagement of its symbolic constitution. The task of philosophy has become, with the work of Lonergan, that of the mediation of immediacy through self-appropriation. This task is not fulfilled primarily by moving from an understanding of human objectifications in language, culture, and action to an understanding of experience, no matter how dialectical, even no matter how accurate, the understanding of these objectifications may be. The essential movement is the other way around, and its cognitive dimensions are expressed in Lonergan's programmatic invitation: 'Thoroughly understand what it is to understand, and not only will you understand the broad lines of all there is to be understood, but also you will possess a fixed base, an invariant pattern, opening upon all further developments of understanding' (ibid. 22). Something similar may be said of the roots of desire and fear in human imagination: *Come to know as existential subject the contingent figures, the structure, the process, and the symbolic spontaneity of your own psyche, and you will come into possession of an expanding base and an intelligible pattern illuminating the vouloir-dire of human desire as it is brought to expression in the cultural and religious objectifications of human history.*

Secondly, and relatedly, as we shall discover in detail in the next chapter, a far more generous evaluation can be provided of the role of the dream than that accorded it by Ricoeur. The Jungian understanding of the dream is, I believe, far more accurate than the Freudian interpretation preserved by Ricoeur. Dreams are anything but the revival of sedimented symbols that have nothing but a past.

Finally, this more generous evaluation of the dream is bound up with a notion of the psyche itself which is explicitly teleological in part. Thus the dialectical counterpart to Freud in understanding the archeological-teleological unity-in-tension of even the most spontaneous dream symbols should be, not Hegel, but a philosophically criticized Jung. While I must severely criticize Jung's lack of serious philosophic underpinnngs, I believe his notions of the structure and dynamics of the psyche, when coupled with Freud's, will provide us with a better understanding of the unity-in-tension that is the concrete symbol than can be afforded by placing Freud and Hegel in dialectical relationship to one another or by finding Freud's problematic in Hegel and Hegel's in Freud. The authentic symbol is a spontaneous psychic production. It is not a matter of *Geist* except insofar as the latter, reinterpreted as the existential subject, has influenced or failed to influence psyche. While the ultimate dialectic of the existential subject is that between intentionality and psyche, the ultimate dialectic of the symbol itself is located within psyche.

I am maintaining, then, that the appropriated dispositional immediacy which is Ricoeur's second naivete is not precisely the result of the dialectic which Ricoeur elaborates, a dialectic of opposed hermeneutics, but of another dialectic, a specifically therapeutic dialectic, a dialectic within the psyche. Philosophy as we have known it cannot bring one to appropriated immediacy in the dispositional realm, but can only point the way, open possibilities, and discuss eventualities. This, of course, Ricoeur has done, and he has done so in masterful fashion. But the process of moving forward to an existential appropriation of dispositional immediacy is a different kind of process. It is, indeed, dialectical and hermeneutical, and it is also reflective in Ricoeur's sense of this word. But it is not philosophy as we have known philosophy, or even as Ricoeur understands philosophy. It is a different kind of mediation. With Lonergan philosophy has become method. But method can sublate psychic analysis and psychic synthesis. Within the methodical exigence, as one of its constituent features, there is the therapeutic exigence.

The therapeutic dialectic of the psyche may be understood, then, as a principal dimension in the achievement of
self-transcending existential subjectivity. It may be placed
into the more inclusive context of the dialectic of intentionality and psyche. But the fact that an archeologicalteleological
unity-in-tension pertains to the most elemental spontaneous
symbolic productions of the psyche of the dreaming subject
indicates a dialectical suspension or tension within the psyche
itself. There is the potential, suggested and *almost* sufficiently
disengaged by Jung (whose psychology collapses on the final psychic complex of the negotiation of evil), that the psyche
may be brought to join in the dynamism of intentionality toward value, indeed toward the upper reaches of an ascending scale of values. And there is the opposed possibility that
the psyche may drift in the direction of the loss of the existential subject as the potential for self-transcending authenticity, that the subject may simply come to drift in the direction of the now harsh and now seductive rhythms of psyche
and nature and thus fail to achieve genuine humanity. I do
not believe Ricoeur highlights strongly enough the fact that
the tension within sybmolism points to a tension within the
mythopoetic core of imagination itself. There seems to be in
the psyche itself a teleological orientation toward joining the
dynamism of intentionality toward being, truth, and value,
as well as an archeological regressive tendency toward the
inertness of non-living matter. The psyche, it is true, cannot
resolve the tension. That is the formidable task of the existential subject finding out for oneself that it is up to oneself
to decide what one is to make of oneself, asking oneself the
most crucial of all questions, What do I want to make of
myself? The conscious mind, or better, the ego is all too often
'reluctant to see or admit the polarity of its own background'
so that incompatible contents remain nonobjectified or are
habitually and assiduously overlooked. 'The more this is so,

the more the [psyche] will build up its counterposition' (Jung 1963, xviii). But the conscious mind can also take stock of psychic polarity, and then there can occur a progressive articulation and differentiation of the inner space of the psyche and a progressive though dialectical conscription of the psyche into the thrust of intentionality to the freedom of originating value.

Thus, within what Jung calls 'the unconscious' itself, there are tendencies which are opposites. The two most inclusive of these we may call the tendency to matter and the tendency to spirit. Because of the dialectic present in a psyche which is human, *both* are to be consciously realized, and not on an intermittent *ad hoc* basis—now matter, now spirit—a basis which could be specified only by a process of deduction from so-called principles. Rather, their realization is to be consistent and permanent, through a psychic reconciliation of one with the other, a process which individuates both of these tendencies. This is the therapeutic dialectic. While it is effected by the existential subject's engaging the symbolic manifestations of dreams, which are intentions without fulfilments, in a continual process of coming to terms, this dialectic of intentionality and psyche is conditioned by a dialectic within the psyche itself. The symbolic manifestations of dreams undergo a story of development or aberration according as they are dealt with by the consciousness of the existential subject, and they take on a particular flavor from the individual existential subject whose dispositional immediacy they represent, whose story they narrate. Since they are relatively autonomous, however, they cannot be integrated into conscious life through philosophy, but only by a different kind of dialectical procedure which often takes the form of a dialogue. 'Usually the process runs a dramatic course, with many ups and downs. It expresses itself in, or is accompanied by, dream symbols that are related to the "representations collectives," which in the form of mythological motifs have portrayed psychic processes of transformation since the earliest times' (Jung 1969, 41).

As a way of expressing the therapeutic exigence as a part of the new movement of historical Western mind of which I spoke in the first chapter, we might say that for Hegel the unity of opposites is conceptual and its comprehension is speculative knowledge, whereas in concrete method, when the latter is extended to the psyche, the unity of opposites is psychic, the progressive result of a dialectical process that is lived while and according as it is comprehended.

4 Mystery and Myth

I accept from Ricoeur, then, both the possibility of a second naivete and the characterization of this naivete as involving the ambiguity of symbolism, though I place the latter more radically in the realm of the preverbal and spontaneous elemental psyche. From Ricoeur I accept also one further qualification of the symbolic realm of which one becomes more aware as the therapeutic dialectic goes forward: symbols are exploratory rather than etiological or explanatory. Such a distinction is entailed in Riceour's well-known phrase, 'the symbol gives rise to thought' (Ricoeur 1969, 374; 1970, 38). To interpret symbols as exploratory is, on Ricoeur's analysis, to reenact them in sympathetic imagination, not through an immediate belief but through the dialectical recovery of their intentionality. In this way the elemental symbol is found to be an interpretation of oneself as existential subject, of one's background, potential future, and present status. Such a relation to symbols I designate as *mystery*. To reenact a symbol through immediate belief, on the other hand, would be to accept it as explanatory. This relation to symbol is *myth*, in the pejorative sense of this plurivocal word. I accept from Ricoeur the notion of symbols as intentions without fulfilments, and would add that this unfulfilled nature of the symbol as such is itself expressive of its archeological-teleological unity-in-tension, of its concrete, dynamic, and dialectically contradictory possibilities. Only the existential subject can resolve the dialectic. What do I want to make of myself?

Jung speaks of a tendency which leads us either to regard symbols as explanatory or to neglect them in favor of concepts:

> We all have an understandable desire for crystal clarity, but we are apt to forget that in psychic matters we are dealing with processes of experience, that is, with transformations which should never be given hard and fast names if their living movement is not to petrify into something static. The protean mythologem and the shimmering symbol express the processes of the psyche far more trenchantly and, in the end, far more clearly than the clearest concept; for the symbol not only conveys a visualization of the process but—and this is perhaps just as important—it also brings a re-experiencing of it, of that twilight which we can learn to understand only through inoffensive empathy, but which too much clarity only dispels (Jung 1967, 162-63).

Of what is the symbol exploratory? Can we be more precise on this point without falling into the conceptualism indicted by Jung? I find helpful some distinctions offered by Lonergan in *Method in Theology* and already discussed in our first chapter (Lonergan 1993, 96, 108). If we insist that the symbol is to be accepted as exploratory rather than explanatory, then we may say that a post-critical symbolic consciousness would understand the elemental symbol as a manifestation of what is interior rather than exterior, as referring to the temporal before the spatial, the generic before the specific, and as related to the divine and the anti-divine, to grace and sin, and not simply to the human. The concrete symbol is exploratory of our affective interiority, of the dispositional aspect of primordial immediacy. It is exploratory of our journey through time and, when produced spontaneously by the psyche of an individual, indicative of one's present stance in time. To say that it refers to the generic before the specific would be to indicate that spontaneously produced symbols function rather as barometer than thermometer.[10] That is, they are indicative of the atmosphere, of its pressures and potentialities, rather than explicative of the precise temperature and of its causes. Finally, to say that symbols are related to the realm of transcendence is to indicate that they are ciphers of the existential subject's relation to the upper levels of the scale of values, where the authenticity of self-transcendence is the fruit of the gift of God's love.[11] Thus the symbols spontaneously produced in the dreams and fantasies of the existential subject are to be regarded in the first instance as opening up for appropriation some element of the psychic constitution of their author, of the temporal relations in terms of which he or she is this concrete man or woman at this point in his or her personal history, and of the stance that he or she is adopting or can adopt to the movement of intentionality toward self-transcendence. The attentive presence to this complex congeries beckons thoughtful reflection, hermeneutic reflection, dialectical reflection, but also therapeutic reflection.

---

10. I am indebted for this formulation to Rev. Charles Goldsmith, Ph.D., clinical psychologist.

11. 1993 note: In my later formulations of this point, I speak of the ultimate anagogic context of symbols.

Finally, I must relate my distinction between mystery and myth to Lonergan's (Lonergan 1992, 554-72). Lonergan later rearticulated this distinction: 'My contrast of mystery and myth was between symbolic expressions of positions and of counterpositions.'[12] Mystery for me is a posture vis-à-vis symbols which searches for the intention of intelligibility, truth, and value in the symbolic revelations themselves. Myth is an opposite posture which regards the symbol itself as fulfilment, which does not intelligently, reasonably, and responsibly discriminate the dialectic of the symbol, and which thus runs the risk of the capitulation of intentionality to psyche that is the romantic agony. While the former attitude is the condition of possibility of the symbolic expression of positions, the latter is the inevitability of the symbolic expression of counterpositions.[13]

5 Individuation

Jungian psychology makes an acute and very important distinction between the first half of life and the second half of life. During the first half of life, which extends at least through one's early 30s, one seeks one's natural self-expression in external life. Thus a conscious ego is developed, which, together with its 'outward face,' the persona, determines for better or for worse an individual's position in regard to what

---

12. Lonergan, '*Insight* Revisited' 275.

13. The tension of the symbol is also dealt with by Matthew L. Lamb, 'Myth and the Crisis of Historical Consciousness,' paper presented for discussion at the convention of the American Academy of Religion, November, 1974.

is exterior, spatial, specific, and human. In the second half of
life, one seeks new channels and new sources of self-expression and meaning. On our analysis, one can then cultivate
the world of interiority, and consequently can come to value
time before space and what is generic as the condition of
what is specific, and to discriminate the psyche in terms of
what Christian spirititual tradition has called the discernment
of spirits. The inner law of the second half of life manifests
itself in the movement to what Jung calls individuation. The
transition from the first half of life to the second half of life is
a very difficult affair. It demands the relativization of the
outer-directed ego and thus of one's relations to what is exterior, spatial, specific, and human. It demands that the ego
surrender its position as the supposed center of the total personality—a position it *had* to adopt during the first half of
life—and that it give way to a deeper center, a more mysterious center, a center which can never be completely circum-
scribed and grasped but which can, at best, be circumambulated. This deeper center Jung refers to as the self. I find no
reason for not identifying it with what Ricoeur calls the *Sum*
of the *Cogito*. For Jung, it is symbolized—inadequately and
abstractly, I believe—by such figures as a mandala, a stone,
or a steadily burning flame.[14] On the other hand, once the
ego gives way to the self as center, there are further and seemingly more treacherous difficulties to be negotiated, which
only time and determination enable one to resolve. For one
can then identify one's ego consciousness with the self, resulting in 'an inflation which threatens consciousness with

---

14. 1993 note: In later writings I rely on Lonergan's distinction of
integrator and operator, posit the mandala as symbolic of the self as integrator, and claim that Jung does not adequately discuss symbols of the
self as operator.

dissolution.'[15] In these moments, as Erich Neumann warns, the 'ecstatic demolition' of the ego may occur, either through a negative introversion or, by projection, through an outward mysticism culminating in a pantheistic seizure. In either case the ego would be overpowered and one would be on the borders of psychosis. *Tertium datur.* There is the possibility, achieved only by ever greater approximation, of being attached to the numinous and at home in oneself, at rest and in creative motion, in the world and outside it at the same time, and of being thus self-consciously, through individuation (see Neumann 1959, 44).

The individuating aspects of such a task are difficult. 'The self is the hero, threatened already at birth by envious collective forces; the jewel that is coveted by all and arouses jealous strife; and finally the god who is dismembered by the old, evil power of darkness. In its psychological meaning, individuation is an *opus contra naturam*, which creates a *horror vacui* in the collective layer and is only too likely to collapse under the impact of the collective forces of the psyche.'[16] These collective forces could be those to which the persona responds, in which case the movement into the second half of life would not occur psychically at all; or they may be what Jung has called the collective unconscious, in which case the psychoses referred to by Neumann are imminent.

The notion of the self is a permanently heuristic notion which is appropriately described only in symbolic language. Jung speaks of the self as 'psychic totality and at the same time a centre, neither of which coincides with the ego but includes it, just as a larger circle encloses a smaller one (ibid.

---

15. C.G. Jung, 'Concerning Rebirth,' in *The Archetypes and the Collective Unconscious* 145.

16. Jung, 'Concerning Rebirth' 146-47.

142). Insofar as it is the sum of conscious and unconscious processes, it is by definition beyond conceptual grasp (Jung 1963, 63). The notion of the self is the type of notion which James Hillman qualifies as indefinable (Hillman 1972, 79). I am convinced that the type of religious meditation represented in, for example, Sebastian Moore's discovery of the image of the Crucified at the far end of the psyche (Moore 1977) may help to specify what Jung was reaching for in his notion of the self at least insofar as the true self emerges out of one's negotiation of the problem of evil and more specifically out of one's progressive discovery of the meaning for oneself of the divinely originated solution to the problem of evil. How am I to participate in this solution?

The Jungian notion of individuation, then, is quite susceptible of reinterpretation within the context of the self-appropriation of the existential subject. Individuation is the psychic complement of the self-appropriation of intentionality aided by Lonergan. It is the movement of an individual to the appropriation of the dispositional aspect of immediacy. The movement from the ego to the self is a movement toward the appropriation of dispositional primordial immediacy. Ironically enough, however, it would appear that this movement toward the appropriation of immediacy is a movement away from naive consciousness. For it is a movement toward centering oneself in what can only be circumambulated, and it takes place through a process of relativizing naive consciousness. It is a movement from what is exterior, spatial, specific, and human, to what is interior, temporal, generic, and in the realm of the divine solution to the problem of evil. It involves a withdrawal of those projections which enable one to find one's realization and meaning in the 'already out there now real.' This movement thus affects the heart of one's desire to be, of one's striving toward existence. It is a movement, if you wish, toward an autonomy not only of one's cognitional being, such that my knowledge is a matter of my raising and answering questions, but also of one's source of desire and *conatus*. The existential and psychic complement to the disinterestedness of the pure desire to know is a movement toward the second innocence of agape. It is, perhaps, Western humanity's way of moving toward what the *Bhagavad Gita* calls 'acting while renouncing the fruits of one's actions,' toward the innocence which the ancient Chinese scripture, the *I Ching*, describes in this way: 'If one does not count on the harvest while plowing nor on the use of the field while clearing it, then it furthers one to undertake something.' It is a movement toward the nonalienation of those who are free to seek only the reign of God and God's righteousness, confident that everything they need for their life will be given them. This movement can be aided symbolically.

Failures to achieve individuation, on the other hand, are a matter radically of the 'loss of the "symbolical attitude,"' of 'a break in the spontaneous relationship between the conscious mind and its matrix, the unconscious' (Adler 1961, 9). For Jung, '… the collective unconscious … does not understand the language of the conscious mind. Therefore it is necessary to have the magic of the symbol which contains those primitive analogies that speak to the unconscious. The unconscious can be reached and expressed only by symbols, and for this reason the process of individuation can never do without the symbol. The symbol is the primitive exponent of the unconscious, but at the same time an idea that corresponds to the highest intuitions of the conscious mind.'[17]

---

17. C. G. Jung, 'Commentary on "The Secret of the Golden Flower,"' in *Alchemical Studies* 28. This passage from Jung highlights the dialectic within the psyche itself.

Joseph Henderson contrasts the Jungian notion of the self with the Hindu conception of Atman and shows the supreme importance of the symbol for the former.

> For the East the supreme ground of Being, Atman, is suprapersonal and completely transcendent, rendering its possessor capable of maintaining an attitude of selfless non-attachment to all wishes or compulsions of the ego. The Western Self, in contrast, is personal as well as impersonal. Through the ego it is attached to life in a meaningful and fateful way, while its transcendent aim relates it to the higher goal of individual differentiation from collective social patterns. In this sense individuation, therefore, involves the experience of conflict between the claims of the ego and the claims of the Self. Resolution occurs only at the nodal points of life where harmony can be established between these two claims by the creation of a reconciling symbol which performs its work by joining in a totally spontaneous or unexpected fashion the images of attachment with images of what is liberating for transcendent experience. In those significant moments a man may become, as Wordsworth says, 'true to the kindred points of heaven and home' (Henderson, 1963, 14).

From this perspective, appropriated dispositional immediacy involves a knowledge of one's own most spontaneous conditions and roots through an appropriation of the symbolic determinants or qualifications of one's own inner order and meaning. The symbolic revelations of dreams are for Gerhard Adler "'living symbols" representing "the inexpressible in an unsurpassable way"' (Adler 1961, 9). Adler quotes Ruth Monroe, *Schools of Psychoanalytic Thought*: 'The living symbol does not merely *represent* wider experience on the *pars pro toto* principle ... Nor is it the agreed-upon sign for highly abstract relationships as in mathematics and the natural sciences. It is creative ... Jung's major point is that the symbols are used *creatively* in dreams, in art, in psychosis, in many social phenomena.'[18]

More important for Jung than the forgotten, the repressed, the subliminally perceived, thought, and felt acquisitions of one's personal existence, retrieved through a reduction to the original infantile situation, is the appropriation of the transpersonal source of imaging itself, which he refers to variously as the collective unconscious and the objective psyche, and which I shall rename the archetypal function. James Hillman has identified it with Augustine's *memoria* (Hillman 1972, 171). This source of transpersonal images is identical also, I believe, with the transcendental imagination which lured Kant and captured Heidegger. Thus psychic self-appropriation is the differentiation and appropriation of the *primordial time structure* of one's dispositional immediacy. This time structure is not only the form of inner sense, as with Kant, but the very constitution of *Befindlichkeit* in its primordiality, unity, and totality, as with Heidegger. To say that the transcendental imagination *captured* Heidegger means that for him it constitutes not only *Befindlichkeit* but intentionality as a whole. This I deny, strongly and emphatically. But it *is* the condition of the possibility of the archeological-teleological unity-in-tension of the concrete symbol. The transcendental time structure of imagination (*Einbildungskraft*—the word is important) and thus of our primordial concern for 'world' is fragile. When one is out of touch, it is because the imaginal constitution of dispositional immediacy has been fractured or distorted, so that one's future does not beckon one's 'having been' into one's present. Genuine psychotherapy

---

18. Ibid. In continuity with Ricoeur's analysis of the dialectic of the symbol, may we suggest that the dream is both a wish and an indication of a pathway to self-realization through what Gaston Bachelard has called dialectical sublimation? (See Bachelard 1964, 99-100.)

is the recovery of the primordial time structure of *Befindlichkeit* through a release of the creative potentialities of the archetypal function which gives rise to primordial time. This recovery occurs in a progressive reconciliation of previously undifferentiated psychic opposites. In each case these opposites take the form of future and 'having been,' of teleology and archeology. Their reconciliation is in each instance a progressive emergence of the authentic, self-transcending existential subject. Only when the opposites are those of good and evil, grace and sin, is reconciliation impossible. This is the subtle point missed by Jung. The solution to the problem of evil is not integration of evil into the psyche; it is not reconciliation or integration of evil with good. The assertion that it is so may well have something to do with the blasphemy against the Holy Spirit of which Jesus accused those who charged that he was possessed by the devil (Mark 3.29). The solution to the problem of evil *is* embodied in a symbol of reconciliation, but it is the symbol of the reconciliation of archeology and teleology, alpha and omega, origin and destiny, creation and eschaton—the Crucified. The impossibility of a reconciliation of good and evil psychically as well as speculatively is the best cipher of the moment calling for total surrender to God's love, for the movement to the soul beyond psychology. God's love deals with evil, not by reconciling it with good nor by integrating it psychically, but by transcending it in the Crucified and in the collaboration set loose upon the world by that Figure, by the historical incarnation both of God's Son and of the self at those farthest reaches of the human psyche where Psyche becomes Wisdom in the act of surrender to God.

4 Sublations

Being is 'what is to be known by the totality of true judgments' (Lonergan 1992, 374). There are various spheres of being. The true judgments of mathematics comprise a sphere of being as do the true judgments intended in the various sciences and those made in cognitional analysis. When true judgments are made concering the symbolic constitution of *Befindlichkeit*, they concern a sphere of being which I call *the imaginal*.

The continuity of the psychic self-appropriation of the imaginal with the self-appropriation of intentionality in method must be further specified. Thus, the differentiation and appropriation of imaginally constituted dispositional immediacy are enabled to come to pass by a sublation on the part of conscious intentionality that is additional to the sublations explained by Lonergan. In addition to the sublation of sensory experience by understanding, of experience and understanding by reasonable judgment, and of experience, understanding, and judgment by the moral responsibility and cooperative-intersubjective consciousness of the existential subject, there is a sublation of the imaginal, and principally of the symbolic revelations of dreams, on the part of the whole of attentive, intelligent, reasonable, responsible, cooperative-intersubjective existential consciousness. Thus, in addition to the attentive, intelligent, reasonable, and responsible appropriation of one's rational self-consciousness, there is the

attentive, intelligent, reasonable and responsible appropriation and negotiation of one's psychic spontaneity.

1 The Imaginal as Operator: A First Determination

The possibility of such a sublation is implicit in
Lonergan's reference to the approach of existential psychology, which 'thinks of the dream, not as the twilight of life,
but as its dawn, the beginning of the transition from imper-
sonal existence to presence in the world, to constitution of
one's self in one's world' (Lonergan 1993, 69). My analysis
extends this reference to an explicit utterance, by speaking
of an additional sublation, through which the symbolic constitution of 'how one is' is mediated to the existential subject.
The imaginal elucidation of one's dispositions is released to
consciousness in dreams. Second immediacy results in part
from the capacity to objectify the imaginal structure of dispositional primordial immediacy through the interpretation
of dreams, through which the dispositional aspect of immediacy is released from muteness and confusion. The concrete
symbols revealed in dreams are to be taken as a kind of text
or story whose meaning can be delineated by interpretive
understanding, reasonable judgment, and evaluative deliberation.

I borrow the term 'the imaginal' from some recent articles in Jungian publications (Durand 1971; Corbin 1972),
but not without changing its meaning. For the authors of
these articles, the term is used in an overly Platonic sense, so
that there is a *mundus imaginalis* somewhere in suspension
between the *mundus sensibilis* and the *mundus intelligibilis*. This
world is highly archetypal and is experienced in dreams and

fantasy. I am using the term to refer instead to what becomes known when one learns to relate disposition to elemental symbolization through the interpretation of the symbols spontaneously produced by the psyche in dreams and fantasies. As we shall see, these symbols, far from constituting an independent world in themselves, are *operators* effecting a sublation of neural and psychic process into the realm of recognition and interpretation, and as such are the most primordial signals of one's orientation as existential subject in the world mediated and constituted by meaning. Again, far from constituting an independent world in themselves, they issue the existential subject into an ever new world of his or her own, if one intelligently, reasonably, and responsibly appropriates their meaning and constitutes one's world on this basis. By using 'imaginal' as a qualification of immediacy, then, and by speaking of appropriation, I am in fact speaking of a fuller entrance into appropriation of the feelings which constitute the primordial apprehension of value. Primordial immediacy is always dispositionally qualified, but this disposition is frequently inarticulate. It becomes articulate in dreams. Dreams are the story of dispositional immediacy. The hermeneutic and dialectical interpretation of dreams is an appropriation of the dispositions which permeate one's immediacy to the operations by which the world is mediated by meaning and to the contents of those operations. Such an appropriation gives access to the symbolic constitution and possibilities of existential subjectivity.

I have already referred to Eugene Gendlin's notion of 'experiencing,' which is his term for what I have been calling dispositional immediacy. It is 'that partly unformed stream of feeling that we have at every moment ... the flow of feeling, concretely, to which you can every moment attend inwardly, if you wish' (Gendlin 1962, 3). Gendlin has, in effect, attempted to delineate other ways besides dream interpreta-

tion of symbolizing dispositional immediacy, by proposing
techniques by which symbols can be reciprocally related to
felt experiencing. When symbolic meanings occur in inter-
action with experiencing, they can change, and when one
employs symbols to attend to a feeling, it can change. In fact,
Gendlin proposes seven different kinds of functional relationships between feelings and symbols. In an effort to high-
light what I mean by the symbolic structure of feeling, I shall
summarize these relationships. Three of them are called parallel relationships and four creative relationships. My only
caution regarding the employment of Gendlin's techniques
is that dispositional immediacy is adequately symbolized only
when the symbols issue from and reflect the same depth dimension from which dreams proceed. Gendlin's techniques,
I believe, can be quite effective if one has already learned the
connection between feelings and the elemental symbolization of the dream.

The first parallel functional relationship, the one least
relevant to our discussion, is called *direct reference*. It involves
directly referring to the felt meaning; it is an individual's reference to a present felt meaning and not to any object, concept, or anything else that may be related to the felt meaning.
Verbal articulations, such as 'this feeling,' refer but *without
naming* the felt meaning to which they refer. They depend for
their meaning on direct reference to the felt meaning, just as
demonstratives depend on present sense perception. Thus
the felt meaning in direct reference is meaningful independently of representative conceptualization. Without at least
some kind of demonstrative reference, of course, there cannot be 'a' felt meaning; feeling would be permeated, but not
at all mediated, by meaning. But without felt meaning, such
demonstrative reference would have no function to perform.
Meaning in direct reference is defined as that which is set off
in some sense as 'one,' 'a' or 'this' felt meaning.

The second parallel functional relationship is *recognition*. Here, what Gendlin calls symbols adequately objectify and *call forth in us* the felt meanings that constitute our recognizing the meanings of the symbols. We hear or see or think a symbol, and in that act feel its meaning. We recognize, not the having of the meaning, but the felt meaning itself. Without such recognition, the symbol would be meaningless. The relationship of feeling and symbol is the reverse of that operative in direct reference, for the symbol means and calls forth feeling. A meaning is a recognition feeling capable of being called forth.

The third parallel functional relationship is *explication*. Here felt meaning, once called forth, gives rise to symbols which further explicate it. These symbols appear as a result of concentrating on the felt meaning itself. Part at least of the technique which Jung calls active imagination, I believe, is based on this process, for in active imagination a feeling or disposition gives rise to an image, and imaginative dialogue with the image gives rise to insight into the image and, if sufficiently pursued, may explicate and even modify both the disposition and the image. Thus the disposition has the independent power to be meaningful and to select the symbols. The latter are instruments of recognition, which in turn have the power to call out and fill out the disposition which gave rise to them.

In the creative functional relationships, symbols already meaningful in parallel relationships enter into relation with dispositions or feelings which have as yet no parallel symbols. A creative functional relationship is one between a partly unsymbolized felt meaning and a symbol that usually means something else.

The first of these creative functional relationships is *metaphor*, a term used by Gendlin in a perhaps more general sense than is usually employed by literary critics. Thus in metaphor a new meaning is achieved by drawing on old experience and by using the symbols for this familiar experience to refer to a new and otherwise unsymbolized experience. These symbols thus have two felt meanings, the old and the new.

The second creative functional relationship is *comprehension*. Here one concentrates on a felt meaning, as in explication, but, finding no extant symbols to express it exactly, one *invents* metaphor for its expression. The felt meaning is itself active, enabling us to feel whether the invented expression succeeds in symbolizing it. It changes in the process, since it becomes a meaning in a new sense and in a new functional relationship with the symbol. Its implicit content remains but becomes explicit. Comprehension differs from metaphor in that the novel creation of the relationship begins with the felt meaning, not with the old, extant symbol.

The third creative functional relationship is *relevance*. Here felt meanings are appealed to in order to make symbolizations understandable, even though these may refer to only a few specific felt meanings. It is an appeal to experience, to the context which renders a given symbol understandable. The set of symbols may be understood differently and to a different degree, given different felt meanings in terms of which they can be understood.

The fourth creative functional relationship is *circumlocution*. This is the creative modification and creative building up of the felt meaning needed for understanding a symbol. Each of the symbols employed already has an associated felt meaning. These interact creatively to give rise to new felt meanings. Circumlocution is related to relevance, in that it creates a felt context out of which other symbolizations will be understandable.

2 Two Clarifications

My interpretation of the term 'the imaginal' as operator leads me to suggest two other alterations of familiar psychological terminology. I suggest that we replace the term 'the unconscious' with the term 'the undifferentiated' and the Jungian term 'the collective unconscious' with the expression 'the archetypal function.' The first alteration is suggested for two reasons. First, as the term 'the unconscious' has come to be used in both Freudian and Jungian literature, it obfuscates the matter by suggesting an 'already down there now real' to be known by looking—but of course by looking down! It is reifying in a naively realistic and ultimately mystifying and mythic manner. Secondly, the replacement of this term with 'the undifferentiated' highlights the fact that primordial affective immediacy, however nonobjectified, is direclty pertinent to consciousness. It is, I believe, a more accurate English rendition of the German *Unbewusstsein*, which literally means 'not known,' 'not objectified,' or undifferentiated. Consciousness is not knowledge. Moreover, it is partly differentiated and partly undifferentiated. The basic psychotherapeutic distinction is not that between consciousness and 'the unconscious,' but that between the self as objectified and the self as conscious. The self as conscious includes the self as differentiated and the self as undifferentiated. The psychotherapeutic intention is to render the self as differentiated approximate to the self as conscious.

The second alteration is suggested for much the same reasons. It is not a denial of the truth Jung was reaching for in his speaking of the collective unconscious: namely, that there are certain universal symbolic patterns expressive and determinative of much that is human. But we must demystify

the substantialist and reifying associations too easily joined
to the term 'collective unconscious.' As Gendlin insists, our
psychological categories must reflect process if they are to
refer to direct experience (ibid. 32). The specific value of the
term 'the collective unconscious' is that it emphasizes the
potential social relevance of Jung's psychology, indeed its
crosscultural relevance. It points to the fact that, through
negotiation of archetypal images, the existential subject is at
the farthest possible remove from solipsism. But the cognitional confusion attendant upon the terminology of 'unconscious' is nonetheless strong enough to warrant a change of
vocabulary. The confusion is reflected in the following passage from Jung:

> Empirically ... [consciousness] always finds its limit when it
> comes up against the *unknown*. This consists of everything we do not
> know which, therefore, is not related to the ego as the centre of the
> field of consciousness. The unknown falls into two groups of ob-
> jects: those which are outside and can be experienced by the senses,
> and those which are inside and are experienced immediately. The
> first group comprises the unknown in the outer world; the second,
> the unknown in the inner world. We call this latter territory the
> *unconscious* (Jung 1973, 3).

It is true that Jung speaks of the inappropriateness of
the term 'subconscious' because of its connotations of
something 'down there,' but his suggested alternatives are
still given in spatial terms. '... how inept it is to designate
[the unconscious] as the "subconscious": it is not merely
"below" consciousness but also above it.'[1] The truth is that
'it' is not *anywhere*, is not some spatially located thing.
	Thus I suggest that we speak of the undifferentiated to

---

1. C.G. Jung, 'Phenomenology of the Spirit in Fairytales,' in *The
Archetypes and the Collective Unconscious* 239.

refer to most of what is included under what has been called the unconscious, whether personal or collective, and of the archetypal function to further designate what Jung calls the collective unconscious. The former we might also call the unknown psychic (Jung 1969a, 185). Jung includes under this notion 'everything of which I know, but of which I am not at the moment thinking; everything of which I was once conscious but have now forgotten; everything which, involuntarily and without paying attention to it, I feel, think, remember, want, and do; all the future things that are taking shape in me and will sometime come to consciousness; ... the Freudian findings ... [and] the psychoid functions that are not capable of consciousness and of whose existence we have only indirect knowledge.'[2]

My suggested changes were confirmed in a personal experiment of reading Jung while substituting 'the undifferentiated' for 'the unconscious,' 'the archetypal function' for 'the collective unconscious,' and 'differentiated consciousness' or 'ego' for Jung's 'consciousness.' The latter term, then, is to be used exclusively in Lonergan's sense of the subject's self-presence, inclusive of what is differentiated and undifferentiated.

---

2. Ibid. 1993 note: Jung includes under 'psychoid functions' the dynamics that promote spiritual operations. One of the central problems in his formulation revolves around his Kantian insistence that we can have no real knowledge of these dynamics. Lonergan's intentionality analysis provides precisely such knowledge.

3 The Symbolic *A priori*

My initial intention was to rename the collective unconscious as the symbolic *a priori*. Properly understood this
designation is quite correct and acceptable. But a proper understanding of the *a priori* elements of human subjectivity is
hard to come by. Perhaps it would be well, then, to examine
the question of the *a priori* first in terms of cognition. Giovanni
Sala has studied the *a priori* of human knowledge in Imman-
uel Kant's *Critique of Pure Reason* and Lonergan's *Insight*.[3] I
shall summarize his findings in order to aid me in discussing
the notion of the symbolic *a priori* and in arriving at a notion
of it in continuity with Lonergan's notion of the *a priori* rather
than, as Jung does, with Kant's.

3.1 The Cognitional A Priori

Kant's *Critique of Pure Reason* is in quest of the *a priori*
component of human knowledge. Kant wished to ground the
synthetic *a priori* judgments in which scientific knowledge
consists. Now for Kant scientific knowledge is knowledge of
the universal and necessary. Such knowledge cannot arise a
posteriori from experience and therefore must be *a priori*. 'Experience' is given at least two meanings in the *Critique of Pure*

---

3. Sala 1971. My quotations are from a summary of this work presented at the 1970 International Lonergan Congress and published in *The
Thomist* 60:2 (1976) 179-221. The paper is entitled 'The *A priori* in Human
Knowledge: Kant's *Critique of Pure Reason* and Lonergan's *Insight*.' This paper
is reprinted as the first chapter in Sala (1994). My quotations are taken
from the *Thomist* publication.

Reason: pure sense knowledge (*Empfindung*) and human knowledge in the full sense, which is sensible and intellectual together. If experience is taken in the first sense, necessity and universality do not originate in experience.

Now *a priori* elements are required to give universality and necessity because the object of knowledge for Kant is given to us through the senses and only through them. Thus the cognitive phases which follow upon experience as pure sensation cannot raise the representation of the sense object to a universal and necessary representation, because they do not contribute a partial object of their own to the constitution of the final and total object of knowledge. '… to understand the sensed object and to reflect on what has been understood, is not, in the Kantian view, to add a further, different content to our knowing; the content of knowledge is simply repeated in shifting from the sense level to the level of understanding, *Verstand*' (Sala 1976, 183). Sala qualifies this statement in a footnote, where he notes an inconssistency, in that 'Kant's *a priori* has its own objective content.' This will be seen further in what follows. In general, for Kant, intuition, *Erfahrung* taken as mere sense experience, tells *what is* but not that it must necessarily be so. For the latter we need the *a priori*.

Now, from Lonergan's perspective, knowledge of the universal and necessary represents the classicist, not the modern, ideal of science. Also, the notion that the object of knowledge is given us through the senses and only through them, that the following phases of cognitive process do not contribute a partial object of their own to the constitution of the final and total object of knowledge, reflects an unacceptable intuitionist principle. '… experience itself is knowledge neither of the "what" nor of the "is"; it is purely and simply presentation. To know "what" is presented and whether this "what" really "is" belongs to the intelligent and rational phases which follow the sensible phase' (ibid.). Universality and necessity, such as they are, are also seen to have a different origin from the Kantian *a priori*. 'As formal determination is added through understanding to an object which is otherwise a mere datum , and as existence is then added through judgment, so the universality of the formal determination as well as the factual necessity of existence are added to the same sense object. We have to consider the entire structure of knowledge in order to grasp how a process, which clearly has its empirical side too, can also have contents and qualifications which are not empirical—not empirical, at least, if one restricts "empirical" to the first level of the cognitional structure' (ibid. 183-84).

There is a tension in the Kantian notion of the *a priori* between attributing to it too little, by insisting on the empirical character of our knowledge, and attributing to it too much, by underlining its constitutive-formal function, such that, according to Kant, 'we can know *a priori* of things only what we ourselves *put into them*.'[4] On Sala's analysis, this tension can be overcome only by 'bringing to completion that turn to the subject (*Hinwendung zum Subjekt*) which is the purpose of transcendental analysis' (ibid. 184). Benefiting from Kant's famous metaphor of the judge, Sala clarifies what this complete *anthropologische Wendung* would reveal.

The evaluation of a given criminal case is confined to a judge because the judge possesses juridical science, which enables one to pose precise questions to the witnesses. The judge promotes the data provided by the witnesses to the level of understanding and then, by reflection on all pertinent factors from the standpoint of juridical science, to evidence sufficient to give knowledge of a juridically determined fact, which is precisely what the judge set out to know.

---

4. Ibid. 184, quoting Kant, *Critique of Pure Reason* B xviii.

The *a priori* of the judge is juridical knowledge. But rather than saying with Kant that the judge has 'put into' the juridically determined *fact*, it is more accurate to say that he or she has drawn something else from himself or herself and put it into the *data*. This something else consists of *questions*, through which alone one comes to know the facts.

Now, from the standpoint of Lonergan's cognitional theory, the juridical knowledge of the judge would be a particular specification of a 'unique, basic preunderstanding, the same for everyone, by which everyone, whether he knows under this aspect or that, always knows being or the real' (ibid. 186). This basic *Vorverständnis* is not any knowledge of objects, of nature or of the human world, but the presence of the subject to himself or herself, *consciousness*, in its immanent orientation toward the universe to be known. This orientation is the *a priori* in the basic sense; particular a prioris such as the judge's juridical science, are constituted a posteriori, 'within the cultural components of the environment in which one is born and raised, and through the personal experiences which constitute the life of the individual in its unicity. The first *a priori*, on the contrary, is the *a priori* in an absolute sense' (ibid.).

While it is in virtue of a particular *a priori* that the judge is able to pose specific questions, we are all able to ask the question about *what is* in virtue of the basic *a priori*. While Kant maintains that we can know *a priori* of things only what we ourselves put into them, it is more correct to say, 'what we ourselves *ask* about them' (ibid. 187). The basic *a priori*, consciousness in its orientation to the universe to be known, is not itself a category of any kind; rather it renders possible every determination of whatever is known, every category. The questions for understanding are the *operators* moving the object as datum to the object as understood; the questions for reflection are the *operators* moving the object as understood to the object as known. 'Human spirit betrays a total poverty at the very same time that it reveals a total capacity for discerning and judging by itself everything in the range of the true' (ibid. 188). Consciousness, the basic *a priori*, is normative of the entire cognitional process. The primordial question is the principle of the cognitional process, giving rise to specific single questions; at the same time, it penetrates the whole process, regulates everything, renders every single act meaningful (see ibid. 191).

> Our radical questioning, then, is a dynamism towards knowledge, an intelligently and rationally conscious dynamism, and one of unlimited scope. Because of these characteristics Lonergan names our pure desire to know *the notion of its objective*, that is to say, the notion of being. The characteristics found in the object of this intention, when it is realized in a manner faithful to its immanent norms, are anticipated by the subject itself, which is not content with data alone, but confronted by the data poses questions in order to understand and to reflect (ibid. 191-92).

The two kinds of questions establish a structure for knowledge so that it moves from experience through understanding to judgment. 'The many acts which introspective analysis brings to light arrange themselves on three essentially different levels, each one adding a new and quite distinct dimension both to knowledge as immanent activity and to the objective content known, until we reach on the one hand rational judgment and on the other the corresponding object' (ibid. 192). Our cognitive activities thus have different relations to the object. This variable relation is determined, not by intuition but by our desire to know, our intention of being.

The scope toward which our intention of being, as primordial question, tends is unrestricted. The way in which we tend to the object is unconditional. This unrestrictedness and unconditionality are interdependent. Being is 'the correlative of an unrestricted intentionality capable of tending towards its object without any qualification or condition' (ibid. 192-93).

Such a notion, however, implies the intelligibility of being, the rationality of the real. These notions, according to Sala, are missing in Kant. 'Man understands, conceives, and—according to a certain meaning of the word—judges; he performs all these activities in a manner coherent with their immanent norms. But for all that, what does he know of reality? Nothing. The intelligent and rational fulfillment of the cognitional dynamism is not [for Kant] the means of knowing reality' (ibid. 193). The reality called Noumenon is 'something absolutely beyond our intelligent inquiry and our critical reflection' (ibid.).

For a rational notion of the real, on the other hand, understanding would have to grasp a *new content* not given through intuition, the intelligible of the sensible grasped in the sensible. 'Understanding thinks, or brings to the concept, or subsumes under the concept, the object of sense, by adding to it an objective element which is not sensible' (ibid. 194). 'Instead [of the intuition principle] we must say that sense intuition has its own content, that the understanding of *Verstand* has its own content, and, going beyond the binary structure, that the judgment of *Vernunft* has its own content … Each cognitional act gives us a partial object. It is the task of the entire structure, which is brought to term in rational judgment, to give us the proper object of knowledge, that is, being' (ibid.). In Kant's assumption, however, the intellectual contributions of *Verstand* and *Vernunft* refer to reality only through the sensible intuition. In fact, *Vernunft*, as tendency toward the unconditioned, will be doubly mediated, through both intuition and understanding. On the other hand, in Lonergan's account, there is an immediate relationship to reality as intended; there is a mediate relation to reality in understanding and conceiving; and there is a transparent medium of the read in judgment—the medium of truth.

Sala now considers each of the elements in knowledge—sensibility, *Verstand*, and *Vernunft*—according to its *a priori* element in each system of thought under investigation. This enables him to distinguish sharply beteween an *operative-heuristic a priori* and *a content-constitutive or object-constitutive a priori* at each of the stages in the process of knowledge. Both of these notions are found in Kant, thus indicating an inconsistency. Only the operative-heuristic notion is found in Lonergan. As Sala will find valid the operative-heuristic *a priori* accounted for in Lonergan's *Insight*, and invalid the contentconstitutive *a priori* in Kant's *Critique of Pure Reason*, so I am seeking an elucidation of the symbolic *a priori* that is continuous with the operative-heuristic *a priori* governing cognitional process, a notion that does not reflect the Kantianism of the content-constitutive *a priori* sometimes found in Jung's writings. This reflected Kantianism is connected, I believe, with Jung's reified 'collective unconscious' and with the mystifying connotations of the recent discussions of the *mundus imaginalis*.

First, then, sensibility. The forms of space and time are considered by Kant *both* as systems of relationship among the contents of experience (operative-heuristic) *and* as containing contents of their own independent of the a posteriori content of experience and capable of being considered in this independence (content-constitutive). The operativeheuristic notion states that the *a priori* is *the law of sensitive receptive operativity* in relation to sense impressions. Space and time are nothing if we prescind from the operativity of the senses when confronted with sense data. The sense representation conforms to the constitution of the sensing subject.

There is also a twofold presentation of the *a priori* of understanding in the *Critique of Pure Reason*. The operative-heuristic *a priori* lies in the categories considered purely and simply as *functions of the synthetic unity*, functions of a judgment without content. By their synthetic activity exercised upon the contents of sensibility, they bring sense knowledge up to the level of human knowledge. As subjective forms of the unity of understanding, they are not objective contents but 'the ability of *Verstand* to add an intelligible content to the sense object by operating a synthesis upon it' (ibid. 202). The *Verstand* is a spontaneity, an original synthetic capacity. Sala maintains that Kant does not extend far enough his analysis of this synthetic capacity of intelligent consciousness, not so much because the categories are fixed at twelve—a common criticism of Kantian scholars—but because they are regarded in too formalistic and logical a manner, in that Kant's discussion of them is infected also with a content-constitutive notion of the *a priori*. 'Actually the spontaneity of understanding cannot be pigeon-holed into any set of concepts. Every concept, no matter how general, is *a posteriori*; but the operative intelligibility of understanding, that which makes it an intelligent intelligible, is *a priori*. The concept, every concept, is the product of this intelligence in operation, never the norm of its operation' (ibid. 202-03).

Kant's content-constitutive conception of the categories highlights the rigidity of his notion of the *a priori* of understanding. This *a priori* is an addition by the cognitive faculty to the raw material of the sense impressions, an addition in the form of an objective content.

> ... the entire problematic of the application of the pure concepts of understanding to a corresponding intuition, makes sense only because the pure concept of understanding is precisely a content to be applied. Likewise, the description of the *a priori* as of something which lies ready in the mind (*Gemüt*), or in the *Verstand*, obviously indicates it to be an object. Finally, the affirmation that the *a posteriori* of empirical intuition is only the occasion or the opportunity for

the mind to draw forth from itself the formal *a priori* elements which it already possesses, points in the same direction, for as regards a heuristic *a priori*, the given is much more than a mere occasion (ibid. 204-05).

Kant's own inconsistency on this point makes it difficult to interpret his doctrine. But the Transcendental Deduction of the Pure Concepts of the Understanding denies that objects can be given in intuition independently of functions of the understanding.

> The appearances that enter our field of consciousness are already fruits of the synthetic activity of understanding, which works on the appearances through the imagination. This is the final word of the Kantian critique ... The unifying moments of the pure concepts of understanding, as well as of the pure intuitions, are the result of the synthetic unity of consciousness which operates from the very beginning of the cognitional process, and finds progressiely in the *a posteriori* datum what it has put there itself, and thus goes ahead creating, on different levels of the structure, the conditions of possibility of objectively valid knowledge (ibid. 206).

Thus even the empirical itself is actually a consequence of the synthetic activity of the imagination. On Sala's interpretation, this represents an attempt to find a substitute for the act of understanding in the sensible. It makes the final direction of Kant's epistemology to be 'towards a totally thetic knowledge.' That is to say:

> The *a priori* either posits or is itself constitutive of the reality which it enables us to know ... On this thetic activity, which extends to the *Anschauung*, depends the ontological status of known reality. The obscurity, the tortuousness, and even the incoherence of the [*Critique of Pure Reason*], are due to the aim of recovering empiricist realism within this idealist perspective. What we consider to be the final word of [the *Critique of Pure Reason*], whenever it is said and as soon as it is said, is subject to correction and reinterpretation within the empiricist perspective—in a to and fro movement which shows in

itself no criterion for settling on any one definitive position (ibid. 207-08).

We move now to the *a priori* of the *Vernunft*. There is a tendency in the human mind to the unconditioned, a tendency which for Kant necessarily forces us to transcend the limits of experience and thus of objectively valid knowledge. There are two aspects of the unconditioned, constituting two modes of the *a priori* functioning of the *Vernunft*. The unconditioned is either the totality of conditions or it is the absolute *simpliciter*.

Thus there is an operative-heuristic *a priori* of reason, rationality on the part of the subject, which requires and seeks unconditionality on the side of the objective content presented by experience and understanding. For Kant, this exigence is satisfied only by an indefinite regressive *discursus*, an infinite regress of prosyllogisms, which never attains the unconditioned; the latter is rather the infinite series in its totality. 'There is no sense in which [the unconditioned] can be said to occur also at each link of the chain' (ibid. 210).

The *a priori* of reason for Lonergan, on the other hand, is the same exigence of consciousness for the unconditioned, but it operates by means of the question for reflection, Is it so? 'Such a question expresses the dissatisfaction of our mind in respect to any representation whatever which does not bear the mark of the absolute, that is, does not claim the same value as our dynamic orientation itself, which is unrestricted and therefore unconditioned' (ibid.). The function of the *a priori* in respect to judgment lies not only in the fact that judgment gives the answer to our tendency to the unconditioned, but also and much more in the fact that this tendency to the unconditioned 'constitutes the operational power of the subject which enables it to act on every level' (ibid. 212).

Neither of the two modes of the unconditioned in Kant's Transcendental Dialectic—the totality of the conditions and the absolute *simpliciter*—is able to acquire objective reference and thus become constitutive of our knowledge. There are also two modes of the unconditioned in *Insight*: the formally unconditioned, which has no conditions whatever, and the virtually unconditioned, which has conditions which are, however, fulfilled. The virtually unconditioned, according to Lonergan, can enter into the constitution of our knowledge; the unconditioned as the totality of conditions, according to Kant, cannot. What is the difference between them?

For Kant, reason tends toward the absolute totality of one unified system, for the universe is conceived as one system of natural events deterministically connected. But if the universe is not a pattern of internal relations, such that no aspect of it can be known in isolation from any and all other aspects of it, if the universe is not explanatory system whose single aspects are totally determined by their internal relations with all other aspects, if the existents and occurrences of the universe diverge nonsystematically from pure intelligibility such that statistical knowledge is true knowledge and the universe a universe of facts, then a judgment is a limited commitment. As Lonergan says, 'so far from resting on knowledge of the universe, it is to the effect that, no matter what the rest of the universe may prove to be, at least this is so' (Lonergan 1992, 368). A true judgment affirms a single unconditioned which has a finite number of conditions which are, in fact, fulfilled. Sala summarizes:

> The Kantian *Unbedingtes* is the comprehensive coherence which embraces the entire universe and towards which we tend by asking questions *for intelligence* ... There is no doubt that in this sense the unconditioned has a purely normative function in our knowledge. In fact what we grasp with the understanding is always a partial intelligibility, which therefore is not unconditioned; in itself, as in-

telligibility of such a nature, it implies merely the possibility of being, not being simply. But our cognitional structure brings forward questions of another kind, those *for reflection*, which turn precisely on those intelligibilities which embrace a limited sphere of the universe. Now the reflexive inquiry subsequent to these questions is capable of attaining an unconditioned which is the result of the combination of a conditioned (expressed by the concept) with the fulfilment of its conditions. It is the virtually unconditioned or *de facto* absolute (Sala 1976, 213-14).

The peculiar contribution of judgment to the process of knowledge is thus the absolute positing of synthesis, the knowledge of what in fact is so.

A mental synthesis which has the character of the absolute is a true synthesis, and the true is the 'medium in quo ens cognoscitur.' The true meaning mediates reality for man. To speak of an absolute positing of a synthesis is not to speak of perception alone, nor of perception plus concept, but rather of an act which is at once empirical, intelligent, and rational. There is only one way to safeguard the role which the senses as well as the concept play in our knowledge of reality, and that is to recognize that both intuition and concept are assimilated by that absolute grounding by means of which the cognitional process passes from thinking to judging (ibid. 217).

This process seeks a self-transcendence which is found neither in experience nor in intelligibility but only in judgment, where 'relativity to the subject is identical with transcendence in respect to the same subject and in respect to any restrictive qualification whatever, because in this case, and only in this case, the subject is defined by a tendency to the transcendent' (ibid. 218). The content of a true judgment is not relative to me.

To ask whether we know being is the same as to ask whether we are capable of a representation whose character, formally as representation, is unconditionality. Our answer is yes, since we saw that the cognitional process is capable of representing the virtually un-

conditioned, by thinking of a conditioned and grasping the fulfillment of its conditions. The delicate point is, How is the content of
our representation grasped as absolute? And our answer is: Not by
the direct way of formal content, but by the indirect way of the virtually unconditioned (ibid. 219).

Thus functions the *a priori* of human consciousness as
quest of the unconditioned. The reflective recognition that
the affirmation of the virtually unconditioned, and this alone,
brings about the transcendence of human knowledge is what
is meant by 'intellectual conversion.' It is a conversion 'from
the animal extroversion with which our psychic life first develops and which perseveres as a valid function throughout
our entire life, to the intellectuality and rationality constitutive of our spirit, recognized and accepted as the immanent
norm of our knowledge of the universe of being' (ibid.).

Ultimately, then, on this analysis, the *a priori* of human
subjectivity is our intrinsic endowment of meaning, 'the dynamism, intelligently and rationally conscious, which lies at
the source of the cognitional process and penetrates it
throughout, setting up principles normative of the different
phases of the structure in which it is realized' (ibid. 220).
Such an analysis eliminates a content-constitutive a priori in the
Kantian sense. 'It does not seem to us that an attentive analysis of knowledge, particularly in its character of receptivity
and development confirms the *a priori* as a knowledge of an
object, or of a partial object, which lies ready in the mind'
(ibid.).

But, as we have emphasized throughout this work, the
proper analysis of human subjectivity extends beyond scientific knowledge to every other field and even reveals that the
operative-heuristic intelligible which we are *creates, constitutes*
the meaning of ourselves and our world. At this point, which
involves the subject as existential and as culturally constituted, and not at the point of the objective knowledge of na-

ture, we can restore the Kantian thetic conception of the *a priori*.

> As regards the human world, the affirmation that objects must conform to our knowledge, i.e., to our intentionality or to our capacity of giving a meaning, or that we know of things only what we ourselves put into them, must be taken literally. Here truly the spirit gives the law to reality, raising nature to the ontological level of human reality. Here knowledge of reality is essentially interpretation, that is, knowledge of the meaning understood and realized by others from the horizon of their own meaning (ibid. 221).

Such interpretation is an *evaluative hermeneutic*. That is to say:

> The expansion of consciousness to the rational level is ultimate for cognitional activity, but not for the conscious activity of man as a whole. Our *a priori* is not only a dynamism which demands the truth of knowing in order to attain being, but also requires, beyond that, consistency between knowing and doing, in order to constitute authentic human living on the basis of true meaning (ibid.).

After this lengthy summary, and with this final constitutive operation of consciousness in the forefront of our minds, we must turn to Jung and seek light on the status of what he calls the archetypes. Jung never seems to have attained to a sufficiently clear distinction between these two modes of understanding the *a priori* element at the symbolic level—the operative-heuristic and the content-constitutive *a priori*. It is obvious, nonetheless, that he wrestled strenuously with this precise problem. It will be our task to refine his notion so as to render it continuous with Lonergan's treatment of the cognitive and existential subject.

3.2 The Psychic A Priori

In one essay Jung speaks of the archetypes as 'autonomous elements of the unconscious psyche which were there before any invention was thought of.' They are representations of the unalterable structure of 'a psychic world whose "reality" is attested by the determining effects it has upon the conscious mind.'[5] This description is vague. *What is unalterable, the structure or the representations, the structure or the psychic world itself?*

In another volume, Jung's description would seem to indicate that it is the representations of the psychic world itself, its contents, that are unalterable: 'Within the limits of psychic experience, the collective unconscious takes the place of the Platonic realm of eternal ideas. Instead of these models giving form to created things, the collective unconscious, through its archetypes, provides the *a priori* condition for the assignment of meaning' (Jung 1983, 87). Yet even here there is a vagueness, for what is explicitly called *a priori* is a *condition of significance*. But in the same volume there is reference to 'primordial images' which 'can rise up anywhere at any time quite spontaneously, without the least evidence of any external tradition' (ibid. 88), and these primordial images are called 'symptoms of the uniformity of *Homo sapiens*' (ibid. xiii).

In his 'Commentary on "The Secret of the Golden Flower,"' Jung speaks of the collective unconscious as 'a common substratum transcending all differences in culture and consciousness,' comparable to the common anatomy of the hu-

---

5. Jung, 'Phenomenology of the Spirit in Fairytales,' 250.

man body through all racial differences. He tells us that this common substratum consists not merely of contents which can become conscious, but of 'latent predispositions towards identical reactions.' Thus the collective unconscious is 'simply the psychic expression of the identity of brain structure irrespective of all racial differences. This explains the analogy, sometimes even identity, between the various myth motifs and symbols, and the possibility of human communication in general. The various lines of psychic development start from one common stock whose roots reach back into the most distant past. This also accounts for the psychological parallelisms with animals' (Jung 1967, 11-12). Jung goes on to present the psychological meaning of this physiological 'common stock.'

> In purely psychological terms this means that mankind has common instincts of ideation and action. All conscious ideation and action have developed on the basis of these unconscious archetypal patterns and always remain dependent on them. This is especially the case when consciousness has not attained any high degree of clarity, when in all its functions it is more dependent on the instincts than on the conscious will, more governed by affect than by rational judgment (ibid. 12).

Thus, as long as circumstances do not arise that call for higher moral effort, a 'primitive state of psychic health' is assured. When these patterns are assimilated by a higher and wider consciousness, however, an autonomy from the old 'gods' develops; they are recognized as 'nothing other than those mighty, primordial images that hitherto have held our consciousness in thrall' (ibid.).

There is still no clear distinction between structure and content. The confusion is a bit less, however, in 'Psychological Aspects of the Mother Archetype.' At first, it appears that

Jung will clearly opt for a direction in which we would prefer not to go, for he places his discussion in a context of what he calls a 'rebirth of the Platonic spirit' prepared, paradoxically, by Kant's destruction of naive metaphysics. But then he immediately focuses his attention on *a priori structure.* 'There *is* an *a priori* factor in all human activities, namely the inborn, preconscious and unconscious individual structure of the psyche' (Jung 1969b, 77). This structure consists of *patterns of functioning* which Jung calls 'images.' The term 'image' now designates a *form* of activity in a given situation. These patterns are primordial in that they are peculiar to the whole human species. The products of dream and fantasy render these patterns visible, 'and it is *here* that the concept of the archetype finds its specific application' (ibid. 78). While there is still some confusion in Jung's exposition, it is clear that what is *a priori* consists at least of 'living predispositions … that preform and continually influence our thoughts and feelings and actions' (ibid. 79). And, at least according to the formulation of this essay, it is mistaken to think of these dispositions on the analogy of 'unconscious ideas.' Most clear and explicit of all is the following statement: 'Archetypes are not determined as regards their content, but only as regards their form and then only to a very limited degree. A primordial image is determined as to its content only when it has become conscious and is therefore filled out with the material of conscious experience … The archetype in itself is empty and purely formal, nothing but a *facultas praeformandi*, a possibility of representation which is given *a priori*' (ibid.). Jung distinguishes between the archetype as such and its representations in images and ideas. The representations are 'varied structures which all point back to one essentially "irrepresentable" basic form. The latter is characterized by certain formal elements and by certain fundamental meanings, although these can be grasped only approximately ... Everything archetypal which is perceived by consciousness seems to represent a set of variations on a ground theme' (ibid.).

The way to remove the abiding confusion between two different notions of the symbolic *a priori* in Jung's writings, it seems, is by clarifying this ground theme. The ground theme is the emergence or failure of emergence of the authentic existential subject as free and responsible constitutive agent of the human world. The basic *a priori* which is human consciousness determines the theme. It is an intention of intelligibility, truth, and value, and it is to be realized only in self-transcending cognitional and existential subjectivity. This basic *a priori* is operative-heuristic. As such, it promotes human experience to human understanding by means of questions for intelligence, and human understanding to truth by means of questions for reflection. This same *a priori* dynamism promotes truth into action in a thetic manner, for the action is constitutive of the human world. The promotion of truth into action consistent with truth occurs through questions for deliberation. The primordial apprehension of the data for these questions occurs in feelings. These feelings structure various patterns of experience. These patterns of experience are imaginally or archetypally meaningful. The archetypal images revealed in dreams, then, promote both neural and psychic process, which permeates the various patterns of experience, to the status of a recognizable and intelligible narrative. The narrative has to do with the ground theme. When the patterns of experience have been released from their more or less customary muteness through symbolic images, they can be interpreted. When the interpretation is affirmed to be true, the images have functioned helpfully in the process of bringing the existential subject to genuine self-knowledge. *The symbolic function is part and parcel of the basic a priori which is human consciousness.*[6]

This account is faithful to the process of analysis. With the aid of an analyst, I interpret the symbols of my dreams; I affirm the meaning interpreted; I thus come to a knowledge of my present condition, situation, and possibilities, through the illumination of 'how I find myself' afforded by the symbolic images. The word 'possibilities' is important. The image is an aid, not only to what we might call a symptomatic hermeneutic, but also to an evaluative hermeneutic. As Jung rightly insists, the image is creative. Psychotherapy aims not only at self-knowledge but also, beyond the affirmation of an interpretation as true, at the constitution and transformation of the subject and the subject's world through authentic praxis. At this point the knowledge gained in the affirmation of a dream interpretation as true becomes thetic knowledge. What am I going to do about it? The interpretation of the image ought not to be affirmed as true, is not correctly so affirmed, unless it includes an interpretation of the creative possibilities revealed in the image. Genuine dream interpretation thus consists in the attentive reception of the dream as exploratory of the dispositional aspect of immediacy in its temporal constitution; in the understanding of what is thus laid open; in the judgment that the understanding is accurate; and in the responsible appropriation and negotiation of this self-knowledge in the ongoing transformation of the human world and in the constitition of myself as a free and responsible subject. *The ultimate intentionality of authentic psy-*

---

6. 1993 note: I have highlighted this sentence in this edition, though it was not emphasized in the first edition. Whether or not one accepts this affirmation will determine whether or not one will agree with the complement to Lonergan's intentionality analysis that I have suggested and on which all of my work to date has been built.

*chotherapy is coextensive with the total sweep of the conscious inten-
tionality of human subjectivity which is our basic a priori.* The
psychotherapeutic function is to conscript the psyche into
the single transcendental dynamism of human consciousness
toward the authenticity of self-transcendence. This function
is rendered capable of being executed because the symbolic
spontaneity of the psyche directly pertains to and is part and
parcel of this single transcendental dynamism. The execution of this function is, as we have seen, dialectical, for there
is also a resistance factor in the psyche parallel to the tendencies to bias on the part of cognitional and volitional subjectivity. But the genuine intention of authentic psychic self-
appropriation is to enable one to achieve the capacity to discover the symbolic meanings through which one's world is
both mediated and potentially constituted at any given time,
the symbolic meanings through which one's own story un-
folds, so as to facilitate the development of the story as a
reflection of the ground theme of human existence. The contents of the images are a posteriori, even when they are found
commonly across cultural, racial, and historical barriers. Their
operative-heuristic function is *a priori*, and it is what determines their ground theme, the emergence of the existential
subject as originative value. The common features found, it
would seem, universally, reflect the structure of the ground
theme, which in every case is the primordial struggle between
the dynamism to truth and value on one side and the flight
from genuine humanity on the other.

There is a sense, then, in which it is quite legitimate to
speak of a symbolic *a priori*. Nonetheless, I prefer to use also
the expression 'the symbolic function' or, when referring to
that dimension that Jung called the collective unconscious,
'the archetypal function,' so as to discourage the possibility
of the content-constitutive understanding of the psyche still
too prevalent in the writings of Jung.

5 Psyche and Intentionality

In this chapter, I wish to present a more detailed understanding of the sublation of the psyche into the dynamism of intentionality. We have already seen that the mediation of cognitive and dispositional immediacy issues in second immediacy; that symbols structure and reflect dispositional immediacy; and thus that a release of the symbolic function aids the mediation of dispositional immediacy; that this is a dialectical process whose principal protagonists are intentionality and psyche; that this dialectic is necessitated by a further dialectic within psyche itself; and that psychic process is continuous with intentionality process because of the operative-heuristic *a priori* function of symbols as operators, so that the sublations which structure the emergence of intelligent, rational, and responsible consciousness are complemented by a sublation raising dreaming consciousness to existential significance. Now we must detail further the relationship between psyche and intentionality, by speaking, first, of the therapeutic context; secondly, of psychic energy; thirdly, of the mutual qualifications of intentionality and psyche; fourthly, of psychic conversion; and fifthly, of the psychic and the psychoid.

1 The Therapeutic Context

The sublation of the imaginal by existential subjectivity
is achieved in a psychotherapeutic context, in the general
case. It is effected in a cooperative-intersubjective milieu, with
the aid of a professional guide to lead one to the discovery
and negotiation of the symbolic function. Thus, for Gerhard
Adler, the actual interview with an analyst plays the decisive
part in establishing familiarity with the symbolic function as
a permanent conscious capacity on the part of an individual.
'A great deal of impressive unconscious material may be
thrown up by the unconscious without ever being "realized;"
the concreteness of the relationship, of the encounter with
an "opposite," plays an integral part in the assimilation of
unconscious imagery, which otherwise may remain mere
unutilized raw material.'[1]

Is the analytic situation needed? Adler comments:

> This process can, and does, take place outside and with-
> out analysis. But it is such a dificult process, full of pitfalls at
> every step, that analysis seems often the only way. Similarly,
> in the East there is also the possibility of achieving by one's
> own effort insight into the nature of Brahman and into its es-
> sential unity with the individual Atman; this is, however, a
> rare alternative to the general way of achieving such insight
> with the help of a guru (ibid.).

---

1. Adler 1961, 8. A number of the quotations in this chapter will contain terminology which I have tried to replace with what I believe to be
more accurage language. An effort must be made to read these quotations
with my suggested changes in mind.

We might also use the analogy of the experience of making the Ignatian *Spiritual Exercises* with and without a competent director. In this case, the danger of self-delusion, of simply reinforcing one's religious inauthenticity, is so great that the attempt to proceed without competent direction, no matter what the extent of one's experience in prayer, is at best highly suspect. So too, it would seem, a guide to the attainment of familiarity with the complexity of the symbolic function is necessary until one has reached the point of quick and accurate access to the process of the ongoing appropriation of dreams. When this point is reached, I believe, the analysis is to be terminated. Otherwise one runs the risk of courting in a psychic fashion what Ivan Illych has called 'iatrogenic disease.'[2]

Particularly persistent in the analytic process is the almost inveterate habit of failing to realize that in the general case, *the figures revealed in dreams are aspects of the dreaming subject*. This habitual failure is, I suspect, not unrelated to the extraversion responsible for the cognitive myth that the real is a subdivision of the 'already out there now.' Furthermore, it entails the subsequent tendency to view dreams as thermometers rather than barometers, as explanatory rather than exploratory, as referring to space before time and to the specific before the generic. An uncritical engagement in the analytic process could very easily mire one further in myth and, depending on the atmospheric pressure, can eventuate in either temporary or permanent psychosis. Psychosis is a resto-

---

2. Illych 1974. The termination of the analysis is not the end of the psychic journey. In one sense, the latter never ends, in that one is certain to continue to have dreams as long as one lives. In another sense, though, it does end in the discovery of the soul beyond psychology which is the movement into the realm of transcendence.

ration to one's roots in the rhythms and processes of nature, but in such a way that nothing remains *but* the roots, entangling one another and eventually choking each other's avenue to differentiated consciousness. The return to the roots must be in terms of time rather than space, the interior rather than the exterior, the generic rather than the specific, and with reference to the self-transcendence of the existential subject in the constitution of the real human world. For such a process to be successful, in the general case, it is helpful that one be warned by the admonitions of one well aware of these differences.

This is not to say that there are not dreams which are directly prophetic of external situations which may have either a great deal or seemingly very little to do with one's own responsibility as constitutive agent of the human world. Thus Bishop Joseph Lanyi of Grosswardein, Hungary, dreamed of the assassination of Archduke Ferdinand of Austria several hours before the event took place. He was awakened by the dream and immediately drew a picture of the event of which he dreamed. The picture corresponded almost point by point to the details of the assassination (Whitmont 1969, 54-55). Needless to say, such dreams are the exception and indicate the limited range of our scientific knowledge of the sphere of being I have called the imaginal. But even those dreams which are prophetic of as yet unfamiliar places, people, and existential situations in one's own life, while not symbolically overdetermined in the same sense as most of the dreams which we can remember, and thus while quite specific, are appropriated by intentional consciousness only to the extent that they are understood as bearing upon interiority, the temporal, the generic, and one's stance vis-à-vis the scale of values.

The psychotherapeutic context must also respect the archeological-teleological unity-intension of the concrete symbol insisted on by Ricoeur in his critique of Freud. The psychotherapeutic context will thus be closer to that suggested by Jung than to that inspired by Freud, for Jung was more aware of this tension within symbolic process. The analytic process is reductive in the same way that the hermeneutic of suspicion is an intrinsic and integral part of the dialectical interpretation of symbols, and thus in the same way that extreme iconoclasm belongs to the restoration of meaning. The analytic process should further a gradually emerging pattern of inner order, a continuous process of integration, a sense-giving factor in the psyche (Adler 1961, 4), but it must do so in part by mercilessly destroying the mythic reenactment of symbols in terms of immediate belief, by moving their intentionality from the exterior, spatial, specific, and human, to the interior, temporal, generic, and religious, and from the explanatory to the exploratory.

This notion of the analytic process is more readily available in Jung's writings than in those of Freud. These two pioneers of the psychotherapeutic revolution are not to be viewed simply as opposed to one another, however, with Freud concerned only with reduction and Jung solely with the teleological moment that is only implicit in Freudian analysis. Jung speaks of a reductive moment in the analysis which he proposes. This reductive moment 'breaks down all inappropriate symbol-formations and reduces them to their natural elements'[3], while the synthetic moment would consist in the integration and appropriation of the archetypal spontaneity of one's psyche. As Adler says, 'Indeed, it is possible to lose sight of the fact that there are analyses in which the therapeutic goal appears to be reached almost exclusively by a

---

3. Jung, 'On Psychic Energy,' in 1969a, 49.

process of *symbolical transformation.*'[4] Jung comments on the complementarity of reduction and teleology in this transformative process:

> In psychology as in biology we cannot afford to overlook or underestimate [the] question of origins, although the answer usually tells nothing about the functional meaning. For this reason biology should never forget the question of purpose, for only by answering that can we get at the meaning of a phenomenon … There are a number of pathological phenomena which only give up their meaning when we inquire into their purpose. And where we are concerned with the normal phenomena of life, this question of purpose takes undisputed precedence …
>
> To supplement the causal approach by a final one therefore enables us to arrive at more meaningful interpretations not only in medical psychology, where we are concerned with individual fantasies originating in the unconscious, but also in the case of collective fantasies, that is, myths and fairytales.[5]

There is another major difference between Freud and Jung which decisively calls for favoring Jung, namely his recognition of archetypes. For many people, Jung maintains, religious symbols have lost their nunimosity, their thrilling power. The compensating primordial images which appear in dreams are for Jung wrongly reduced by Freud to purely personal experiences in much the same way as the alchemists misplaced them onto chemical substances.

> Both of them act as though they knew to what known quantities the meaning of their symbols could be reduced …

---

4. Adler 1961, 3. On Jung and Freud, see Lonergan 1993, 67-68, and especially footnote 4 on p. 68.

5. Jung, 'On the Psychology of the Trickster Figure,' in 1969b, 260, 266.

The result of this reduction ... is not very satisfactory—so little, in fact, that Freud saw himself obliged to go back as far as possible into the past. In so doing he finally hit upon an uncommonly numinous idea, the archetype of incest. He thus found something that to some extent expressed the real meaning and purpose of symbol production, which is to bring about an awareness of those primordial images that belong to all men and can therefore lead the individual out of his isolation.

But Freud failed to realize the ulterior meaning of this insight and 'succumbed to the numinous effect of the primordial image he had discovered.' That is, he allowed himself to become a victim of what I have called myth by personalizing the archetype in the Oedipal complex and historicizing it in the murder of the primal father.[6] He made the symbol explanatory and etiological rather than exploratory and hermeneutic.

On Jung's view, then, Freud missed the nature of the symbol. Freud's method consists in collecting a series of clues pointing to an unconscious background and interpreting this material in such a way as to reconstruct a set of elementary instinctual processes. Freud referred to these conscious clues as symbols, but in reality they function for him as no more than signs or symptoms of 'already there' subliminal processes.

The true symbol differs essentially from this, and should be understood as an expression of an intuitive idea that cannot yet be formulated in any other or better way. When Plato, for instance, puts the whole problem of the theory of knowledge in his parable of the cave, or when Christ expresses the idea of the Kingdom of Heaven in parables, these are genuine and true symbols, that is, attempts to express something for

---

6. Jung, 'The Philosophical Tree,' in 1967, 301-302.

which no verbal concept yet exists. If we were to interpret Plato's metaphor in Freudian terms we would naturally arrive at the uterus, and would have proved that even a mind like Plato's was still stuck on a primitive level of infantile sexuality. But we would have completely overlooked what Plato actually created out of the primitive determinants of his philosophical ideas, we would have missed the essential point and merely discovered that he had infantile sexual fantasies like any other mortal (Jung 1966, 70).

Jung is not denying a partial validity to the Freudian therapeutic method, however. Pathological psychic formations must be broken down, so as to prepare the way for normal, healthy adaptation. But Jung denies the adequacy of Freud's method, and highlights its unsatisfactoriness by pointing to the poverty of Freud's critique of culture. When the Freudian point of view is applied, for example, to a work of art, it

> ... strips the work of art of its shimmering robes and exposes the nakedness and drabness of *Homo sapiens*, to which species the poet and artist also belong. The golden gleam of artistic creation ... is extinguished as soon as we apply to it the same corrosive method which we use in analyzing the fantasies of hysteria. The results are no doubt very interesting and may perhaps have the same kind of scientific value as, for instance, a postmortem examination of Nietzsche, which might conceivably show us the particular atypical form of paralysis from which he died. But what would this have to do with *Zarathustra*? Whatever its subterranean background may have been, is it not a whole world in itself, beyond the human all-too-human imperfections, beyond the world of migraine and cerebral atrophy? (Ibid. 69)

It is the exclusiveness of Freudian reductionism, then, to which Jung objects. 'Freud's only interest is where things come from, never where they are going ... Many psychological facts have explanations entirely different from those based on the *faux pas* of a *chronique scandaleuse*.'[7]

The validity of Freudian method for Jung lies primarily in its appropriateness to the historical situation in which it emerged. Freud

> ... preaches those truths which it is of paramount importance that the neurotic of the early twentieth century should understand because he is an unconscious victim of late Victorian psychology. Psychoanalysis destroys the false values in him personally by cauterizing away the rottenness of the dead century ... But in so far as a neurosis is not an illness specific to the Victorian era but enjoys a wide distribution in time and space, and is therefore found among people who are not in need of any special sexual enlightenment or the destruction of harmful assumptions in this respect, a theory of neurosis or of dreams which is based on a Victorian prejudice is at most of secondary importance ... Freud has not penetrated into [the] deeper layer which is common to all men. He could not have done so without being untrue to his historical task. And this task he has fulfilled—a task enough for a whole life's work, and fully deserving the fame it has won (ibid, 39-40).

In terms of our present analysis, we might say that Freud's exclusivistic reductionism is due to a propensity to interpret dream images in a content-constitutive rather than operativeheuristic way. Causal exclusivism is parallel with a tendency to view 'unconscious' processes as causing distorted content images which influence conscious life, culture, and religion. An operative-heuristic notion, on the other hand, is by definition bound to teleology in some fashion.[8]

---

7. Jung, 'Sigmund Freud in His Historical Setting,' in 1966, 37-38.

8. 1993 note: More accurately, an operative-heuristic notion implies a finalistic account, in Lonergan's sense of finality as an upwardly but *indeterminately* directed dynamism. Finality in this sense is quite distinct

2 Psychic Energy

What seems to be at stake in this discussion is the nature of psychic energy. Jung distinguishes between a mechanistic, purely causal standpoint and an energic, finalistic standpoint. The assumption of the latter is that 'some kind of energy underlies the changes in phenomena, that it maintains itself as a constant throughout these changes and finally leads to entropy, a condition of general equilibrium,' which can be called its direction or goal. This energic standpoint is for Jung 'an indispensable explanatory principle,' functioning as 'the logical reverse of the principle of causality.'[9]

Now such a standpoint is valid for Jung only if some kind of 'quantitative estimate' of psychic energy is possible. Jung finds one source of such 'quantitative estimates' in an individual's conscious system of values. 'Values are quantitative estimates of energy' (ibid. 9). Thus, we can determine the relative strength of our evaluations by weighing them against one another in terms of different intensities of value in relation to similar qualities or objects. But—a caution very pertinent to our present discussion—such a process has minimal applicability once we realize how much of our orientation to the world is undifferentiated or, in Jung's terms, in relation to unconscious value intensities. Here another point

---

from 'final cause,' the overtones of which can be heard in some of Jung's pronouncements quoted above and in some of those which we are yet to see.

9. Jung, 'On Psychic Energy,' 3-5.

of departure is required, one that will allow some indirect estimate.

Jung maintains that his early studies in word association showed the existence of groupings of psychic elements around feeling-toned contents or complexes, whose psychological significance is frequently 'unconscious.' Each complex has a nucleus consisting, first, of an experientially and environmentally determined factor and, second, of an innate and dispositional factor in the individual. The feeling-toned complex is a 'value quantity.' An indirect estimate of this quantity is possible, based on the constellating power of its nuclear element, which can be estimated in terms of the relative number of constellations it effects, the relative frequency and intensity of the reactions indicating a complex, and the intensity of the accompanying affects. The symbolic images of dreams are ciphers for such an estimate.

Psychic energy for Jung is a specific part of a broader energy called life energy or libido. The main principle governing an understanding of its functioning is the principle of the conservation of energy, especially as considered under the rubric of the principle of equivalence: 'For a given quantity of energy expended or consumed in bringing about a certain condition, an equal quantity of the same or another form of energy will appear elsewhere'(ibid. 18). Freud has clearly shown the psychological applicability of this principle in his account of repressions and their consequent substitute formations. But for Jung, while libido never leaves one structure, e.g., the sexual, to pass over into another without taking the character of the old structure over into the new, the idea of psychic development demands the possibility of change in various systems of energy capable of theoretically unlimited interchangeability and modulation under the principle of equivalence. In other words a theory of psychic development demands the teleological point of view, according to which *causes are also means to an end*. The theory of the symbol is the key to this teleological point of view.

From a purely causal point of view, the whole edifice of civilization becomes a mere substitute for the impossibility of incest. But the teleological point of view takes seriously the difference, for example, between the personal mother and the mother *imago* and regards regression to the latter as a means of finding the memory associations by means of which further development can take place — e.g., from a sexual system into an intellectual or spiritual system. Thus, 'what to the causal view is *fact* to the final view is *symbol*, and vice versa … The symbolic interpretation of causes by means of the energic standpoint is necessary for the differentiation of the psyche, since unless the facts are symbolically interpreted, the causes remain immutable substances which go on operating continuously … Cause alone does not make development possible. For the psyche the *reductio ad causam* is the very reverse of development; it binds the libido to the elementary facts' (ibid. 24).

Thus, when psychic development has occurred it is because the causes have been (operatively and heuristically) transformed into 'symbolical expressions for the way that lies ahead. The exclusive importance of the cause … thus disappears and emerges again in the symbol, whose power of attraction represents the equivalent quantum of libido' (ibid.). In the context of our previous discussion of mystery and myth, a reenactment of the symbol through immediate belief is a reduction of the symbol to a cause, while the reenactment through sympathetic imagination holds fast to the symbolic quality and follows its direction toward development. The attitude of mystery alone is in accord with the principle of equivalence, which for Jung is the basic law of psychic energy.

The direction of psychic energy's symbolic proces is towards entropy, or, far better I believe, toward an equaliza-
tion of differences or a unity of opposites. Thus, Jung's
alchemically inspired understanding of a unity of opposites
cumulatively yielding a new attitude whose stability is the
greater in proportion to the magnitude of the initial differences is an expression of the teleological point of view.

> The greater the tension between the pairs of opposites,
> the greater will be the energy that comes from them; and the
> greater the energy, the stronger will be its constellating, at-
> tracting power. This increased power of attraction corresponds
> to a wider range of constellated psychic material, and the fur-
> ther this range extends, the less chance is there of subsequent
> disturbances which might arise from friction with material not
> previously constellated. For this reason an attitude that has
> been formed out of a far-reaching process of equalization is
> an especially lasting one (ibid. 26).

Jung refers to the process of the transformation of energy as 'the canalization of libido,' a phrase which refers to
the 'transfer of psychic intensities or values from one content to another' (ibid. 41). Culture results from and then further enables the conversion of natural instincts into other
dynamic forms productive of work. Instinctual energy is chan-
neled into an analogue of its natural object. 'Just as a power-
station imitates a waterfall and thereby gains possession of
its energy, so the psychic mechanism [the symbol] imitates
the instinct and is thereby enabled to apply its energy for
special purposes' (ibid. 42).

It is only a small part of our total psychic energy that
can be thus diverted from its natural flow, a relative surplus
of energy not used to sustain the regular course of life. It is
the symbol that makes this deflection of excess libido possible. An energy-converting symbol is called by Jung a 'li-

bido analogue' (ibid. 48). It 'can give equivalent expression
to the libido and canalize it into a form different from the
original one' (ibid.). These symbols have never been devised
consciously, but have always been produced spontaneously.
Most of the symbols used throughout history for the conversion of psychic energy probably derive directly from dreams.
Today we are witnessing a recrudescence of such individual
symbol formations parallel to the fading away of those religious forms which tended to suppress individual symbol formation as a matter of central significance for life.

    Reductive psychoanalysis is called for, then, when one's
psychic libido flows off unconsciously along too low a gradient. This is the moment which 'breaks down all inappropriate symbol-formations and reduces them to their natural elements' (ibid. 49), restoring the natural flow of life energy.
But another gradient than the merely natural one will be
sought for one's excess libido. 'When the unsuitable structures have been reduced and the natural course of things is
restored, so that there is some possibility of the patient living
a normal life, the reductive process should not be continued
further. Instead, symbol-formation should be reinforced in a
synthetic direction until a more favourable gradient for the
excess libido is found.'[10] 'Reversion to nature must therefore
be followed by a synthetic reconstruction of the symbol'(ibid.
50) in a spiritual, cultural, and religious direction.

> Freudian theory consists in a causal explanation of the
> psychology of instinct. From this standpoint the spiritual prin-
> ciple is bound to appear only as an appendage, a by-product
> of the instincts. Since its inhibiting and restrictive power can-

---

10. Ibid. 50. Jung is here expressing his understanding and conviction of what I would call the intention of truth and value, of self-transcendence, within the psyche itself.

not be denied, it is traced back to the influence of education, moral authorities, convention, and tradition. These authorities in their turn derive their power, according to the theory, from repression in the manner of a vicious circle. The spiritual principle is not recognized as an equivalent counterpart of the instincts (ibid. 55).

When useless symbols are broken down by reduction and life is returned to its natural course, a damming up of libido occurs. This condition can be the beginning of an individual religion, which is the way to further development.

> … an advance always begins with individuation, that is to say with the individual, conscious of his isolation, cutting a new path through hitherto untrodden territory. To do this he must first return to the fundamental facts of his own being, irrespective of all authority and tradition, and allow himself to become conscious of his distinctiveness. If he succeeds in giving collective validity to his widened consciousness, he creates a tension of opposites that provides the stimulation which culture needs for its further progress (ibid. 59).

The transformation of energy from biological forms to cultural forms, aside from the forced sublimations of convention and collective religion, is always an individual one and is achieved by means of the symbol.

James Hillman goes so far as to say, correctly I believe, that Jung's psychology is a psychology of creativity. For Jung the creative is the essence of being human. In addition to the 'instincts' of hunger, sexuality, activity, and reflection, there is the 'instinct of creativity,' the *quintessentia*. 'His major concern in both his therapy and his writing was with the manifestations and vicissitudes of the creative instinct and with disentangling it from the other four. Consequently, we are led to state that Jungian psychology is based primarily upon the creative instinct and in turn to infer that Jungian psychology is primarily a creative psychology' (Hillman 1972 33-34). Thus, 'his insistence upon finality in regard to the libido, upon the final point of view toward all psychic phenomena and upon the prospective interpretation of the dream—all have as basis a creative psychology' (ibid. 35). On our analysis, then, Jung's concern with an archeology of the subject is within a broader dialectical and operative-heuristic context concerned with the fulfilment of psychic infrastructure in its incorporation into the dynamism of intentionality.

3 Intentionality and Psyche

We are offering here, though, not Jungian psychology, but a new interpretation of what psychotherapy can become. My specific points of difference with Jung have already been indicated, and those that are epistemological have, I believe, been at least partly settled. Let me add simply that by 'inappropriate symbol formations' I would mean those formations which sponsor a reenactment of the symbol through immediate belief or an acceptance of the symbol as explanatory, and which orient the subject immediately to the exterior, the spatial, the specific, and the human. The process of symbolic transformation would involve the turn to the interior, the temporal, the generic, and the transcendent.

In addition, though, I am insisting that the process of intentional self-appropriation toward which Lonergan leads one should be regarded as the first and indispensable moment in a total mediation of immediacy within the context of method. The appropriation of one's cognitional being through the aid of *Insight* is the first stage of a more inclusive process. When joined with Lonergan's later analysis of the existential subject, it is the stage of the discrimination of spirit, of active mind, of *logos*, word, idea, intellect, principle, abstraction, meaning, *ratio*, *nous*, *animus*. A second stage is that of the cultivation of soul. It is the stage of psyche, *mythos*, image, symbol, atmosphere, feeling, relation, earth, nature, rhythm, *anima*. A third stage then follows, beyond *logos* and psyche, reason and imagination, *animus* and *anima*, beyond common sense, theory, and interiority. It is the progressive discovery of the realm of transcendence. It is the religious journey under the cloud of unknowing. It is the agapic stage of the surrender of discriminated spirit and cultivated soul to the *mysterium tremendum et fascinans*. The movement of self-appropriation in the context of method should pass through these stages in this order, for the cultivation of soul without the discrimination of spirit is the romantic agony, and religion without psyche is rootless. In contrast, the process of self-appropriation I am suggesting would provide, as I will argue in the next chapter, the inclusive horizon for the theological enterprise in our emerging epoch and the key to dialectic and foundations as functional specialties within both the *scienza nuova* in general and theology in particular. When method takes the step into the domain of psyche, when self-appropriation becomes appropriation first of intentionality and then of psyche, theological foundations consist of a patterned set of judgments of cognitional fact and of value cumulatively heading toward the full position on the human subject.

Nonetheless, intelligence, reason, and intentionality can also be understood archetypally from the standpoint of the psyche. The psyche seems to insist on this input, as a matter of fact. Not only does Jung speak of a 'thinking function,' but he adds that a change has come over our consideration of understanding and reason since Kant's *Critique of Pure Reason*, a change which for me is valid irrespective of whether one accepts Kantian epistemology, a change which reflects the dynamic thrust of the *anthropologische Wendung* toward radicalization. Understanding and reason are no longer regarded as independent processes subject only to the eternal laws of logic. Rather, they are 'co-ordinated with the personality and subordinate to it.' This means the addition of a 'personal equation' in every intellectual investigation.

> We no longer ask, 'Has this or that been seen, heard, handled, weighed, counted, thought, and found to be logical?' We ask instead, 'Who saw, heard, or thought?' ... Today we are convinced that in all fields of knowledge psychological premises exist which exert a decisive influence upon the choice of material, the method of investigaion, the nature of the conclusions, and the formulation of hypotheses and theories ... Not only our philosophers, but our own predilections in philosophy, and even what we are fond of calling our 'best' truths are affected, if not dangerously undermined, by this recognition of a personal premise ... Can it be possible that a man only thinks or says or does what he himself *is*?[11]

Thus not only does the destruction of the cognitional myth that the real is a subdivision of the 'already out there now' also aid one toward the dissolution of the affective dimensions of this myth and thus toward turning from inappropriate symbolic formations to appropriate symbolic formations, from myth to mystery, so that the specifically psychic part of the total process of self-appropriation is greatly aided to the extent that one is self-consciously attentive, intelligent, reasonable, and responsible; but we must also attend to the reciprocal dynamics of these two movements. *Befindlichkeit* is meaningful independently of any representative conceptual menaing (Gendlin 1962, 96). While self-appropriation begins with the appropriation of one's cognitional

---

11. Jung, 'On the Psychology of the Mother Archetype,' 76-77.

process, such an appropriation is itself a therapeutic contribution, and as such helps in the construction of a more inclusive semantics of human desire. Not only does it determine the movement from *logos* to *methodos* but it also foreshadows the movement of method into and through psyche. This latter movement affects method's understanding of itself, makes it accept humbly the symbolic significance which psyche insists it bears. For the conclusion of this movement is a kind of *coniunctio* in second immediacy of *animus* and *anima*, of the two interlocking and equiprimordial constitutive ways of being *Dasein*.

It might be helpful to understand the point we are here making if we turn to Jung's notion of four psychological functions: thinking, feeling, sensation, and intuition. In normal psychological development, aided by no such reflective technique as psychotherapy or cognitional analysis, only one of these functions is truly successfully differentiated. This Jung refers to as an individual's superior function. Depending on whether an individual's orientation is extraverted or introverted, this function determines one's personality type. Now, one or two of the other functions may be partially differentiated, and, to this extent, aid the superior function. The latter is one's most reliable function, the one most amenable to one's conscious intentions. The fourth, inferior function, around which one's 'shadow' is constellated, proves to be inaccessible to conscious willing. Thus even the differentiated functions have only partially freed themselves from the undifferentiated, for the psyche is one. The three more or less differentiated functions are confronted by the fourth, more or less undifferentiated function. The latter disturbs the former, to the extent that the worst enemy of the superior function is in truth another aspect of the same psyche to which it itself belongs. 'Like the devil who delights in disguising himself as an angel of light, the inferior function secretly and mischievously influences the superior function most of all, just as the latter represses the former most strongly.'[12]

This whole matter would be better understood within a context more sensitive to intentionality and its differentation from the psyche. Jung tends to swallow all the functions into the psyche and frequently speaks as though a human being were *only* a psychic being. Lonergan's *Insight* is an aid to the differentiation of what Jung is reaching for in his notions of the thinking function and the intuitive function. The existence of other influences is acknowledged by Lonergan, either aiding or disturbing insightful and reasonable performance. But these latter influences are not the principal concern of *Insight* and so they are not described in such a way as significantly to further their differentiation. It may well be that *Insight*'s appeal has been largely to those whose normal development has issued in a differentiation of what Jung calls the thinking function as one's superior function. But even the further and more self-conscious differentiation aided by *Insight* will not free the thinking function from the deleterious interference of what is undifferentiated (which is likely, in this case, to be one's feeling function). Further self-appropriation is called for, and it is the task of authentic psychotherapy, as understood within this context, to get 'all systems going' in a harmonious unity through the cumulative reconciliation of opposites.

On the other hand, for one whose normal psychological development has seen the differentiation of another function, psychic wholeness will demand the differentiation also of the thinking function, which, in this instance, is liable to be the function most neglected. May I be so bold as to suggest that a complete therapeutic process could do no better, for such a

---

12. Jung, 'Phenomenology of the Spirit in Fairytales,' 238.

purpose, than to stress intentionality and even to encourage cognitional self-appropriation as aided by *Insight*? For in such an instance, perhaps what is therapeutically most important is the mediation of active mind, of spirit, *logos*, word, idea, intellect, principle, abstraction, meaning, *ratio, nous* —of *animus* as archetype of intentionality.

4 Psychic Conversion

The conscious capacity for the sublation of the imaginal is effected by a conversion on the part of the existential subject. This conversion I call psychic conversion. Psychic conversion is integrally related to the religious, moral, and intellectual conversions specified by Lonergan as qualifying authentic human subjectivity.

Lonergan first began to thematize conversion in his search for renewed foundations of theology. In a lecture in 1967, he describes the new context of theology in terms of the demise of the classical mediation of meaning and the struggle of modern culture for a new maieutic, only to conclude that this new context demands that theology be placed on a new foundation, one distinct from the citation of Scripture and the enunciation of revealed doctrines characteristic of the foundation of the old dogmatic theology. What was this new foundation to be?

Lonergan drew his first clue from the notion of method, considered as 'a normative pattern that related to one another the cognitional operations that recur in scientific investigations.'[13] The stress in this notion of method is on the

---

13. Lonergan, 'Theology in Its New Context,' 1988, 65.

personal experience of the operations and of their dynamic and normative relations to one another. If a scientist were to locate his or her operations and their relations in one's own experience, maintained Lonergan, one would come to know oneself as scientist. And, since the subject as scientist is the foundation of science, one would come into possession of the foundations of one's science.

Of what use is such a clue to one seeking a new foundation for theology? Lonergan says: 'It illustrates by an example what might be meant by a foundation that lies not in a set of verbal propositions named first principles, but in a particular, concrete, dynamic reality generating knowledge of particular, concrete, dynamic realities' (ibid.).

Lonergan then draws a second clue from the phenomenon of conversion, which is fundamental to religious living. Conversion, he says, 'is not merely a change or even a development; rather, it is a radical transformation on which follows, on all levels of living, an interlocked series of changes and developments. What hitherto was unnoticed becomes vivid and present. What had been of no concern becomes a matter of high import' (ibid. 65-66). Conversion of course has many degrees of depth of realization. But in any case of genuine conversion, 'the convert apprehends differently, values differently, relates differently because he has become different. The new apprehension is not so much a new statement or a new set of statements, but rather new meanings that attach to almost any statement. It is not new values so much as a transvaluation of values' (ibid. 66). Conversion is also possible as a change that is not only individual and personal but also communal and historical; and when viewed as an ongoing process, at once personal, communal, and historical, it coincides, Lonergan says, with living religion (ibid. 66-67).

Now if theology is reflection on religion, and if conversion is fundamental to religious living, then not only will theology also be reflection on conversion, but reflection on conversion will provide theology with its foundations. 'Just as reflection on the operations of the scientist brings to light the real foundation of the science, so too reflection on the ongoing process of conversion may bring to light the real foundation of a renewed theology' (ibid. 67). Such is the basic argument establishing what is, in fact, a revolutionary recasting of the foundations of theology.

For the moment, however, my concern is not theology but conversion. The notion is significantly developed in *Method in Theology*, where conversion is differentiated into its religious, moral, and intellectual varieties. I am maintaining that the emergence of the capacity to disengage the symbolic constitution of the feelings in which the primordial apprehension of values occurs satisfies Lonergan's notion of conversion but also that it is something other than the three conversions of which he speaks. As any other conversion, it has many facets. As any other conversion, it is ever precarious. As any other conversion, it is a radical transformation of subjectivity influencing all the levels of one's living and transvaluing one's values. As any other conversion, it is 'not so much a new statement or a new set of statements, but rather new meanings that attach to almost any statement' (ibid. 66). As any other conversion, it too can become communal, so that there are formed formal and informal communities of men and women encouraging one another in the pursuit of further understanding and practical implementation of what they have experienced. Finally, as any other conversion, it undergoes a personal and arduous history of development, setback, and renewal. Its eventual outcome, most likely only asymptotically approached, is symbolically described by Jung as the termination of a state of imprisonment through a cumulative unity of opposites (Jung 1963, 65), or as a resolution of the contradictoriness of 'the unconscious' and consciousness in a nuptial *coniunctio* (ibid. 81), or as the birth of the hero issuing 'from something humble and forgotten.'[14] But, like any other conversion, psychic conversion is not the goal but the beginning. As religious conversion is not the mystic's cloud of unknowing, as moral conversion is not moral perfection, as intellectual conversion is not methodological craftsmanship, so psychic conversion is not unified affectivity or total integration with intentionality or immediate release from psychic imprisonment. It is, at the beginning, no more than the obscure understanding of the nourishing potential of the psyche to maintain the vitality of conscious living by a continuous influx of energy; the hint that one's psychic being can be transformed so as to aid one in the quest for individual authenticity; the suspicion that coming to terms with one's dreams will profoundly change one's ego by ousting it from its central and dominating position in one's conscious living, by shifting the birthplace of meaning gradually but progressively to a deeper center which is simultaneously a totality, the self (Jung 1969a, 141). Slowly one comes to discover the ambiguity of the psyche and to affirm the arduousness of the task to which one has committed oneself. Slowly one learns that the point is what is interior, temporal, generic, and indeed religious, and not what is exterior, spatial, specific, and human. Slowly a system of internal communication is established between intentionality and psyche. Slowly one learns the habit of disengaging the archetypal symbolic significance of one's feeling-toned responses to situations, people, and objects. Slowly one learns to distinguish symbols which further one's orientation to truth and value from those which mire one in myth and ego-centered satisfactions. One becomes attentive in a new way to the data of

---

14. Jung, 'Concerning Rebirth,' in 1969b, 141.

sense and the data of consciousness. One is aided by this new symbolic consciousness in one's efforts to be intelligent, reasonable, and responsible in one's everyday living and in one's pursuit of truth and value. Some of the concrete areas of one's own inattentiveness, obtuseness, silliness, and irresponsibility are revealed one by one, and can be named and quasi personified. They are complexes with a quasi personality of their own. When personified, they can be engaged in active imagination, in imaginative dialogue where one must listen as well as speak. The dialogue relativizes the ego and thus frees the complexes from rigidity. Some of them can then even be befriended and transformed. When thus paid attention to and, in a sense, compromised with, they prove to be sources of conscious energy one never before knew were at one's disposal. Such is psychic conversion. In itself it is not a matter of falling in love with God or of shifting the criterion of one's choices from satisfactions to values or of reflectively recognizing that knowing is not looking but the affirmation of the virtually unconditioned. It is not religious conversion or moral conversion or intellectual conversion. It *is* conversion, but it is something other than these. In the next chapter I shall describe its relation with these other conversions. For the moment, I am satisfied with establishing its uniqueness, with putting it on the map.[15]

---

15. 1993 note: I later came to define psychic conversion as the transformation of the psychic dimension of the censorship vis-à-vis neural demand functions from a repressive to a constructive functioning in one's development. I think this is a precise definition. However, the effects of psychic conversion also need to be spelled out more clearly than they are in the present volume. Some of this occurs in *Theology and the Dialectics of History*, chapters 2 and 6-10. But the notion of *embodiment* (theologically, of course, linked with Incarnation) still needs to be developed. Our operative Christology is still monophysite, and there is a corresponding mono-

5 The Psychic and the Psychoid

Psychic conversion heads toward what Jung, in his own vocabulary, calls 'the achievement of a synthesis of conscious and unconscious, and the realization of the archetype's effects upon the conscious contents' (Jung 1969a, 210). Such an achievement represents the 'climax of a concentrated spiritual and psychic effort, in so far as this is undertaken consciously and of set purpose' (ibid.).

The achievement is described as a movement from psychic dissociation to psychic integration. Psychic dissociation arises from the conditional nature of the link between psychic processes. Not only are there the rare cases of split personality or double consciousness, but much more frequently we find smaller fragments of the personality which have been broken off from the larger psychic totality to form autonomous complexes. The original state of the psyche contains very loosely knit processes and 'it often takes only a little to shatter the unity of consciousness so laboriously built up in the course of development and to resolve it back into its original elements' (ibid. 174).

A dissociated element or 'secondary subject' owes its separation to one of two definite causes.

> In the one case, there is an originally conscious content that became subliminal because it was repressed on account of its incompatible nature: in the other case, the secondary subject consists essentially in a process that never entered into

---

physitism to the rejection of the notion of psychic conversion on the part of some students of Lonergan.

> consciousness at all because no possibilities exist there of
> appperceiving it. That is to say, ego-consciousness cannot ac-
> cept it for lack of understanding, and in consequence it re-
> mains for the most part subliminal, although, from the energy
> point of view, it is quite capable of becoming conscious (ibid.
> 174-75).

On Jung's account, as opposed to Freud, the latter case, which is not pathological, is the most frequent.

Both kinds of undifferentiated material have an effect on consciousness and manifest themselves first in symptoms which are in part semiotic rather than symbolic. That is, to a certain extent we are to identify their causes rather than follow their direction. But these symptoms are in part also symbolic, since they are 'the indirect representatives of unconscious states or processes whose nature can be only imperfectly inferred and realized from the contents that appear in consciousness' (ibid. 175). To the extent that we cannot strictly identify causes, we may explore through sympathetic imagination the direction opened up by these manifestations, which then play a symbolic role.

Jung calls the sphere of these complexes 'the psychic.' It is an intermediate sphere with an upper and a lower threshold, both of which mark its differentiation from what he calls 'the psychoid.' 'The psychic' is the sphere uncovered when 'the disturbances emanating from the unconscious, the effects of spontaneous manifestations, of dreams, fantasies, and complexes, [are] successfully integrated into consciousness by the interpretative method' (ibid. 178). The lower threshold of the psychic is the boundary between the compulsive functioning, the all-or-none reaction, of physiological drives, and the more or less emancipated functioning of energy which is capable of more extensive and varied application. The upper threshold marks the boundary where the intrinsic energy of the function ceases altogether to be oriented by original instinct and attains a spiritual form. It is the sphere between these two more or less flexible boundaries that is called the psychic. It is the sphere affected by psychic conversion. Within this sphere, psychic functions can be voluntarily modified in a number of ways. While the differentiation of psychic function from physiological compulsion is indispensable for the maintenance and promotion of human life, such psychic flexibility or disposable energy increases the possibility of collision and produces dissociations which jeopardize the unity of consciousness.

There are, then, for Jung three systems: instinct, psyche, and spirit. The first and the third are autonomous and cannot be voluntarily coerced. But between them is a sphere of disposable energy based on, but relatively free from, specific instinctual compulsion and capable of either harmony or disharmony with the outer limits of instinct and spirit. Psychic conversion may be understood as the gaining of the capacity of intentional consciousness to integrate this flexible psychic system and even to effect a cumulative harmony with instinct and spirit, in such a way that 'all systems are working' and working more or less in harmony. It is a self-appropriation of the psychic system on the part of the existential subject, an appropriation based on the dialectic of the symbol and its more than purely personalistic intentionality.[16]

---

16. 1993 note: Jung's insistence on the autonomy and inflexibility of the realm that he calls spirit is based in a Kantian understanding of the spirit as an unknowable thing-in-itself. This, of course, is precisely what Lonergan has transcended in his intentionality analysis, where the operations of the spirit as intentional are brought to bear on the same operations as conscious, to yield an understanding of the realm of spirit that can be verified and so proclaimed correct. Jung's Kantianism leads to a neglect of the notion of pneumopathology, of a sickness that is rooted, not in the psyche, but in the spirit dimension of the person. Often enough, the healing of pneumopathology is required before the healing of psychopathology can take place.

Thus, when undifferentiated feeling-toned complexes are attended to, they can be transformed. 'They slough off their mythological envelope, and, by entering into the adaptive process going forward in consciousness, they personalize and rationalize themselves to the point where dialectical discussion becomes possible' (ibid. 187). When not integrated, and with increasing dissociation, undifferentiated psychic process approximates the underlying instinctual pattern of 'autonomous non-susceptibility to influence, all-or-none reaction' (ibid.). This analysis of Jung's thus corroborates our notion of a dialectic within the psyche itself. For Jung, the cumulative harmony of all three systems is possible because of the archetypes. While they represent the authentic element of spirit, and while 'archetype and instinct are the most polar opposites imaginable,' yet archetype and instinct 'belong together as correspondences, which is not to say that the one is derivable from the other, but that they subsist side by side as reflections in our own minds of the opposition that underlies all psychic energy' (ibid. 206).

These opposites of instinct and spirit are 'never incommensurables; if they were they could never unite. All contrariety notwithstanding, they do show a constant propensity to union' (ibid. 207). The symbol, appropriately dealt with by existential consciousness, is the function of their unification, precisely because of its archeological-teleological unity-in-tension. The moral significance of the opposites is found not in either taken singly, but depends on conscious integration and negotiation of symbolic processes—i.e., attentive, intelligent, reasonable, responsible, cooperative-intersubjective discrimination. Conscious confrontation with a representative of an instinct or with an archetype is 'an *ethical* problem of the first magnitude'(ibid. 208). Jung provides a helpful example:

> A poorly developed consciousness … which because of
> massed projections is inordinately impressed by concrete or
> apparently concrete things and states, will naturally see in the
> instinctual drives the source of all reality. It remains blissfully
> unaware of the spirituality of such a philosophical surmise,
> and is convinced that with this opinion it has established the
> essential instinctuality of all psychic processes. Conversely, a
> consciousness that finds itself in opposition to the instincts
> can, in consequence of the enormous influence then exerted
> by the archetypes, so subordinate instinct to spirit that the
> most grotosque 'spiritual' combinations may arise out of what
> are undoubtedly biological happenings. Here the instinctuality
> of the fanaticism needed for such an operation is ignored (ibid.
> 207).

It is the capacity of the existential subject for a symbolic dialectical disengagement of psychic process that will see one between these symbolic counterpositions to a genuine harmony of instinct and spirit in incarnate authentic subjectivity. This perhaps is one way of phrasing the potential result of the events constituting what I call psychic conversion.

I close this chapter by repeating in a new context something I have said before. Jung's notion of individuation as a cumulative process of the reconciliation of opposites under the guidance of responsible consciousness and with the aid of a professional guide is an extraordinarily accurate and fruitful one. Furthermore, Jung's insistence that neither of the polar extremes of instinct or spirit is in itself good or evil, that moral significance attaches rather to the process of reconciliation, is correct. Nonetheless, there *is* a problem of evil. Jung's researches help us enormously in rejecting a falsely spiritualistic tendency to locate the root of evil in instinct. But Jung did not adequately treat the problem of evil, and his psychology cannot handle it. What is worse, however, is the tendency of his psychology to *try* to handle it on the analogy of the process of the unity of opposites which determined the therapeutic dialectic. The divine and only solution to the problem of evil radically affects and transforms the psyche, but not by making it the locus where good and evil, grace and sin, embrace. Perhaps this tendency alone in Jung's psychology is sufficient to render intelligible the accusation of gnosticism to which he is subject. Psychology is not the source of answers to our ultimate problem, and it never will be. With sufficient understanding of the limited range of its concern, depth psychology can be conscripted into the far more extensive collaboration of human beings with God in working out the solution to the problem of evil in concrete circumstances. But when it insists on originating the solution, it joins the ranks of the contributors to the problem, and is ever so subtly coopted by the counterphilosophies which deny the ulterior finality of existential subjectivity.

6 Psyche and Theology

In the introduction to this work, I stated a twofold aim. My intention was, first, to contribute to our understanding of the existential subject by using Lonergan's thought to help generate categories appropriate to a methodological understanding of depth psychology; and, secondly, to use this latter understanding to fill out our notion of theological foundations. The first intention has been fulfilled, and I turn now to the second. I must clarify the relation of the psyche both to foundational reality and to the functional specialty 'foundations.' I discuss first foundational reality in *Insight* and in the later Lonergan; second, psyche and foundational reality; third, the functional specialties of dialectic and foundations; and fourth, psyche and foundations.

1 Foundational Reality: The Early Lonergan and the Later Lonergan

A discussion of foundations in *Insight* occurs within the context of an attempt to outline a method of metaphysics. This problem is raised by Lonergan immediately after the establishing of what he calls the basic positions: the position on the subject in chapter 11, the position on being in chapter

12, and the position on objectivity in chapter 13. The problem is raised in the following terms: while these three basic positions are accounted for in terms of the intellectual pattern of experience, human consciousness is polymorphic, and thus other patterns of experience may give rise to different views concerning the human subject, being, and objectivity. The intellectual pattern of experience is not the only pattern of experience, nor has Lonergan ever expressly argued that it is the privileged pattern of experience. Human experience can also be patterned in biological, dramatic, practical, aesthetic, artistic, and mystical modes. Furthermore, though,

> These patterns alternate; they blend or mix; they can interfere, conflict, lose their way, break down. The intellectual pattern of experience is supposed and expressed by our account of self-affirmation, of being, and of objectivity. But no man is born in that pattern; no one reaches it easily; no one remains in it permanently; and when some other pattern is dominant, then the self of our self-affirmation seems quite different from one's actual self, the universe of being seems as unreal as Plato's noetic heaven, and objectivity spontaneously becomes a matter of meeting persons and dealing with things that are 'really out there' (Lonergan 1992, 410-11).

Thus:

> Against the objectivity that is based on intelligent inquiry and critical reflection, there stands the unquestioning orientation of extroverted biological consciousness and its uncritical survival not only in dramatic and practical living but also in much of philosophic thought. Against the concrete universe of being, of all that can be intelligently grasped and reasonably affirmed, there stands in a prior completeness the world of sense, in which the 'real' and the 'apparent' are subdivisions within a vitally anticipated 'already out there now.' Against the self-affirmation of a consciousness that at once is empirical, intellectual, and rational, there stands the native

bewilderment of the existential subject, revolted by mere animality, unsure of his way through the maze of philosophies, trying to live without a known purpose, suffering despite an unmotivated will, threatened with inevitable death and, before death, with disease and even insanity (ibid.).

Lonergan maintains that a philosophy of philosophies can be developed, according to which 'the many, contradictory, disparate philosophies can all be contributions to the clarification of some basic but polymorphic fact,' i.e., human consciousness (ibid. 412). It is toward this philosophy of philosophies that his four chapters on metaphysics head. These philosophies share a twofold unity: they *originate* in inquiring intelligence and reflecting reasonableness, and they *ambition* truth. This twofold unity 'is the ground for finding in any given philosophy a significance that can extend beyond the philosopher's horizon and, even in a manner he did not expect, pertain to the permanent development of the human mind' (ibid.). It is in the mind of any given philosopher that contradictory contributions attain their complex unity. This unity is heuristically structured by the principle that the positions invite development and the counterpositions reversal.

It is in explicating this principle that Lonergan discusses foundations. He distinguishes between the *basis* of any philosophy, which lies in its cognitional theory, and the *expansion* of that philosophy in its pronouncements on metaphysical, ethical, and theological issues. In the basis, he distinguishes further between two aspects: the *determination* of cognitional theory in an appeal to the data of consciousness and to the historical development of human knowledge, and the inevitable inclusion, in one's *formulation* of cognitional theory, of one's judgments on basic issues in philosophy. That is to say, first, that one will arrive at one's cognitional theory by an analysis of the data of one's own conscious knowing performance and by an appeal to the discovery and development of mind; and, secondly, that one cannot articulate one's cognitional theory without committing oneself in advance on certain basic philosophic questions.

It is with respect to these philosophic commitments necessarily immanent in the formulation of cognitional theory that there arise for Lonergan in the first instance the notions of position and counterposition. The philosophic issues concerning which one must take a stand in the formulation of cognitional theory concern reality, the subject, and objectivity. What determines whether one's basic philosophic commitments are positions open to development or counterpositions inviting reversal is their agreement or discrepancy with the judgments concerning the subject, reality, and objectivity expressed, respectively, in the eleventh, twelfth, and thirteenth chapters of *Insight*.

> ... the inevitable philosophic component immanent in the formulation of cognitional theory will be either a basic position or else a basic counterposition.
>
> It will be a basic position, (1) if the real is the concrete universe of being and not a subdivision of the 'already out there now'; (2) if the subject becomes known when it affirms itself intelligently and reasonably and so is not known yet in any prior 'existential' state; and (3) if objectivity is conceived as a consequence of intelligent inquiry and critical reflection, and not as a property of vital anticipation, extroversion, and satisfaction.
>
> On the other hand, it will be a basic counterposition if it contradicts one or more of the basic positions.
>
> ...any philosophic pronouncement on any epistemological, metaphysical, ethical, or theological issue will be named a position if it is coherent with the basic positions on the real, on knowing, and on objectivity; and it will be named a counterposition if it is coherent with one or more of the basic counterpositions (ibid. 413).

The second of these basic positions needs a brief clarification. The subject becomes known when it affirms itself intelligently and reasonably. Now, *nothing* is known unless it is intelligently grasped and reasonably affirmed. The self-affirmation inevitably included in the basis of one's philosophy, however, is the intelligent and reasonable affirmation of one's own intelligence and reasonableness. It is the judgment 'I am a knower,' where knowledge is the compound of experience, understanding, and judgment. Thus the basic position on the subject in *Insight* is the position on the knowing subject. The selfknowledge of the subject is true if it is based in one's intelligent grasp and reasonable affirmation of one's own intelligence and reasonableness. This affirmation, along with positions on the real and objectivity, are the positions which constitute the foundations or basis (to use the term employed in *Insight*) of metaphysics, ethics, and philosophical theology.

In the terminology of the post-1965 Lonergan—I take 'Dimensions of Meaning' as signalling the transition to the 'later Lonergan'—these positions are attained as a result of a basic philosophic *conversion*, which Lonergan calls intellectual conversion. But now, intellectual conversion is seen usually, though not necessarily, to follow upon and to be conditioned by the conversions which he calls religious and moral. We have seen in chapter 1 what Lonergan means by religious and moral conversion. In the general case, religious conversion occurs first, and gives rise to moral conversion, in that it is on the basis of one's religious experience that one is moved to self-transcendence in one's actions. Intellectual conversion, in the general case, is consequent upon and conditioned by religious and moral conversion, in that there is a realism implicit in one's religious and moral self-transcendence which conditions the recognition of the realism of knowing that is intellectual conversion. On the other hand, the latter conversion is that which Lonergan prefers to explicate first, since this articulation helps him to say what is meant by the self-transcendence of moral goodness and of authentic religion.

> I should urge that religious conversion, moral conversion, and intellectual conversion are three quite different things. In an order of exposition I would prefer to explain first intellectual, then moral, then religious conversion. In the order of occurrence I would expect religious commonly but not necessarily to precede moral and both religious and moral to precede intellectual. Intellectual conversion, I think, is very rare (Lonergan 1972b, 233-34).

This developed understanding of conversion is concomitant with the emergence of a distinct notion of the good. Thus, in the 1968 lecture 'The Subject,' as we have seen, a primacy is assigned to the subject trying to be good, to the existential subject. Nothing that was accorded the cognitional subject in *Insight* is denied in the later works. But the basic position on the subject would seem to be more than the basic position on knowing, for the subject as deciding, deliberating, evaluating is granted a primacy. The basic position on the subject would now seem to be a compound position, consisting not only of judgments of cognitional fact, but also of judgments of value. Furthermore, if the intellectual conversion which issues in the basic positions which are foundational for philosophy is somehow consequent upon religious and moral conversion, then the foundations of one's metaphysics, ethics, and theology would seem to lie in the objectification of all three conversions in this patterned set of judgments concerning the subject as cognitional and as existential. Such is the crucial significance of the emergence of a distinct notion of the good. My present concern is not with the very serious question of what this means philosophically and especially for metaphysics, but with what it means for theology. At the present moment, the jury in my own mind is still out on the question of whether it is valid for Lonergan to proceed to a metaphysics on the foundations laid in *Insight*.[1] But it is a fact that he does *not* proceed to a theology on these foundations alone. The foundations of theology include but go far beyond *Insight*'s basic positions on knowing, the real, and objectivity. And they transcend these positions not by denying them in the least, but by affirming that the position on knowing is not the full position on the human subject. The authentic human subject is the subject who is self-transcending in knowing, doing, and religion. This subject is the foundational reality of theology. The functional specialty 'foundations' consists in an objectification of self-transcending subjectivity in its cognitional, existential, and religious dimensions. The subject's intelligent and reasonable affirmation of his or her own intelligence and reasonableness may be the beginning of a foundational position on the subject, so that Lonergan prefers to discuss intellectual conversion before moral and religious conversion; but it is not the full position on the subject. This is quite clear from Lonergan's later writings. It is not simply my interpretation of Lonergan, but rather necessarily is included in Lonergan's affirmation of the primacy of the subject as existential. Foundational reality consists not only of a subject who intelligently and reasonably affirms his or her own intelligence and reasonableness, but also of an existential subject for whom the criterion of decision has been shifted from the satisfactions spontaneously desired by biological extraversion to the values prized by a consciousness which is not only intelligent and reasonable but also responsible, and finally of a religious subject in love with an otherworldly *mysterium tremendum et fascinans*. The intentionality of human consciousness itself, the primordial

---

1. 1993 note: I now believe that this move is valid.

infrastructure of human subjectivity, is a dynamism heading toward self-transcendence in knowing, morality, and religion. The subject whose conscious performance is in accord with this dynamism is foundational reality. The objectification of this dynamism in a patterned set of judgments of cognitional fact and of value constitutes foundations in theology.

This development settles for me what has been a very persistent problem ever since my first reading of *Insight*. Human experience is variously patterned. As we have seen, Lonergan discusses its various patterns. In *Insight*, he highlights its intellectual pattern for, as he has said, his purpose was a study not of human life but of human understanding. But the overall impression conveyed by *Insight* — an impression which will, of course, find no verification in Lonergan's explicit utterance but which is nonetheless communicated — is that the intellectual pattern of experience is the privileged pattern of experience. But with the emergence of a distinct idea of the good, cognitional analysis becomes intentionality analysis. Then, what is privileged is not some one pattern of experience but a *self-transcendence* that can be attained in any of several patterns of experience — in the dramatic pattern of experience of common sense, in the aesthetic and artistic patterns of experience, in the mystical pattern of experience, and of course in the intellectual pattern of experience. Lonergan is probably quite correct that this self-transcendence is best grasped in a discussion of the intellectual pattern of experience, and thus probably quite justified in his preference to discuss intellectual conversion before moral and religious conversion. But the emergence of the distinct notion of the good in Lonergan's later writings, when sufficiently appreciated for its radical importance in his development, decisively changes the atmosphere and shifts the balance present in his thought taken as a whole. As self-transcending subjectivity defines human authenticity, so Lonergan's thought as a whole is not primarily cognitional theory but an elucidation of the drama of the emergence of the authentic subject. It is a basic semantics of human desire. Such is, I believe, the most accurate interpretation and assessment of his achievement.

2 Psyche and Foundational Reality

For the author of *Insight*, counterpositions invite reversal because they are incoherent, not with one another, but with the activities of grasping them intelligently and affirming them reasonably. Thus they prompt the intelligent and reasonable inquirer to introduce coherence. The activities themselves of intelligent grasping and reasonable affirmation contain the basic positions on the real, on knowing, and on objectivity. But if the position on the subject is not coincident with the self-affirmation of the knower, with the position on knowing, can it be said that the activities of intelligent grasping and reasonable affirmation of one's own intelligence and reasonableness contain the basic position on the subject? Or does that basic position find enunciation only when judgments of cognitional fact are joined with judgments of existential fact and of value? If the latter is the case, and if judgments of value are mediated with judgments of fact by feelings, then does not the basic position on the subject demand not only the functioning of intelligence and reasonableness grasping and affirming intelligence and reasonableness, and not only a satisfactory transcendental analysis of the human good, but also a set of judgments detailing the authentic development of feelings? If the story of the development and aberration of feelings or of dispositional immediacy can be told by disengaging the spontaneous symbols produced in dreams, if the habit of such disengagement is mediated to the subject by psychic conversion, if conversion is foundational reality, if the objectification of conversion is the functional specialty 'foundations,' then is psychic conversion not an aspect of foundational reality and will not an objectification of psychic conversion constitute a genuine aspect of foundations? There are counterpositions on the real, on knowing, and on objectivity that are incoherent with the activities of intelligent grasping and reasonable affirmation. But there are also counterpositions on the subject that are incoherent, not specifically with these activities alone, but with the emergence of the authentic existential subject. Only in this latter incoherence are they suspected of being counterpositions, for they are apprehended as articulations of countervalues in the feelings of the existential subject striving for self-transcendence, and they are judged to be such in the same subject's judgments of value. They are incoherent, not specifically with the self-transcendence intended in the unfolding of the desire to know, but with the self-transcendence toward which the primordial infrastructure of human subjectivity as a whole is headed. The subject who contains implicitly the full position on the subject is not the intelligent and reasonable subject, but the experiencing, intelligent, reasonable, responsible, religious subject. In fact, we would even have to say that, if one is looking for the full position on the human subject by scrutinizing only one's intelligence and reasonableness, one is heading for the articulation of a counterposition. One is the victim of an intellectualist bias too easily confirmed by the writings of the early Lonergan in those readers whose spontaneous subjective development has been characterized by a preference for the superiority of what Jung has called the thinking function. I cannot emphasize too much that the emergence of the notion of the good as distinct from, though not contradictory to, the intelligent and reasonable in the writings of the post-1965 Lonergan decisively shifts the atmosphere—yes, the archetypal significance—of his work as a whole. Human authenticity is a matter of self-transcendence. Self-transcendence can be achieved in one's knowing, in one's free and responsible constitution of the human world, and in one's religious living as a participation in the divine solution to the problem of evil. The struggle between the dynamism for self-transcendence and the flight from authenticity is the archetypal struggle which provides the ground theme unifying the various aspects of this achievement. The articulation of this struggle in an objectification of conversion constitutes a semantics of human desire.

This ground theme itself is invested with a symbolic or archetypal significance. Not only does intentionality in its dynamic thrust for self-transcendence have the potential of conscripting psyche into its service through the dialectical disengagement of the intention of truth and value present in the psyche, but the psyche insists on stamping the entire drama with its own characteristic mark by giving it an archetypal representation, by releasing in dreams the ciphers of the present status of the drama, by indicating to the existential subject how it stands between the totality of consciousness as primordial infrastructure intending self-transcendence and the subject's explicit self-understanding in his or her intention of or flight from truth and value. The articulation of the story of these ciphers, the disengagement of their systematically intelligible pattern in a dialectical hermeneutic phenomenology of the psyche, would constitute a transcendental aesthetic. This aesthetic would, I wager, follow Jung's phenomenology of the psyche quite closely until one comes to the farthest reaches of the psyche, which also constitute its center. There the dialectic becomes that of good and evil, grace and sin, and at that point dialectic itself breaks down. Just as a dialectical analysis of human progress and decline is not adequate for meeting the problem of evil, so dialectical reconciliation of opposites is not the process for engaging this ultimate psychic struggle. Intentionality and the psyche it has conscripted into its adventure must at this point surrender to the gift of God's love poured forth in our hearts by the Holy Spirit who has been given to us. The transcendental aesthetic issues in kerygma, manifestation, proclamation, in the return to the fullness of language simply heard and understood, in the return to the homeland of one's own life from the journey to the mountaintop and the sojourn in the forest. This is the second naivete intended by Paul Ricoeur. It is mediated by the process of self-appropriation in its entirety, by the objectification of the primordial infrastructure of cognitional and existential subjectivity in a twofold mediation of immediacy by meaning.

Psychic conversion, like religious and moral conversion, is an event which normally takes place outside and independently of method. But I must now attempt to articulate a better understanding of its role within method, by stating its relation to the three conversions specified by Lonergan as constituting the authentic subjectivity which is foundational reality. We have already seen that, in the order of occurrence, religious conversion generally precedes moral conversion, and both religious and moral conversion generally precede intellectual conversion. But that is not the complete story of their existential interrelationships. For in *Method in Theology*, Lonergan tells us that subsequent to the occurrence of these events, intellectual conversion is sublated by moral conversion, and that both intellectual conversion and moral conversion are sublated by religious conversion (Lonergan 1993, 241-43). It is within the context of these sublations that I understand the foundational significance of psychic conversion. Lonergan understands sublation along the lines suggested by Karl Rahner, and not in a fashion inspired by Hegel.

Sublation, then, is in no sense a negating or nihilating of what is sublated. Rather, 'what sublates goes beyond what is sublated, introduces something new and distinct, puts everything on a new basis, yet so far from interfering with the sublated or destroying it, on the contrary needs it, includes it, preserves all its proper features and properties, and carries them forward to a fuller realization within a richer context' (ibid. 241). Thus the achievement of a familiarity with the self-transcending capacities of human knowing that is intellectual conversion is needed, included, preserved, elevated to a new level, and carried forward to more precise specification by the self-transcending capacities of the existential subject in the free and responsible constitution of the human world. And the same happens to each of these in the movement of deepening one's commitment to collaboration with God in the divine solution to the problem of evil. While intellectual conversion may be the rarest of the conversions, it is not the final answer, for it is not the solution to our ultimate problem. It is a facet of the collaboration of some in working out the concrete and specific details of the solution. But there is no way in which one can claim that Lonergan proposes a sublation of religion into knowing, of religious conversion into intellectual conversion, or of the divine solution to the problem of evil into a human understanding of human understanding. This Hegelian trap is avoided at every step in the writings of both the early and the later Lonergan. In the later formulation, what happens to the subject in the specifically philosophic conversion which provides one with familiarity with the self-transcending capacities of human judgment is taken up by the more extensive dynamic orientation to self-transcendence in human responsibility and human openness to the gift of God's love. How does psychic conversion affect this double movement of sublation?

First, let me state that psychic conversion does not occur necessarily either before or after the three conversions spoken of by Lonergan. It is the emergence of a capacity to disengage the symbolic constitution of immediacy. It can conceivably occur with or without religious faith, with or without the existential self-transcendence usually consequent upon religious faith. It obviously occurs quite frequently without even the suspicion that there may be something like a philosophic conversion through which one comes to affirm what one is doing when one is knowing, why doing that is knowing, and what one knows when one does that. Since its finality is determined by the ground theme of the emergence of the self-transcending existential subject, it is highly doubtful whether it can be carried to any fruitful conclusion without at least moral resolve and something resembling religious faith and trust in God. But in itself it is an independent event, and I would not want to state where it usually occurs in the temporal sequence of the conversions. My concern is rather with its role in method, and thus with its function in the interrelationship of all the conversions through sublation.

The orientation of intentionality toward self-transcendence in knowing, doing, and religion includes an exigence for psychic self-appropriation. The precise room for the methodological understanding of this exigence is provided by the emergence of a distinct notion of the good in the writings of the later Lonergan. As the good is apprehended in feelings and as feelings are symbolically certifiable, so psychic conversion is an aid to the discrimination of one's stance regarding the good. The story of one's own personal engagement in the drama of the existential subject is enabled to be told by psychic conversion. Thus I locate psychic conversion methodologically as facilitating the sublation of intellectual conversion by moral conversion and of both by religious conversion; as facilitating the richer context within which one's familiarity with the self-transcending capacity of human judgment is carried forward by the self-transcending capacity of human action, and the still richer context within which both of these are carried forward by the soul beyond both cognitional analysis and psychology, the soul in love with God, the soul moving toward the God wrapped in the cloud of unknowing. Psychic conversion functions in aid of the self-appropriation of the existential subject. It enables such a subject to narrate the drama of his or her own struggle against the flight from authenticity. This drama is primal. It is archetypal. It is the ground theme of human history and of personal life. It is the story of one's salvation or of one's loss. It is the story of the human good writ large in the pages of history, the story of the progress or decline of groups, of cultures, of nations and polities, of civilization, of the world. While it is the story of human beings from our origins to the present day, of myth through logic to the recapitulation of both logic and myth in method, it is ontogenetically reproduced in the individual story of contemporary men and women as they struggle for release from the flight from authenticity or succumb to that flight at the expense of their humanity. The gate that leads to life is a narrow gate, as we are well aware. Familiarity with the psyche can be brought to aid one in the recognition of the contours of that gate, of its distinctiveness from the avenues to destruction, and of the path along which one is walking oneself. As there are philosophies which deny the self-transcending finality of human knowing and doing, so there are psychologies which deny the moral and religious significance of psychotherapy. It is only within the context of a thoroughgoing intentionality analysis that depth psychology can discover its own inner meaning and finality. Depth psychology cannot answer the question, What is a human being? For an objectification of the transcendetnal infrastructure of human subjectivity will include far more than a knowledge of the human psyche. But depth psychology can contribute to the answer to the question, Who am I? when the psychic journey is undertaken as an aid to the quest for self-transcendence on the part of the existential subject; and it can figure in a transcendental anthropology when the psychic journey itself is objectified as a transcendental aesthetic with a place of its own within the overarching context of transcendental method.

I have related psychic conversion to moral conversion and religious conversion within the context of the sublations affirmed by Lonergan. I have said little of its relation to intellectual conversion. I have spoken of its moral and religious finality, but I have not yet indicated how it aids in the sublation of intellectual conversion into this ulterior dynamism of human intentionality. To that question I must now turn. My comments are offered within the context of the contention that, with the emergence of a distinct notion of the good, Lonergan's thought in its entirety is no longer primarily cognitional analysis but rather intentionality analysis, that the full position on the subject is not the position on knowing but a patterned set of judgments of cognitional fact and of value, and that the privileged domain of human subjectivity is not the intellectual pattern of experience but self-transcendence in one's knowing, doing, and religion.

In its full sweep intellectual conversion is the mediation of immediacy which occurs when one answers correctly and in order the three critical questions. The answer to the first question, What am I doing when I am knowing? reveals the dynamic structure, promoted by questioning, of human cognitional process. The answer to the second question, Why is doing that knowing? reveals that structure to be transcendental and in principle not subject to revision. The answer to the third question, What do I know when I do that? is that what I know when I faithfully pursue the process is what I intended to know when I began the process: what is, being, the real, the true. Concomitant with answering these questions is the elimination of the cognitional myth that the real is a subdivision of the already out there now and that it is to be known by looking.

What I wish to emphasize is that an objectifiction of intellectual conversion plays a role within an articulated semantics of human desire, for intellectual conversion, when sublated by existential subjectivity, has a distinctly therapeutic value. It is a step, and perhaps methodologically the first step, in the displacement of the origin and home of meaning and value away from naive consciousness. It is a contribution to the movement of subjectivity toward the deeper center, the self. It is a shift in the center of human significance away from the near-animal extraversion of untutored consciousness and toward the infolding of human desire in a unified and self-appropriated subjectivity. It achieves this shift by rendering a thematization of something that was previously quite undifferentiated, the dynamic structure-in-process of the subject's orientation to truth. It is a self-conscious appropriation of what otherwise is left inarticulate. The three critical questions are an aspect of the exigence for appropriation in terms of interiority that has given rise to the third epoch in human conscious evolution. In its deepest significance, this exigence is existential. It is an exigence to heal the rift between the self as conscious and the self as known. It is an exigence for self-knowledge, and one of its dimensions calls for an understanding of one's own understanding.

I have called intentionality analysis as articulated by Lonergan the appropriation of *logos*. As such it is the thematization of the emergence of *logos* from *mythos*. This description is particularly apt for Lonergan's cognitional analysis. The emergence of *logos* from *mythos* involved a release and liberation of human consciousness from the domination of the maternal imagination, from the hegemony of psyche. It was the announcement of intentionality that psyche is not the horizon of Being, that the transcendental time structure of imagination may be the form of inner sense and the institution of *Befindlichkeit* in its primordiality, unity, and totality, but that the transcendental imagination does not constitute intentionality as a whole. It was the heroic severing of the umbilical cord which binds mind to maternal imagination. It was archetypally represented in the drama of Orestes. It was the condition of the possibility of the systematic control of meaning which found its first secure triumph in the Socratic maieutic and expended itself in needless exhaustion in the Hegelian dialectic. It is repeated in the ontogenetic development of the conscious subject who is the heir of Western philosophy and science. The answers to the critical questions thematize for that subject the cognitional significance of the manifesto of *logos*. They render cognitional subjectivity present to itself by thematizing the heroic achievement which some two thousand years have brought to maturity.

The drama of Orestes, however, reflects the fact that, while intentionality may in a self-inflated fashion proclaim that it is now done with psyche, psyche is by no means done with intentionality. There is an existential crisis which results from the heroic victory of intentionality, from its rightful proclamation of hegemony, from its defiance of the pretended totalitarianism of the imagination. Orestes is pursued in a frightful fashion by the darkest powers of the psyche. He is finally vindicated by the combined judgment of the reasonable citizens who represent the positive aspect of his triumph and by the embodiment of psyche as wisdom in the goddess Athena. The judgment of vindication must be a combined judgment. Psyche must have its say in the final outcome, a decisive say. And what were the darkest powers of psychic nature must be *persuaded* by psyche as wisdom to take up their abode in the depths of the earth upon which the city of reasonable people is built, and to lend their powerful support to the advance of cultured humanity. They cannot be disposed of or escaped from. They can be transformed by persuasion. But they will never go away.

The appropriation of *logos*, then, must give way to the appropriation of *mythos*, to the transformation by dialectical persuasion of these otherwise chaotic powers. The answering of the critical questions is only the beginning of a far more extensive process demanded by the existential situation of a consciousness which has brought to some kind of conclusion the demands of its systematic differentation. If this existential crisis is left unattended, it will bring catastrophe to the city of reasonable people, to the scientific community, to the economy, to the polity, to the nations, to the world. It is the same crisis that is manifested cognitively in the split between theoretically differentiated consciousness and common sense. But its existential ciphers are far more dramatic. It is the lonely isolation of the hero from all that has nourished one. It is one's self-chosen separation from the primal ground of one's being. It is the alienation of the light from the darkness out of which it violently broke forth, but without which it cannot remain light. Lonergan's articulation of the necessary victory of *logos* over the uroboric dragon of myth is the methodologically primary step toward the healing of an existential crisis which threatens civilization with destruction. But it is only a beginning. It clarifies what has happened, thematizes what has occurred. But it does not heal the crisis. *Logos* still remains isolated, cut off from the rhythms and processes of nature, separated from psyche, alienated from the original darkness which both nourished it and threatened to smother it, guilty over the primal murder of an ambiguously life-giving power. With Lonergan's help, we now know what we have done in overcoming the gods and claiming a rightful autonomy. But we still do not know how to achieve a differentiated reconciliation with psychic darkness. For a time, we even suspect that all such reconciliation is regression, a cancelling of the victory of *logos*, a repudiation of a bitterly won autonomy. But then we are told that intellectual conversion needs to be sublated by moral and religious conversion, and that the first step in an understanding of moral conversion is a thematization of the primordial apprehension of values in symbolically charged feelings. Perhaps we are on the way, on a road which leads simultaneously to a vindication of the decision of *logos* in favor of understanding and truth and to a transformation of those dark and strange powers which have been overruled by this decision but as yet by no means pacified and conscripted into its ulterior orientation. Self-appropriating *logos* can utilize its own newly discovered resources in the intelligent hermeneutic, reasonable affirmation, and responsible transformation of those imaginal roots out of which these very powers of intelligent grasping, reasonable affirmation, and responsible constitutive subjectivity have violently wrested their birthright. This is the psychic, moral, and religious imperative now manifest in the epochal shift of the control of meaning whose overarching contours have been sketched by Lonergan. It is also the first really secure step in the sublation of intellectual conversion by moral conversion.

3 Dialectic and Foundations

Foundations in theology lie in an objectification of conversion, in a reflective thematization of the movement of conversion in its origins, its developments, its purposes, its acheivements, and its failures (ibid. 131). Such foundations articulate the *horizon* within which the meaning of any doctrinal or theological statement can be understood.

3.1 Perspectives and Horizons

Lonergan distinguishes between perspective and horizon. Perspectives are perhaps best understood in the context of the progress of both historical research and history itself. Historical research may to all intents and purposes regard a given investigation as complete. But then new sources of information are discovered which call for the rewriting of history. 'Archeological investigations of the ancient Near East complement Old Testament study, the caves of Qumran have yielded documents with a bearing on New Testament studies, while the unpublished writings found at Kenoboskion restrain pronouncements on Gnosticism' (ibid. 192). Furthermore, as history itself goes forward, earlier events are placed in new perspectives by later ones. 'The outcome of a battle fixes the perspective in which the successive stages of the battle are viewed; military victory in a war reveals the significance of the successive battles that were fought; the social and cultural consequences of the victory and the defeat are the measure of the effects of the war. So, in general, history is an ongoing process. As the process advances, the context within which events are to be understood keeps enlarging. As the context enlarges, perspectives shift' (ibid.).

Shifting perspectives are not contradictory, and thus they do not invalidate previous work.

> New documents fill out the picture; they illuminate what before was obscure; they shift perspectives; they refute what was venturesome or speculative; they do not simply dissolve the whole network of questions and answers that made the original set of data massive evidence for the earlier account.

Again, history is an ongoing process, and so the historical context keeps enlarging. But the effects of this enlargement are neither universal nor uniform. For persons and events have their place in history through one or more contexts, and these contexts may be narrow and brief or broad and enduring with any variety of intermediates. Only in as much as a context is still open, or can be opened or extended, do later events throw new light on earlier persons, events, processes. As Karl Heussi put it, it is easier to understand Frederick Wilhelm III of Prussia than to understand Schleiermacher and, while Nero will always be Nero, we cannot as yet say the same for Luther (ibid. 192-93).

A horizon is something other than a perspective. The latter is a prior understanding derived, say, from historical sources. The former is derived from elsewhere. To hold for the moment to the historian, a horizon reflects one or several basic options reflected in preconceptions about what must have happened or at least about what could not have happened. A horizon is constituted of basic convictions about humanity and the world, and these convictions are derived from one's upbringing, education, and cultural milieu. It is the notion of horizon, rather than that of perspective, which accounts for histories that are, not more or less comprehensive, but irreconcilable. To change one's horizon is a quite different and far more radical procedure than to change or enlarge one's perspective. While perspectival differences result from the complexity of data, differences of horizon originate in an explicit or implicit cognitional theory, an ethical stance, and a religious outlook. They can be overcome only by the radical transformations effected in intellectual, moral, and religious conversion. There is a functional specialty called dialectic which brings precisely these radical conflicts into the light and objectifies the differences in subjectivity that account for them. Interestingly enough from our present perspective, dialectic and foundations are the two functional specialties correlated with the fourth level of intentional consciousness, the level highlighted in Lonergan's later writings because of the emergence of a distinct notion of the good, the level of existential subjectivity. On my present interpretation, just as it is the emergence of the distinct notion of the good that accounts for the possibility of these two functional specialties, so it is these two functional specialties which contain the key to understanding *Method in Theology*.

3.2 *Dialectic*

Foundations as a functional specialty is best understood, I believe, from the understanding of dialectic. First, then, not all differences in horizon are dialectical. Within a given cultural framework, people from many different backgrounds and with many different occupations and fields of competence will recognize the need in that culture for the competencies of the others. In this sense their different horizons, determined by the different worlds in which they live, will also either include the horizons of the others or at least complement them. 'Singly they are not self-sufficient, and together they represent the motivations and the knowledge needed for the functioning of a communal world. Such horizons are complementary' (ibid. 236). Furthermore, different horizons may be related genetically as successive stages in a process of development. Horizons are dialectically opposed when 'what in one is found intelligible, in another is unintelligible. What for one is true, for another is false. What for one is good, for another is evil' (ibid.). Moreover:

> … the other's horizon, at least in part, is attributed to wishful thinking, to an acceptance of myth, to ignorance or fallacy, to blindness or illusion, to backwardness or immaturity, to infidelity, to bad will, to a refusal of God's grace. Such

a rejection of the other may be passionate, and then the suggestion that openness is desirable will make one furious. But again rejection may have the firmness of ice without any trace of passion or even any show of feeling, except perhaps a wan smile. Both astrology and genocide are beyond the pale, but the former is ridiculed, the latter is execrated (ibid. 236-37).

Any given horizon is a 'structured resultant of past achievement and, as well, both the condition and the limitation of further development ... Horizons then are the sweep of our interests and of our knowledge; they are the fertile source of further knowledge and care; but they also are the boundaries that limit our capacities for assimilating more than we already have attained' (ibid. 237).

From the French Jesuit moral philosopher Joseph de Finance, Lonergan draws the distinction between an exercise of freedom within a given horizon — horizontal freedom — and the exercise of freedom by which we move from one horizon to another — vertical freedom. The exercise of vertical freedom is twofold. Either one moves from one horizon to another in a continuous fashion, so that 'the new horizon, though notably deeper and broader and richer, none the less is consonant with the old and a development out of its potentialities' (ibid.).; or one moves by way of an about-face, by repudiating the characteristic features of the old horizon, by beginning a new sequence that reveals ever deeper and broader and richer dimensions. The latter exercise of vertical freedom is consequent upon a conversion, an intellectual conversion, a moral conversion, or a religious conversion. Each of the conversions is a modality of self-transcendence. 'Intellectual conversion is to truth attained by cognitional self-transcendence. Moral conversion is to values apprehended, affirmed, and realized by a real self-transcendence. Religious conversion is to a total being-in-love as the efficacious ground of all self-transcendence, whether in the pursuit of truth, or in the realization of human values, or in the orientation man adopts to the universe, its ground, and its goal' (ibid. 241). We have already seen Lonergan's account of the occurrence and sublation of these conversions.

If conversion is an about-face in terms of self-transcendence, there is also an aboutface in the direction of inauthenticity. Such an about-face is termed a breakdown. Lonergan's account of breakdown is interesting, and I choose to present here a lengthy quotation.

> What has been built up so slowly and so laboriously by the individual, the society, the culture, can collapse. Cognitional self-transcendence is neither an easy notion to grasp nor a readily accessible datum of consciousness to be verified. Values have a certain esoteric imperiousness, but can they keep outweighing carnal pleasure, wealth, power? Religion undoubtedly had its day, but is not that day over? Is it not illusory comfort for weaker souls, an opium distributed by the rich to quiet the poor, a mythical projection of man's own excellence into the sky?
>
> Initially not all but some religion is pronounced illusory, not all but some moral precept is rejected as ineffective and useless, not all truth but some type of metaphysics is dismissed as mere talk. The negations may be true, and then they represent an effort to offset decline. But also they may be false, and then they are the beginning of decline. In the latter case some part of cultural achievement is being destroyed. It will cease being a familiar component in cultural experience. It will recede into a forgotten past for historians, perhaps, to rediscover and reconstruct. Moreover, this elimination of a genuine part of the culture means that a previous whole has been mutilated, that some balance has been upset, that the remainder will become distorted in an effort to compensate. Further, such elimination, mutilation, distortion will, of course, be admired as the forward march of progress, while the evident ills they bring forth are to be remedied, not by a return to a misguided past, but by more elimination, mutilation, distortion. Once a process of dissolution has begun, it is screened by self-deception and it is perpetuated by consistency. But that does

not mean that it is confined to some single uniform course. Different nations, different classes of society, different agegroups can select different parts of past achievement for elimination, different mutilations to be effected, different distortions to be provoked. Increasing dissolution will then be matched by increasing division, incomprehension, suspicion, distrust, hostility, hatred, violence. The body social is torn apart in many ways, and its cultural soul has been rendered incapable of reasonable convictions and responsible commitments.

For convictions and commitments rest on judgments of fact and judgments of value. Such judgments, in turn, rest largely on beliefs. Few, indeed, are the people that, pressed on almost any point, must not shortly have recourse to what they have believed. Now such recourse can be efficacious only when believers present a solid front, only when intellectual, moral, and religious skeptics are a small and, as yet, uninfluential minority. But their numbers can increase, their influence can mount, their voices can take over the book market, the educational system, the mass media. Then believing begins to work not for but against intellectual, moral, and religious self-transcendence. What had been an uphill but universally respected course collapses into the peculiarity of an outdated minority (ibid. 243-44).

The functional specialty 'dialectic,' then, has a twofold task. Its first task is evaluative. There is a functional specialty called interpretation, whose task is to understand the *Sache* of a text, its words, its author, and oneself; to judge the accuracy of one's understanding; and to determine the best way of expressing what one has understood. There is also a functional specialty called history, whose job is to determine the facts about what was going forward in the various movements being studied. Now, besides a hermeneutic which understands, there is also a hermeneutic which evaluates the constitutive and effective force of the meanings one has understood. And besides a history which detemines facts, there is a history which evaluates achievements in terms of good and evil. Regarding the latter, Lonergan quotes the eminent historian Carl Becker: 'The value of history is … not scientific but moral: by liberating the mind, by deepening the sympathies, by fortifying the will, it enables us to control, not society, but ourselves—a much more important thing; it prepares us to live more humanely in the present and to meet rather than to foretell the future' (ibid. 245, quoting Smith 1956, 117). Evaluative hermeneutic, evaluative history, and the promotion of the specialized research needed for them are one task of dialectic.

The second task of dialectic may be called horizon encounter. We have already seen that dialectic deals with differences of horizon rather than differences of perspective, and with those differences of horizon which depend on opposed and radical convictions concerning the intellectual, moral, and religious infrastructure of human subjectivity. The only remedy to such differences is conversion. When such differences are involved in history, the discovery of new data will not remedy them, for the new data are just as susceptible of opposed readings as were the old data. Regarding interpretation, there is a different self to be understood if one is convinced of the intellectual, moral, and religious capacities for self-transcendence from the self that is understood if one implicitly or explicitly rejects such self-transcendence. Such opposed self-understandings give rise to different understandings of the *Sache* of a text, of its words, of its author, and of the manner of expressing what one has understood. Regarding research, one's horizon determines what one will regard as appropriate data for interpretation and history. 'One easily finds what fits into one's horizon. One has very little ability to notice what one has never understood or conceived. No less than interpretation and history, the preliminary special reseach can reveal differences of horizon' (ibid. 247). Dialectic, then, is a matter of meeting the persons one is studying in history and interpretation, appreciating the values they represent, criticizing their defects, and letting oneself be challenged radically in the process, thus putting one's own self-understanding and horizon to the test (ibid.). Of particular relevance to our present concern is the observation that 'such response is all the fuller, all the more discriminating, the better a man one is, the more refined one's sensibility, the more delicate one's feelings' (ibid. 245).

Dialectic, then, is the completion of the phase of theology which mediates the past. It is a necessary complement to research, interpretation, and history, for while these latter respectively provide data, clarify what the data mean, and narrate what was going forward, it is not their task to promote horizon encounter. But interpretation and history need such encounter, for interpretation depends on one's self-understanding, and history as written depends on one's horizon.

The existence of dialectically opposed horizons gives rise to an enormous problem.

> All three types of conversion may be lacking; any one may be present, or any two, or all three. Even prescinding from differences in the thoroughness of the conversion, there are eight radically differing types. Moreover, every investigation is conducted from within some horizon. This remains true even if one does not know one operates from within a horizon, or even if one assumes that one makes no assumptions. Whether they are explicitly acknowledged or not, dialectically opposed horizons lead to opposed value judgments, opposed accounts of historical movements, opposed interpretations of authors, and different selections of relevant data in special research (ibid. 247-48).

Dialectic, as a functional specialty within theology, is confronted with the formidable task of meeting these problems head on.

Two precepts govern the process of dialectic. Those statements compatible with intellectual, moral, and religious conversion are to be furthered and developed; those statements incompatible with intellectual, moral, and religious conversion are to be reversed. The development of the compatible statements occurs through integrating them with fresh data and further discovery. The reversal of the incompatible statements occurs by expeditiously excising from these statements the elements incompatible with conversion. While these two precepts determine the heuristic structure of dialectic, though, the actual process is obviously far more complicated. Researches, interpretations, histories, events, statements, and movements have to be assembled. Then they have to be evaluated. There follows the task of comparing them, so as to mark out affinities and oppositions. Then the dialectician must try to reduce the affinities and oppositions to an underlying root, determine which of these underlying sources depend on dialectically opposed horizons, and finally select only these as the material to which one devotes one's energies under the guidance of the two heuristic principles. The different results achieved by different dialecticians, furthermore, have to be clarified, and this clarification takes place through a threefold objectification of horizon. First, each investigator distinguishes between those statements compatible with any or all of the conversions and those statements found to be incompatible. Secondly, each investigator indicates the view that would result from the development of compatible statements and from the reversal of incompatible statements. Thirdly, each investigator takes these results as themselves materials to be operated on, to be assembled, evaluated, compared, reduced, classified, selected; that is, each investigator proceeds to the task of developing positions and reversing counterpositions.

Now, if the dialectician is operating from the basis of the conversions, his or her development of statements compatible with the conversions and reversal of statements incompatible with them will result in what Lonergan calls 'an idealized version of the past, something better than was the reality' (ibid. 251). I take this to mean in part that one will find challenges to conversion everywhere. Moreover, one will find oneself in agreement with all other dialecticians operating from the same foundation and supported in part by those operating from the foundation of one or two of the conversions. On the other hand, a dialectician not operating from the foundation of conversion would end up mistaking counterpositions for positions and positions for counterpositions, and developing counterpositions while reversing positions. The result would be that one would present, not an idealized version of the past, but a representation of it as worse than it really was. I think here, for example, of Leslie Dewart's presentation of the deleterious infection of the Christian message by the concerns of Greek philosophy (Dewart 1966). That the problem is real enough does not indicate that it is so blithely to be treated as nothing but a catastrophe. At any rate, while the dialecticians operating from the foundations provided by intellectual, moral, and religious conversion will find themselves in agreement with one another, dialectic carried out without such foundations can produce a further dialectic in seven different ways. For there will be dialecticians without any experience of conversion, those with the experience of only one of the three conversion, and those lacking the experience of only one of the three conversions. Those who present an idealized view of the past will agree with one another in their idealization, while those who represent the past as worse than it really was can disagree with one another in seven dialectically opposed ways. Theoretically, then, dialectic can be performed in eight radically different manners. The problem is not only complicated; it is radical.

> ... it is only through the movement towards cognitional and moral self-transcendence, in which the theologian overcomes his own conflicts, that he can hope to discern the ambivalence at work in others and the measure in which they resolved their problems. Only through such discernment can he hope to appreciate all that has been intelligent, true, and good in the past even in the lives and the thought of opponents. Only through such discernment can he come to acknowledge all that was misinformed, misunderstood, mistaken, evil even in those with whom he is allied. Further, however, this action is reciprocal. Just as it is one's own self-transcendence that enables one to know others accurately and to judge them fairly, so inversely it is through knowledge and appreciation of others that we come to know ourselves and to fill out and refine our apprehension of values.
>
> Inasmuch, then, as investigators assemble, complete, compare, reduce, classify, select, they bring to light the dialectical oppositions that existed in the past. Inasmuch as they pronounce one view a position and its opposite a counter-position and then go on to develop the positions and reverse the counter-positions, they are providing one another with the evidence for a judgment on their personal achievement of self-transcendence. They reveal the selves that did the research, offered the interpretations, studied the history, passed the judgments of value.
>
> Such an objectification of subjectivity is in the style of the crucial experiment. While it will not be automatically efficacious, it will provide the openminded, the serious, the sincere with the occasion to ask themselves some basic questions, first, about others but eventually, even about themselves. It will make conversion a topic and thereby promote it. Results will not be sudden or startling, for conversion commonly is a slow process of maturation. It is finding out for oneself and in oneself what it is to be intelligent, to be reasonable, to be responsible, to love. Dialectic contributes to that end by pointing out ultimate differences, by offering the example of others that differ radically from oneself, by providing the occasion

for a reflection, a self-scrutiny, that can lead to a new understanding of oneself and one's destiny (Lonergan 1993, 252-53).

3.3 *Foundations*

It is dialectic, then, which brings to light the key to *Method in Theology*, for 'the basic idea of the method we are trying to develop takes its stand on discovering what human authenticity is and showing how to appeal to it. It is not an infallible method, for men are easily unauthentic, but it is a powerful method, for man's deepest need and most prized achievement is authenticity (ibid. 254). While dialectic is the functional specialty which makes this basic idea a topic, a question which affects the theologian as theologian, foundations is the functional specialty which thematizes this question. The first question dealt with in foundations is, *What is human authenticity?* The answer to this question provides theology with its foundations. Moreover, an individual theologian's answer to this question reveals the foundations of the theology of which he or she is the author.

3.3.1 Foundational Reality and the Functional Specialties

Besides the phase of theology which mediates the past — the phase of research, interpretation, history, and dialectic — there is the phase in which the theologian articulates his or her own positions, joins them together systematically, relates them to the sciences, to philosphy, and to history, and participates in the collaboration through which what one judges to be true is communicated to different members of different classes in different cultures. Foundations in theology are, for Lonergan, more specifically foundations for this second or mediated phase of theology, for doctrines, systematics, and communications. The foundational reality, conversion, will be operative in research, interpretation, history, and dialectic, but it will not be a prerequisite for engaging in these functional specialties. Its operation will be implicit, in that 'it does not constitute an explicit, established, universally recognized criterion of proper procedure in these specialties.' Even with respect to dialectic, conversion is not necessary for lining up opposed positions, for revealing the polymorphism of human consciousness reflected in opposed interpretations and histories, 'the deep and unreconcilable oppositions on religious, moral, and intellectual issues' (ibid. 268). Conversion indeed functions in taking sides, but the sides are taken not by the dialectician as such but by the converted or unconverted person. The sides are taken in 'a decision about whom and what you are for and, again, whom and what you are against. It is a decision illuminated by the manifold possibilities exhibited in dialectic. It is a fully conscious decision about one's horizon, one's outlook, one's world-view. It deliberately selects the framework, in which doctrines have their meaning, in which systematics reconciles, in which communications are effective' (ibid.). Foundational reality is a deliberate decision in favor of 'total surrender to the demands of the human spirit: be attentive, be intelligent, be reasonable, be responsible, be in love' (ibid.). It is consciousness become conscience which constitutes the foundational reality. Such constitution is anything but the arbitrary drifting into one or another contemporary horizon that marks the unauthentic person. Nor is it a purely private affair based on nothing but intensely personal experience.

> While individuals contribute elements to horizons, it is only within the social group that the elements accumulate and it is only with century-old traditions that notable developments occur. To know that conversion is religious, moral, and intel-

lectual, to discern between authentic and unauthentic conversion, to recognize the difference in their fruits — by their fruits
you shall know them — all call for a high seriousness and a
mature wisdom that a social group does not easily attain or
maintain.

It follows that conversion involves more than a change
of horizon. It can mean that one begins to belong to a different social group or, if one's group remains the same, that one
begins to belong to it in a new way. Again, the group will bear
witness to its founder or founders whence originated and are
preserved its high seriousness and mature wisdom. Finally,
the witness it bears will be efficacious in the measure that the
group is dedicated not to its own interests but to the welfare
of mankind. But how the group is constituted, who was the
founder to whom it bears witness, what are the services it renders to mankind, these are questions not for the fifth functional specialty, foundations, but for the sixth, doctrines (ibid. 269).

The foundations of the mediated phase of theology will
consist in an objectification of this deliberate decision about
one's horizon. What will be paramount for the foundations
of a theology that is an ongoing, developing process will not
be a set of logically first propositions, but the immanent and
operative set of norms guiding each forward step, ensuring
the acceptance and development of positions and the rejection and reversal of counterpositions. The sole and ever precarious guarantee of such process lies in the three conversions. It is provided only if 'investigators have attained intellectual conversion to renounce the myriad of false philosophies, moral conversion to keep themselves free of individual,
group, and general bias, and religious conversion so that in
fact each loves the Lord his God with his whole heart and his
whole soul and all his mind and all his strength.'[2] Such a

---

2. Ibid. 270. 1993 note: To individual, group, and general bias must
be added the dramatic bias that Lonergan treats in chapter 6 of *Insight*. It
is with regard to this element of bias that psychic conversion is most pertinent.

foundation will not provide the premises for deducing all desirable conclusions. It is not a set of propositions uttered by a theologian but 'a fundamental and momentous change in the human reality that a theologian is. It operates, not by the simple process of drawing inferences from premises, but by changing the reality (his own) that the interpreter has to understand if he is going to understand others, by changing the horizon within which the historian attempts to make the past intelligible, by changing the basic judgments of fact and of value that are found to be not positions but counter-positions' (ibid. 270-71).

While the attainment or nonattainment of converted foundational reality will not affect the methods followed in research, interpretation, history, and dialectic, the foundational question is of more than minimal importance to these functional specialties.

> ... one's interpretation of others is affected by one's understanding of oneself, and the converted have a self to understand that is quite different from the self that the unconverted have to understand. Again, the history one writes depends on the horizon within which one is attempting to understand the past; the converted and the unconverted have radically different horizons; and so they will write different histories. Such different histories, different interpretations, and their underlying styles in research become the center of attention in dialectic. There they will be reduced to their roots. But the reduction itself will only reveal the converted with one set of roots and the unconverted with a number of different sets. Conversion is a matter of moving from one set of roots to another. It is a process that does not occur in the marketplace. It is a process that may be occasioned by scientific inquiry. But it occurs only inasmuch as a man discovers what is unauthentic in himself and turns away from it, inasmuch as he discovers what the fulness of human authenticity can be and embraces it with his whole being (ibid. 271).

3.3.2 Foundational Reality and Pluralism

The manifestion of conversion in deeds and words depends on the degree of differentiation of consciousness in the converted subject. Thus the same fundamental stance of faith is expressed in a pluralism of forms and in a multiplicity of theologies. Lonergan distinguishes six differentiations of consciousness: common sense, theory, interiority, scholarship, art, and transcendence. 'Any realm becomes differentiated from the others when it develops its own language, its own distinct mode of apprehension, and its own cultural, social, or professional group speaking in that fashion and apprehending in that manner' (ibid. 272). The mathematically possible combinations of these differentiations are thirty-two in number. Moreover, each of them can be incipient or mature or receding.

> In a devout life one can discern the forerunner of mystical experience, in the art lover the beginnings of creativity, in a wisdom literature the foreshadow of philosophic theory, in the antiquarian the makings of a scholar, in psychological introspection the materials of interiorly differentiated consciousness. But what has been achieved need not be perpetuated. The heroic spirituality of a religious leader may be followed by the routine piety of his later followers. Artistic genius can yield place to artistic humbug. The differentiated consciousness of a Plato or Aristotle can enrich a later humanism though the cutting edge of genuine theory does not live on. High scholarship can settle down to amassing unrelated details. Modern philosophy can migrate from theoretically to interiorly differentiated consciousness but it can also revert to the undifferentiated consciousness of the Presocratics and of the analysts of ordinary language.[3]

---

3. Ibid. 275. Note the aside to Heidegger.

Thus, besides the radical pluralism that is the dialectical resultant of the presence or absence of the conversions, there is the 'more benign yet still puzzling variety that has its root in the differentiation of human consciousness' (ibid. 276). Lonergan discusses the varieties of Christian theology in terms of these differentiations (ibid. 276-81), only to conclude that the theology dominated by theoretically differentiated consciousness is at an end, that theology will no longer turn to metaphysics for guidance and help in clarifying its thought and making it coherent, but that the new source of basic clarification will be found in interiorly and religiously differentiated consciousness. The former differentiation will provide theology with its general categories, those which it shares with other disciplines; the latter differentiation will provide it with its special categories, those proper to theology as such. The theologian engaged in the functional specialty 'foundations' has the task of working out both general and special theological categories on the basis or foundation of the conversions.

3.3.3 Foundations and Categories

Such a basis or foundation is transcultural, not as it may be formulated by a given author, but in the realities represented in the formulations. '… these realities are not the product of any culture but, on the contrary, the principles that produce cultures, preserve them, develop them' (ibid. 282). The base for general theological categories is transcendental method, that of special theological categories God's gift of love. General and special theological categories will be themselves transcultural only to the extent that they refer to the inner core of this twofold base. 'In their actual formulation they will be historically conditioned and so subject to correction, modification, complementation. Moreover, the more elaborate they become and the further they are removed from that inner core, the greater will be their precariousness' (ibid. 284). Nonetheless, as a set of interlocking terms and relations they will have the utility of models. They will be useful in guiding investigations, in framing hypotheses, and in writing descriptions. They may provide the theologian with a basic sketch of what one finds to be the case or they may not; if they do not, the very discovery of their irrelevance may help one uncover the clues necessary for further work. They may provide an adequate language to enable the theologian to discuss known realities. They may greatly facilitate description and communication. To the extent that they are built up from the basic terms and relations provided by transcendental method and religious experience, their validity will be quite real. Only the individual theologian, however, can decide whether any model is to be taken as more than a model, whether in itself it can be taken as a hypothesis or a description.

How are theological categories derived? Lonergan discusses first the generation of general theological categories, those which theology shares with other disciplines. The base or foundation of these categories is the theologian in his or her structured subjectivity as an attending, inquiring, reflecting, deliberating subject, as an intention of truth and value; it is the theologian with the operations of experiencing, understanding, judging, and deciding which one has uncovered within oneself; it is the structure of these operations in their dynamic relations promoting intentionality through the transcendental precepts—Be attentive, Be intelligent, Be reasonable, Be responsible; it is the subject as self-transcending, as one whose operations reveal objects, whose structured operations reveal compound objects and whose self-conscious operations reveal, not objects, but the subject. This basic set of terms and relations can be verified, not only in the theologian, but in the men and women of all ages; and in these men and women, not in isolation, but as living in social groups which through their development and decline generate history. Furthermore, this basic set of terms and relations can be differentiated in many different manners. Each of the different conscious operations occurs in aesthetic, intellectual, dramatic, practical, and religious patterns of experience. There is a different quality of consciousness inherent in the different conscious operations, and there are different manners in which the operations themselves proceed toward their goals—the manner of common sense, that of the sciences, that of interiority and philosophy, that of prayer and theology. These different manners of proceeding give rise to different realms of meaning. The operations proceed toward their goals within different heuristic structures. There is a sharp contrast between the differentiated consciousness that shifts with ease from one manner of operation in one world to another manner of operation in another world, and the relatively or completely undifferentiated consciousness which is at home only in its local manner or variety of common sense. There is another sharp contrast between those that have or have not been converted religiously, morally, or intellectually, and this contrast gives rise to dialectically opposed positions and counterpositions, models, and categories.

These various manners of differentiation vastly enrich the basic and initial nest of terms and relations found in the intention of truth and value that is objectified in transcendental method. This broadened basis alone is what has provided Lonergan with the materials for a sophisticated discussion of the human good, of values and beliefs, of meaning, and of religion. These analyses, along with others—e.g., the elaboration of models of change in scientific knowledge; the analysis of developmental process from global operations through differentiation to integration; the understanding of scientific revolutions on the model of successive higher viewpoints, of the universe of proportionate being as a process of emergent probability, of authenticity as generating progress and unauthenticity as bringing about decline; the understanding of the problem of evil as the introduction to the discussion of religion; the intention of a potential universal point of view providing a general semantics for hermeneutics (all of these from *Insight*) — are what provide theology with its general categories. In every case, the categories are derived from the transcultural base provided by the objectification of the transcendental infrastructure of human subjectivity in its intention of intelligibility, truth, and value. In every case, what is truly transcultural is the infrastructure, not its objectification in method nor the formulation of the categories derived from it. Nonetheless, what Lonergan is saying can basically be summarized by stating that *Insight* and the first three chapters of *Method in Theology* provide examples of what is meant by speaking of general theological categories.

The derivation of special theological categories is quite different today from what it was in medieval theoretical theology. There the starting point was a metaphysical psychology representing the order of nature and founding general theologial categories, and a notion of sanctifying grace framed in terms of this metaphysical psychology and articulated in terms of supernatural entities. Now the starting point is rather intentionality analysis and transcendental method as grounding general theological categories, and a dynamic state of being in love with God, a state manifested in inner and outer acts, as grounding special theological categories. The data on the foundation of these categories are the data on conversion and development. They will provide the functional specialty 'foundations' with its first set of special theological categories. 'There are needed studies of religious interiority: historical, phenomenological, psychological, sociological. There is needed in the theologian the spiritual development that will enable him both to enter into the experience of others and to frame the terms and relations that will express that experience' (ibid. 290). A second set will be derived by moving from the subject to the community, to 'the history of the salvation that is rooted in a being-in-love, and the function of this history in promoting the kingdom of God amongst men' (ibid. 291). A third set is derived by moving from our loving to the loving source of our love. 'The Christian tradition makes explicit our implicit intending of God in all our intending by speaking of the Spirit that is given to us, of the Son who redeemed us, of the Father who sent the Son and with the Son sends the Spirit, and of our future destiny when we shall know, not as in a glass darkly, but face to face' (ibid.). A fourth set of categories will deal, not with authentic or inauthentic humanity, but with authentic or inauthentic Christianity, and a fifth set with the progress and decline which are generated respectively from these. 'Not only is there the progress of mankind but also there is development and progress within Christianity itself; and as there is development, so too there is decline; and as there is decline, there also is the problem of undoing it, of overcoming evil with good not only in the world but also in the church' (ibid.).

In general, then, 'the derivation of the categories is a matter of the human and the Christian subject effecting self-appropriation and employing this heightened consciousness both as a basis for methodical control in doing theology and, as well, as an *a priori* whence he can understand other men, their social relations, their history, their religion, their rituals, their destiny' (ibid. 292). The general theological categories function in any of the eight functional specialties. The use and acceptance of the special theological categories as referring to reality occurs in doctrines, systematics, and communications. The concern of foundations is 'with the origins, the genesis, the present state, the possible developments and adaptations of the categories in which Christians understand themselves, communicate with one another, and preach the gospel to all nations' (ibid. 293).

4 Psyche and Foundations

Foundations, then, would seem to have a twofold task: that of articulating the horizon within which theological categories can be understood, and that of deriving the categories which are appropriate to such a horizon. What is the relationship of my present work to this twofold task?

I have spoken of the first task in terms of framing a patterned set of judgments of cognitional fact and of value cumulatively heading toward the full position on the human subject. I have described my own work as a contribution to this patterned set of judgments and thus to the full position on the subject. Implicit in this description is the claim that the present work is a complement to the work of Lonergan. My question now is whether it is a needed complement. Is psychic self-appropriation an intrinsic part of transcendental method? Is it a necessary feature of the objectification of the transcendental infrastructure of human subjectivity? Can it be dispensed with completely? Can it be politely treated as a useful auxiliary? Or is it demanded by the task set by Lonergan, the task of moving toward a viable control of meaning for a new epoch in the historical evolution of, at least, Western mind? The question is answered, I believe, already by the affirmation that the psyche is no accidental feature of the transcendental infrastructure of human subjectivity and that it does not achieve its integration with intentionality by some kind of higher integration introduced by knowledge, but only by the free and responsible decisions of the existential subject. The integration of psyche and intentionality, to be sure, is not the only task confronting the existential subject. It is a task that for the most part affects one's effective freedom, and there is the more radical question which one must deal with at the level of one's essential freedom. *What do I want to make of myself?* The integration of psyche with intentionality occurs in the framework of one's answer to that question. But occur it must, if this more radical answer is to bear fruit in the effective constitution of oneself and of one's world.

Lonergan speaks of placing 'abstractly apprehended cognitional activity within the concrete and sublating context of human feeling and of moral deliberation, evaluation, and decision' (ibid. 275). Until cognitional activity, no matter how correctly apprehended, is so placed, it remains abstract in its apprehension. The move toward greater concreteness on the side of the subject demands this second mediation of immediacy by meaning. Only such mediation brings transcendental method to its conclusion. I confess that my own experience and my association and collaboration with others who have been profoundly affected by Lonergan's cognitional analysis have prompted me to the conviction that this is no easy task, that it is at least as complicated as comprehending cognitional activity, that equally sophisticated techniques are needed for its execution, and that without it the movement brought into being by Lonergan is left incomplete, and those influenced by this method are left the potential victims of what I must call an intellectualist bias. The shift of the center of attention in Lonergan's work from cognitional analysis to intentionality analysis, from the intellectual pattern of experience to self-transcendence in all patterns of experience as the privileged domain of human subjectivity, has not yet been sufficiently attended to. The underlying assumption is still that intellectual conversion is the last and the rarest of the conversions. But the exigence giving rise to a new epoch in the evolution of human consciousness only begins to be met in the philosophic conversion aided by Lonergan's cognitional analysis. The radical crisis is not cognitional but existential. It is the crisis of the self as objectified becoming approximate to the self as conscious. It is the exigence for a mediation of the transcendental infrastructure of the subject as subject that would issue in a second immediacy. This exigence is only initially met by the appropriation of *logos*. Psyche will never cease to have its say and to offer both its potential contribution and its potential threat to the unfolding of the transcendental dynamism toward self-transcendence. My suspicion is that something along the lines of the psychic self-appropriation proposed in this book is, in the general case, quite necessary if the concrete sublation of appropriated cognitional activity within the context of human feeling and moral decision is to take place. My suspicion is, too, that something like a depth-psychological analysis carried out according to the understanding here offered is a necessary contribution to the maieutic that *is* the self-appropriating subject. It is my conviction, then, that an articulation of psychic conversion is a constituent feature of the patterned set of judgments of cognitional fact and of value cumulatively heading toward the full position on the human subject that constitutes renewed foundations in theology.

There is a second task of foundations. It is that of deriving categories appropriate to the horizon articulated in the objectification of conversion. What is the relation of psychic self-appropriaiton to this foundational task?

All theological categories have an archetypal significance. The general theological categories are those derived from the transcendental base giving rise to the emergence of the authentic cognitional and existential subject. This emergence is archetypally significant. It is the ground theme of the dialectic between intentionality and psyche. It is objecti-

fied in a semantics of human desire. Special theological categories are those proper to a theology which would mediate
between the Christian religion and the role and significance
of that religion within a given cultural context. The cultural
context is a compound of stories reflecting the ground theme
of the emergence of existential subjectivity. The Christian
religion is the fruit of a collaboration between human beings
and God in working out the solution to the radical problem
of this emergence. Both are archetypally significant. As the
emergence of the existential subject is the archetypal drama
of human existence, so the Christian religion in its authenticity is the fruit of the divinely originated solution to that drama.
As psyche will continue to have its say in the drama even
when intentionality has proclaimed its relative autonomy from
imagination, so at the farthest reaches of self-appropriation
there emerges a differentiated surrender to God in which
alone the finality of the psyche as a constituent feature of
human subjectivity is achieved. Psychic self-appropriation is
a part of the objectification of the transcendental and
transcultural base from which both general and special theological categories are derived. It affects the selfunderstanding
in terms of which one mediates the past in interpretation,
history, dialectic, and the special research generated by their
concerns. And it gives rise to the generation of theological
categories appropriate to the mediated phase of theology, the
phase which takes its stand on self-appropriation and ven-
tures to say what is so to the men and women of different
strata and backgrounds in different cultures of the world of
today. It gives rise to the possibility of theological categories,
doctrines or positions, and systems which are legitimately
symbolic or poetic or aesthetic. It makes it possible that such
categories, positions, and systems can be poetic without ceasing to be explanatory, without ceasing to fix terms and relations by one another, without falling into a theology which is

little more than the camouflaged narrative of a given
theologian's autobiography, a purely descriptive theology
relating the things talked about only to the dramatic subjectivity of the given theologian. A hermeneutic and dialectical
phenomenology of the psyche would be the objectification of
psychic conversion that is a constituent feature of theological foundations in terms of which appropriate explanatory
categories can be enunciated. What Ray L. Hart has called a
systematic symbolics (Hart 1968) is an ambition that is methodologically both possible and desirable. But its valid methodological base is found, I believe, only in the mediation of
immediacy in which one discovers, identifies, accepts one's
submerged feelings, only in the kind of depth-psychological
analysis rendered possible by psychotherapy.

Second immediacy will never achieve a total mediation
of primordial immediacy. Complete self-transparency is impossible short of our ulterior finality in the vision of God.
Only in seeing God as God is will we know ourselves as we
are. But there is a poetic enjoyment of the truth about ourselves and God that has been achieved in many cultures, at
many times, within the framework of many differentiations
of consciousness, and related to different combinations of the
various realms of meaning. The second mediation of immediacy by meaning can function in aid of a recovery of this
poetic enjoyment. Methodologically it can function in aid of
the second naivete ambitioned by Paul Ricoeur, the immediacy of the twice-born adult, in which I 'leave off all demands and listen' (Ricoeur 1970, 551). It may well be that, in
Eliot's words,

> ... the end of all our exploring
> Will be to arrive where we started
> And know the place for the first time (Eliot 1971, 59).

In that case, however, the end of all our exploring will be neither intellectual conversion nor even the far more complete mediation of *logos* as intention of self-transcendence aided by the later Lonergan. The mediated return to immediacy demands in addition the satisfaction of a further exigence toward a second mediation of immediacy by meaning. Moral and religious conversion can consciously and consistently sublate intellectual conversion only if they are aided by a further step in the process of the appropriation of human interiority.

As this process of sublation goes forward, one will confirm the suspicion, I believe, that the gift of God's love has been responsible for initiating and sustaining the whole process, that one's own responsibility has been a cooperation with a fated call to a dreaded holiness, with a 'charged field of love and meaning, which at times has reached notable intensity, but more often has been ever unobtrusive, hidden, inviting each of us to join' (Lonergan 1993, 290). One will discover that one has been in love all along, experiencing something analogous to the ups and downs, the misunderstandings and reconciliations of every love relationship. While one may suspect and affirm this relationship all along or at least at intervals, the eye of faith becomes sharpened and its interpretations more sensitive as one learns to confess the extent to which one is loved with an other-worldly, all-embracing, completely gratuitous, and severely jealous love, and to experience the extent to which one can indeed be brought to leave off all demands and listen. Psychic conversion facilitates the sublation of one's commitment to truth into a commitment to all value, and the sublation of both into a state of surrender leaving the unified affectivity of love, joy, peace, patience, kindness, goodness, faithfulness, gentleness, and self-control concerning which there is no law. But this post-critical religious consciousness is quite different from the religious experience which may have initiated the entire process, for it is habitually focused in its immediacy on interiority, time, the generic, and the divine, rather than on exteriority, space, the specific, and the human. The clearing of the possibility of such religious consciousness and the elucidation of its experienced reality would be the first task of foundations in a theology which would mediate a critically conscious and historically sophisticated cultural matrix and the role and significance of a living religion within that matrix. But such a consciousness is attained only in the third stage of the appropriation of interiority: not in the stage of the discrimination of spirit or *logos* in intentionality analysis, nor in the stage of the cultivation of soul in psychological analysis, but in the stage of the self-surrender to the undertow on the part of discriminated spirit and cultivated soul. Then, in the language of the concerns of the new hermeneutic, 'if theology is understood as language *about* God, it is to be asked to what extent its language is *from* God' (Funk 1966, 68). God and ourselves will be, in a sense, together in the one sentence, for God will be thought and affirmed again in strict relation to 'real life,' to the world mediated by meaning through operations experienced immediately. When a transcendental aesthetic becomes a part of foundations in theology, the ultimate religious and theological dialectic will occur in the dialogue of world religions, and it will revolve about the concrete figures of this ultimate dialectic: Gotama, Krsna, LaoTse, Confucius, Mohammed, Abraham and Moses, Jesus. Through this dialogue, perhaps as nowhere else, the common rootedness of the human side of all religion in the symbolic function will be recognized. Moreover, systematic theology can then become, in John Macquarrie's phrase, 'a kind of phenomenology of faith' (Macquarrie 1955, 6). But its basic terms and relations will be explanatory, because derived from the most thoroughgoing fidelity to the methodical exigence. Such fidelity, pursued to its limits, turns truth into poetry. As Vico declared all to begin with poetry, so perhaps there is a way of affirming that all ends with poetry: we end where we began, but we see the place as if for the first time. Perhaps even of the theologian, it may be said with Hölderlin and Heidegger:

> Full of merit, and yet poetically, dwells
> Man on this earth.[4]

---

4. Quoted by Heidegger in 'Hölderlin and the Essence of Poetry,' in 1949, 270.

Bibliography

Gerhard Adler. *The Living Symbol: A Case Study of the Process of Individuation*. Princeton: Princeton University Press, 1961.

Gaston Bachelard. *The Psychoanalysis of Fire*. New York: Beacon Press, 1964.

Ernest Becker. *The Denial of Death*. New York: The Free Press, 1973.

Henri Corbin. 'Mundus Imaginalis, or the Imaginary and the Imaginal,' *Spring* (1972) 1-19.

F. E. Crowe. 'An Exploration of Lonergan's New Notion of Value,' *Science et Esprit* 29 (1977) 124-43.

Joseph Campbell. *The Masks of God*, vol. 1, *Primitive Mythology*. New York: Viking Press, 1970.

Leslie Dewart. *The Future of Belief*. New York: Herder & Herder, 1966.

Robert M. Doran. *Theology and the Dialectics of History*. Toronto: University of Toronto Press, 1990.

John S. Dunne. *The Way of All the Earth*. New York: Macmillan, 1972.

Gilbert Durand. 'Exploration of the Imaginal,' *Anima* (1971) 84-100.

Mircea Eliade. *Cosmos and History: The Myth of the Eternal Return*, trans. William R. Trask. New York: Harper & Row, 1959.

T. S. Eliot. 'Little Gidding,' *Four Quartets*. New York: Harcourt, Brace & World, 1971.

Marie-Louise von Franz. *Number and Time: Reflections Leading toward a Unification of Depth Psychology and Physics*, trans. Andrea Dykes. Evanston: Northwestern University Press, 1974.

Robert W. Funk. *Language, Hermeneutic, and the Word of God*. New York: Harper & Row, 1966.

Eugene Gendlin. *Experiencing and the Creation of Meaning*. Toronto: Free Press of Glencoe, 1962.

Ray L. Hart. *Unfinished Man and the Imagination*. New York: Herder & Herder, 1968.

G. W. F. Hegel. *Sämtliche Werke*, Bd. IV, *Wissenschaft der Logik, Erster Teil: Die Objektive Logik*. Stuttgart: Frederick Fromann Verlag, 1965.

Martin Heidegger. *Existence and Being*, trans. Douglas Scott. Chicago: Henry Regnery, 1949.

________. *Kant und das Problem der Metaphysik*. Frankfurt am Main: Klostermann, 1951.

________. *Being and Time*, trans. John Macquarrie and Edward Robinson. New York: Harper and Row, 1962.

Joseph L. Henderson. *The Wisdom of the Serpent*. New York: Braziller, 1963.

A. Hesnard. *L'Oeuvre de Freud et son importance pour le monde moderne* (1960).

James Hillman, *The Myth of Analysis*. Evanston: Northwestern University Press, 1972.

________. 'Anima,' in *Spring: An Annual of Archetypal Psychology and Jungian Thought* (1973).

Edmund Husserl. *Cartesian Meditations*, trans. Dorion Cairns. The Hague: Nijhoff, 1960.

Don Ihde. *Hermeneutic Phenomenology: The Philosophy of Paul Ricoeur*. Evanston: Northwestern University Press, 1971.

Ivan Illych. *Medical Nemesis: The Expropriation of Health*. Cidoc Cuaderno, No. 89, 1974.

C. G. Jung. *Mysterium Coniunctionis*, trans. R. F. C. Hull, vol. 14 of Collected Works of C. G. Jung. Princeton: Princeton University Press, 1963.

________. 'On the Relations of Analytical Psychology to Poetry,' in *The Spirit in Man, Art, and Literature*, trans. R. F.

C. Hull, vol. 15 in Collected Works of C. G. Jung. Princeton: Princeton University Press, 1966.

______. 'Paracelsus as a Spiritual Phenomenon,' in *Alchemical Studies*, trans. R. F. C. Hull, vol. 13 in Collected Works of C. G. Jung. Princeton: Princeton University Press, 1967.

______. 'On the Nature of the Psyche,' in *The Structure and Dynamics of the Psyche*, trans. R. F. C. Hull, vol. 8 in Collected Works of C. G. Jung. Princeton: Princeton University Press, 1969a.

______. 'Archetypes of the Collective Unconscious,' in *The Archetypes and the Collective Unconscious*, trans. R. F. C. Hull, vol. 9i of Collected Works of C. G. Jung. Princeton: Princeton University Press, 1969b.

______. *Psychological Types*, trans. R. F. C. Hull, vol. 6 in Collected Works of C. G. Jung. Princeton: Princeton University Press, 1971.

______. *Aion*, trans. R. F. C. Hull, vol. 9ii in Collected Works of C. G. Jung. Princeton: Princeton University Press, 1973.

Fred Lawrence. 'Self-Knowledge in History in Gadamer and Lonergan,' in *Language, Truth and Meaning*, ed. Philip McShane. Notre Dame: University of Notre Dame Press, 1972.

Bernard Lonergan. 'Bernard Lonergan Responds. ' in McShane, ed., *Language, Truth and Meaning*, ed. Philip

McShane. Notre Dame: University of Notre Dame
Press, 1972.

______.'Bernard Lonergan Responds. ' in *Foundations of The-
ology*, ed. Philip McShane. South Bend: University of
Notre Dame Press, 1972b.

______. *Philosophy of God, and Theology*. Philadelphia: West-
minster, 1973.

______. 'The Subject,' in *A Second Collection*, ed. William F. J.
Ryan and Bernard J. Tyrrell. London: Darton,
Longman & Todd, 1974.

______. *A Third Collection*, ed. Frederick E. Crowe. Mahwah,
NJ: Paulist Press, 1985.

______. *Insight: A Study of Human Understanding*, vol. 3 of Col-
lected Works of Bernard Lonergan, ed. Frederick E.
Crowe and Robert M. Doran. Toronto: University of
Toronto Press, 1992.

______. *Method in Theology*. New York: Herder and Herder,
1972; latest reprint, Toronto: University of Toronto Press,
1993.

______. 'Dimensions of Meaning,' in *Collection*, vol. 4 of Col-
lected Works of Bernard Lonergan, ed. Frederick E.
Crowe and Robert M. Doran. Toronto: University of
Toronto Press, 1988.

John Macquarrie, *An Existentialist Theology* (London: SCM
Press, 1955)

Sebastian Moore. *The Crucified Jesus Is No Stranger*. New York: Seabury, 1977.

Erich Neumann. 'Mystical Man,' in *Eranos Jahrbuch* 16 (1959)

Ira Progoff. *The Death and Rebirth of Psychology*. New York: McGraw Hill Paperbacks, 1973a.

______. *The Symbolic and the Real*. New York: McGraw-Hill Paperbacks, 1973b.

Paul Ricoeur. *Fallible Man*, trans. Charles Kelbley. Chicago: Henry Regnery, 1965.

______. *Freedom and Nature: The Voluntary and the Involuntary*, trans. Erazim Kohak. Evanston: Northwestern University Press, 1966.

______. *The Symbolism of Evil*, trans. Emerson Buchanan. Boston: The Beacon Press, 1969.

______. *Freud and Philosophy*, trans. Denis Savage. New Haven: Yale, 1970.

Giovanni Sala. *Das Apriori in der menschlichen Erkenntnis:Eine Studie über Kants Kritik der reinen Vernunft und Lonergans Insight*. Meisenheim am Glan: Verlag Anton Hain, 1971.

______. 'The *A priori* in Human Knowledge: Kant's *Critique of Pure Reason* and Lonergan's *Insight*,' in *The Thomist* 60:2 (1976) 179-221.

______. *Lonergan and Kant: Five Essays on Human Knowledge*. Toronto: University of Toronto Press, 1994.

Charlotte Smith. *Carl Becker: On History and the Climate of Opinion*. Ithaca: Cornell, 1956.

Rix Weaver. *The Old Wise Woman*. New York: C. G. Jung Foundation, 1973.

Edward C. Whitmont. *The Symbolic Quest*. New York: C. G. Jung Foundation, 1969.